» BROTHERHOOD TO NATIONHOOD «

# Brotherhood to Nationhood

George Manuel and the Making of
the Modern Indian Movement

Peter McFarlane

between the lines

© 1993, Peter McFarlane

Published by:

Between The Lines
394 Euclid Avenue, #203
Toronto, Ontario
M6G 2S9, Canada

Cover Design: Mary Anne Barkhouse
Frontcover photo courtesy of UBCIC
Typeset with SGML software by Adams & Hamilton, Toronto
Printed in Canada

Between The Lines gratefully acknowledges financial assistance from the
Canada Council, the Department of Communications, the Ontario Arts
Council, and the Ontario Ministry of Culture, Tourism, and Recreation,
through the Ontario Publishing Centre.

**Canadian Cataloguing in Publication Data**

McFarlane, Peter, 1954-
    Brotherhood to nationhood: George Manuel and the making of the
modern indian movement

Includes index.
ISBN 0-921284-67-5 (bound). – ISBN 0-921284-66-7 (pbk.)

1. Manuel, George, 1921-    . 2. Indians of North America – Canada –
Civil rights.  3. Indians of North America – Canada – Government
relations.  4. Indians of North America – Canada – Political activity.
5. National Indian Brotherhood.  6. Assembly of First Nations.  7. World
Council of Indigenous Peoples.  8. Shuswap Indians – Biography.
9. Indians of North America – British Columbia – Biography.  I. Title.

E92.M35  1993   323.1′19702   C93-095138-7

## » CONTENTS «

## IV. Final Days

# ACKNOWLEDGEMENTS

I would like to thank my friend, Dana Williams, who originally suggested I take on this project and who, along with Sonny Williams, helped with the research. Dana also introduced me to Bob Manuel, Arthur Manuel and Wayne Haimila, who made it possible to bring the project to completion. I am grateful to all of them not only for their considerable help, but for their friendship and hospitality.

I would also like to thank Harold Cardinal, Senator Len Marchand, Marie Marule, Walter Rudnicki, Michael Posluns, Ron George, Mary Thomas, Vera Manuel, Marlene Manuel and the dozens of others who patiently answered my questions and offered valuable insights into George Manuel and the development of the First Nations movement.

A special thanks goes to the late Phillip Paul who, even though quite ill, invited me to his home and spent many hours supplying details of George Manuel's life and work I could not have found elsewhere.

Janine Cheeseman of Aurora Artists arranged the publication of the book, and the readers, Heather Ross and David Long, offered insightful suggestions on shaping the manuscript. Marg Anne Morrison of Between the Lines guided the book to completion and the editor, Carroll Klein, laboured long and hard to polish what was a very rough manuscript. I would also like to thank the Canada Council for its support during the first year of research and writing.

Finally, I would like to thank Betsy, who was the first reader and who offered encouragement as well as valuable suggestions throughout the writing process.

The growth of the Indian movement has been one of Canada's most important political developments in the last half century. Since 1951, when an Indian Act revision lifted the restrictions on Indian organizing, the movement has emerged from the political wilderness, where native concerns were addressed by the handful of retired military men who ran the Indian Affairs Department, to become a central issue of the country's political and constitutional life.

These gains did not come easily. It took the efforts of innumerable activists in every region of the country fighting for their rights against all levels of government. And it took leaders who were as skilled at the political manoeuvrings as their opponents in government.

In his day, George Manuel was the greatest of these leaders. In his three decades of active political life, he served not only as the head of the national Indian organization, but also as the main strategist and visionary of the movement.

As a builder of organizations, his contribution is remarkable. When he took command of the newly formed National Indian Brotherhood in 1970, it was a paper organization without a funding source or a clear political direction. George Manuel gave the twelve provincial and territorial native organizations that made up the NIB a common "national Indian philosophy" aimed at winning sovereignty for the First Nations, and built the organization into the largest lobbying force in Ottawa.

George Manuel's vision took him further; he sought the unity of indigenous peoples of North, Central and South America and Eurasia. He called this collection of indigenous societies, which had been swamped under successive waves of European expansion, the Fourth World. To give that world a voice he launched the UN-affiliated World Council of Indigenous Peoples in 1975.

Through these two organizations and his writings and speeches, George Manuel gave shape to today's native movement. Yet despite these accomplishments, which earned him three Nobel Peace Prize nominations, he never stopped seeking new ways to push the struggle forward. When he became convinced that he had reached the end of his effectiveness as what he described as an "establishment Indian," he returned to British Columbia to build and lead a "peoples' movement." In BC, he legitimized (and even institutionalized) native radicalism and in tribute to his leadership his young followers, caught up in the heady excitement of the times, adopted the name of Manuelistas.

Ironically, it was during this period, when he was operating from his BC base, that George Manuel had his greatest single impact on the national scene. During the constitutional debate of 1980, he led a thousand of his supporters to Ottawa and forced the government to include aboriginal rights provisions in the constitution, thus opening the door for future breakthroughs.

Throughout his life, however, George Manuel's political battles were accompanied by difficult personal ones. He endured the physical and mental abuse of the residential school system and a long childhood battle with tuberculosis that left him with a twisted hip and life-long limp. He also lived with the day-to-day racism of Canadian society that saw him, even as the leader of the National Indian Brotherhood in the mid-1970s, refused a room in a Halifax hotel.

None of these challenges diverted George Manuel from his passion to organize indigenous people. Despite his international profile, he never forgot who he was or where he came from. He was a man of the people, and on a personal level his story is that of a generation of native people in Canada who, through their tireless efforts, have forced Canadians to look at the historical injustices on which their society is founded.

George Manuel may be Canada's greatest prophet and to refuse to consider his words of advice may be the ultimate folly of our times.

Vine Deloria, Jr.
American Indian activist

George Manuel's grandparents,
Dick and Macreet Andrew

George, left, and his wife Marlene, camping in spring 1979

Pierre Trudeau and George Manuel in 1978

George Manuel, centre, with Rodrigo Contreras
in Peru in 1979

George Manuel with Julius Nyerere in Tanzania in 1971.

# PART ONE

# The Neck of the Chicken

I get the neck of the chicken
I get the rumble seat ride
I get the leaky umbrella
Everyone casts me aside

George Manuel's party piece

## CHAPTER ONE

# Paradise, Paradise Lost
## 1960

Is that what you people are afraid of – that the Indians will be a self-supporting nation?

George Manuel, to the Joint Committee on Indian Affairs
26 May 1960

George Manuel limped into the oak-panelled hearing room on 26 May 1960 and set his battered briefcase down on the table.

At his side was Genevieve Mussell, a non-native woman who had gained status through marriage and who served as his vice-president on the native rights committee of the Interior Tribes of British Columbia. In front of him, framed by the Red Ensign on one side of the room and a portrait of the young Queen Elizabeth II on the other, were a dozen MPs and senators who had been given the task of reforming Canada's Indian policy.

George Manuel had been preparing for this meeting for the past two years. He and a group of activists had travelled the BC interior spreading the gospel of resistance and eliciting their peoples' grievances. The result was a one-hundred page brief detailing the desperate straits of BC Indians and criticizing the Department of Indian Affairs for a century of crimes and misdemeanours.

The parliamentary committee had allotted Manuel only two hours to express a hundred years of frustration. Even in that limited time, the MPs and senators would not be an easy audience. The Joint Committee had been sitting for a year and the members were clearly bored by the endless parade of witnesses. Noel Dorion, the MP who was chairing the hearings, had begun to focus his energies on merely keeping the process moving – in, out, next – with a minimum of discussion.

When George Manuel took his seat in the witness chair that morning, Noel Dorion didn't think he would pose much of a problem. Manuel was wearing a new blue suit that the people of his community had bought for him, but the fabric was stretched uncomfortably across his boom man's shoulders. Dorion had also noted that the Shuswap Indian had entered the room with a pronounced limp and when he smiled his round face and crooked grin made him look a bit like a beaming jack-o'-lantern. Dorion was obviously unimpressed by the figure he cut; he assumed that the white woman had been brought in to speak for him and offered her the floor.

Genevieve Mussell, a strong backer of George Manuel, reacted with surprise to Dorion's invitation. Mr. Manuel, she told the committee, would be speaking for himself.

And speak he did. The smile left his face and George Manuel began in a slow and deliberate voice coloured by a strong Shuswap accent. By the time he finished, he had stretched his allotted two hours into two full days of testimony, and he had delivered the most sweeping indictment of the government's Indian policy the committee had heard.

Manuel described how the lack of an adequate economic and land base on the reserves was driving young people into the slums of the city. He told them how inadequate social services left old people living in dirt-floor huts with only $22 a month in support payments. He told them police harassment was so serious that in some communities the chiefs intentionally let the roads deteriorate so they would no longer be passable for RCMP patrol cars. He berated Colonel Jones, the director of Indian Affairs, for hiring as Indian agents retired military men who had no knowledge or sensitivity to Indian people. And finally, he called on the Diefenbaker government to repair the damage by funding Indian organizations so they could help Indian people rebuild their shattered lives and re-emerge as "self-supporting nations."[1]

In the foggy complacency of the Eisenhower era, the suggestion that the goal of Canada's Indian policy should be to help the First Nations win back their economic and political independence sounded almost heretical. The buzzwords at the time were "assimilation" and "integration," which meant moving people from the reserves into towns and cities where they would eventually disappear as distinct peoples. Noel Dorion quickly chastized George Manuel, warning him that he was "wandering all over the map" with his self-supporting nations comment, and reminding him that the topic at hand was Indian reserves, not nations. [2]

But George Manuel refused to back down. He continued to make his case, shifting his tone with his arguments – moving from thoughtful discourse to humour to the occasional flash of anger to the simple plea that the government of Canada look at the disaster it was wreaking on the lives of his people.

That first day he spoke for almost six hours, and while he did, the mood in the room gradually changed. The objections from the MPs and senators became fewer and fewer and even Dorion began to lean forward in his chair. By the time the marathon session ended on the second day, the parliamentarians were listening to the Shuswap leader with genuine respect. Whatever they thought of his ideas, they recognized that they had met a man of vision and deep conviction and few believed they had seen the last of George Manuel.

The source of the vision that took Manuel to Ottawa that spring, and would take him to the four corners of the world during the next two decades, was not derived from political theory. It was rooted in his own knowledge of who he was and where his Shuswap people had come from.

In many ways, the story of the Shuswap nation could have been told by a Carib Indian in the sixteenth century, a Maliseet in the seventeenth, a Huron in the eighteenth or a Plains Cree in the nineteenth. But for the Shuswap people, the full weight of the European occupation didn't come until the 1860s when George Manuel's own grandfather was in his twenties. George Manuel brought with him to Ottawa, and to all of his political struggles, the memories of the old man who had grown up in a world where the Shuswap were a free people living on the lands the Old One had given to them when the Earth was still young.

» «

During the hearings, one of the MPs referred to reserves as "glorified concentration camps." George Manuel bristled at the statement. [3]

He reminded the politicians that most reserves were the remnants of vast national territories, and he told them that the lands were "rich in memories and traditions."[4] In his case, those memories were reinforced every time he fetched a pail of water from the river in front of his house and passed the deep circular excavation where his grandfather, Dick Andrew, had lived in a *kekuli*, the traditional Shuswap pit-house.

The *kekuli* reminded him of just how recently the Europeans had usurped the land. When Dick Andrew was growing up during the 1840s and 1850s, all the lakes and streams and all the mountains and valleys still had Indian names. The Shuswap lived off the natural abundance of the land and still followed their ancient rhythm of life, with the thirty-seven Shuswap bands travelling between summer and winter hunting and fishing grounds, then coming together in the spring and fall for informal national assemblies to arrange marriages with members of other bands, allocate hunting and fishing areas and discuss relations with the neighbouring tribes and with the newly arrived fur traders.

The closest trading post to Dick Andrew's Neskainlith band was Fort Kamloops, seventy kilometres west at the meeting of the South and North Thompson rivers. Twice a year the people of Neskainlith paddled south to trade their stockpile of furs, dried salmon and dried meat, for European goods like firearms, knives and axes.

If the chief found that the prices at Kamloops were not attractive enough, he would lead his people to other posts, in Gale or Hope, where they could strike a better bargain. Overall, the trade was profitable for the Shuswap and they treated the whites as shopkeepers who were free to carry on their business on Shuswap territory as long as they stayed within carefully proscribed limits.

The calamities of contact for the Shuswap people began in 1861 when smallpox, the scourge that had wiped out millions of North, Central and South American Indians in the previous three centuries, arrived in British Columbia.

After taking a terrible toll on the coast, the epidemic spread into the interior. Estimates of the death rate among the Shuswap run as high as two-thirds of the population; in some cases whole villages were wiped out.

The chief of Dick Andrew's Neskainlith band led his people into the hills to avoid contact with the most badly infected areas. Still the losses were devastating, with almost half the band succumbing to the disease.

After the epidemic ran its course, the survivors were left with a terrible psychic scar. The traditional medicines and practices the people had acquired from their ancestors had proved useless in battling the disease; some historians believe it was the resulting loss of faith in traditional medicine that paved the way to the Indians' conversion to Christianity.

As elsewhere in the Americas, the French Oblate missionaries staged baptisms of entire villages and gave the people Christian names. Along with preaching the Christian gospel, the Oblates worked diligently to undermine the traditional Shuswap religion and customs and encouraged the people to settle down and take up agriculture. By the turn of the century, most of the Shuswap were at least nominally Catholic and only a few, like George Manuel's grandfather, continued to resist Christian teachings.

But even those who held on to the old faith could not resist the next wave of the white invasion. In the late 1860s, settlers began to move into the area to take advantage of a government decree allowing each white man to pre-empt 320 acres of Indian land and to purchase a further 320 acres from the colonial land office at a cut-rate price.

As settlement increased, traditional Shuswap hunting areas were cleared and fenced. Game animals receded further into the forest and the Shuswap were themselves forced to turn to small-scale farming, particularly livestock raising, to supplement the loss of game.

The small scale of the farms was not necessarily a matter of choice. The colonial authorities had awarded only about twenty acres of land to Indian families, compared to the 640 acres set aside for the settlers. When the Shuswap were forced to depend more and more on agriculture for their foodstuffs, each family had access to less than four per cent of the land of their white counterparts. The Shuswap people found themselves paupers on their own land, and by the time George Manuel was born in 1921, all but a fraction of the band's hundreds of square kilometres of land had been annexed. His people were corralled on a small strip of land between the South Thompson River and a steep mountain ridge across from the town of Chase.

All this – the smallpox epidemic, the mass conversions to Christianity and the hordes of settlers who had invaded the Shuswap territory – had taken place in the lifetime of George Manuel's own grandfather, and Andrew passed on to him the story of his people.

For George Manuel, Dick Andrew's stories of the past formed a kind of two-part national epic – paradise and paradise lost. George Manuel, as the parliamentarians had discovered in 1960, was determined to write the third book of the epic – paradise regained – with his deeds. The 1960 hearings were his opening shot. Within a decade, Manuel would be back in Ottawa leading a national Indian organization dedicated to regaining the lost land and liberty of the fifty-two First Nations.

## CHAPTER TWO

# The Hard-Luck Shuswap Kid

## 1920–1932

. . . A hard-luck Shuswap kid from the British Columbia interior, George Manuel had a bagful of excuses to sit out his life in self-pity and let the state support him.

CP wire service report
3 Oct. 1977

On the long winter nights, when the winds whipped the snows against the walls of the log cabin, Dick Andrew told his grandson not only about their peoples' past, but also recounted the rich storehouse of Shuswap legends.

As a child, George Manuel's favourite was about the Shuswap boy who was orphaned at an early age and spent his days wandering the village. At night he would sit close to the tents where the elders were telling their children and grandchildren stories from the past, and in this way the orphan quietly absorbed all the wisdom of his people. When he grew to manhood, he emerged as the wisest person in the village and he became one of the greatest Shuswap leaders of his day.[1]

In later life, George Manuel used a version of the listening-at-the-tents approach in his life-long commitment to self-education. But as a child, the story also spoke to his position in the world. He never knew his father. In fact, little is known about Pierre Rainbow Manuel, except that he was the son of Quimopohian (Rainbow), the band chief of the Shuswap village of Skeechestn, and that he arrived in Neskainlith at the end of the First World War in search of a wife.

In the Shuswap tradition he consulted the local elders about the women of marriageable age and the one he finally approached was Maria, the daughter of Dick Andrew and his wife Macreet.

The young couple wed in early 1920 and settled in Neskainlith on the slopes above the South Thompson River near the bowl-shaped valley called Skunk Hollow. They built a one-room house and Rainbow Manuel began to farm the adjacent hillside.

Their only child, George, was born on 17 February 1921. Just two months later, Rainbow Manuel collapsed in his field and died of what appears to have been a heart attack.

Dick Andrew and Macreet immediately came to the aid of their widowed daughter. They brought her salmon to eat and coal oil for her lamps and as soon as the child was weaned, they began to give the young mother a break by taking him to stay with them for a few days at their log house by the river. [2]

A year or so later, when Maria began to see another man, Louis Manuel (no relation to Pierre) [3], George's stays with his grandparents became longer. When Maria and Louis married and started a family of their own, George found himself living more or less permanently with his grandparents.

In later life, George Manuel would have some difficulty sorting out his relationship with his mother. He saw her often when he was growing up – her house was only a few kilometres away from his grandparents – but they were never close emotionally and George felt like a forgotten son in his mother's eyes. [4]

The fact that George Manuel was raised by his grandparents, however, would have a defining impact on his life. Dick Andrew was a practitioner of Indian medicine, and the world George Manuel grew up in was guided by his grandparents' traditional values and by the basic tenets of the ancient Shuswap culture.

In the interior of British Columbia in the 1920s, the core of that culture was still intact. The town of Chase had been built across the river a few years before George Manuel was born but the peoples' defence was to draw into themselves. Adults went into town only every month or two to sell or trade cord wood or small quantities of farm produce in exchange for a few basic provisions like coal oil, sugar, a pouch of tobacco, a sack of flour and ammunition for hunting. Children were generally kept away from the town altogether. [5]

The isolation was helped by the fact that few of the people spoke

English. Most, like George's grandparents, spoke the Shuswap language at home and with their indigenous neighbours they spoke Chinook, a lingua franca made up of a mixture of BC Indian dialects and a smattering of French picked up from the fur traders. In George Manuel's case, he did not hear a word of English until he was eight years old.

By the 1920s, most of the others in the village were at least nominally Catholic, but the absence of a resident priest prevented the Church from dominating the community's political and spiritual life. When an itinerant priest came to the village, the people attended mass at the church by the river, but after he left, they conducted village councils in the traditional manner.

George Manuel's own memories of growing up in the 1920s were of a simple life where the community still lived and worked closely together. He recalled the "traditional chiefs leading the people into the fields to tend the crops. The men would work at harvesting or planting . . . according to the season. The women cooked for them on open fires . . . No one was idle."[6]

The children also pitched in to help. At home and during the community gatherings they carried water and chopped wood, not because they were told to, but because, as one of today's elders recalls, they simply felt there was an unspoken expectation that they do their share.[7]

As a child, George learned that when you went to visit friends or relatives, you didn't sit down if you noticed the water pail or wood box was empty. You went out and filled them. It was a tradition George later attributed to giving societies, where you returned the gift of hospitality with the gift of your labour.[8]

Boys of eight or nine were also expected to fish and hunt. George's cousin, Mary Pierrish (now Thomas), who spent a great deal of time living at Dick Andrew's house, remembers that the young George Manuel often headed off with his grandfather's rifle early in the morning and hunted all day on the forested slopes on the west side of the mountain ridge.

Even at that age, it was a source of embarrassment to come home empty-handed. As George later told Mary Thomas, he would sometimes get so desperate when he saw the sun beginning to set that he would shoot a rabbit because "at least you can make a pot of rabbit stew. At least it's something you can put on the table."[9]

While George Manuel was living with his grandparents, he was also expected to help his mother and stepfather up at the farm. Louis Manuel drove him hard in field work. One of Mary Thomas's most enduring memories of George as a small boy is the sight of him behind a hand-plough and team of horses with his face so encrusted with sweat and dust that all you could see were his eyes.

Along with learning the tough physical skills they would later need to earn their livelihood, the Shuswap children were given moral training through instructional stories that were repeated over and over again. These stories were not, in themselves, didactic; instead, at the end the storyteller would point out "*Tat a mas,*" which means literally "See that man" to show the child that by following the good or bad actions of the people in the story, they would reap the same good or bad consequences.

The young George also learned about the world from the trips he took with his grandfather to surrounding Shuswap villages to attend councils of elders or to make medicine for those who were still suspicious of white doctors.

George Manuel always spoke with great respect about Dick Andrew's traditional healing. He rejected the term medicine man or shaman, describing his grandfather instead as an Indian doctor or psychologist. "He talked to his patients and he listened to them. . . . The songs and rituals were one way of drawing out the anxiety and pains."[10]

The Shuswap children of George's generation were also exposed to the political discourse of their people in the large community gatherings. One of the provincial leaders who visited Neskainlith was Andy Paull, who later became George Manuel's first political model and mentor. But during the 1920s, the most influential leader on the local scene was George Manuel's great-uncle, William Pierrish, a First World War veteran who had lost an arm in the service of the King and who decided that it was time that the King and the Dominion government paid some of their outstanding debts to the First Nations.

George Manuel and his generation learned about the political struggle in the same way they learned about other aspects of life: by watching and listening.

» «

At the turn of the century, it was widely assumed by the Dominion government that the "Indian problem" would soon solve itself, as native people, who were considered an "inferior race," gradually died off from white man's diseases. The few survivors would then be absorbed into the larger society and the Indian nations would disappear into the mists of time.

These expectations were stated most clearly by the Department of Indian Affairs deputy superintendent, Duncan Campbell Scott, who wrote that his goal was "to continue until there is not a single Indian in Canada that has not been absorbed into the body politic and there is no Indian question, and no Indian Department."[11] The government was confident that the Department would succeed in these goals. In the House of Commons during this period, the Indian question had less to do with the fate of the First Nations than with the division of their lands once they were finally assimilated.

After the First World War, however, it became clear that neither the Indian people nor the Indian land question were about to go away. Indian populations and Indian militancy were growing across the country and the returning Indian veterans, like William Pierrish, were spearheading the movement.

The Pierrishes were one of the most important families in the community. The younger generation of Pierrishes had been deeply influenced by the traditional views of Dick Andrew. William, his brother François and sister Christine had spent several years at his house in the 1890s after their mother, Macreet's sister, died in a canoeing accident.

François Pierrish was the first to rise to a position of leadership; he was elected as Neskainlith band chief in 1914. But when the First World War broke out he and his brother William, and Dick Andrew and Macreet's three sons, Joe, Harry and Aleck, all enlisted in the 42nd Forestry Brigade and were sent overseas to the battlefields in France.

François returned without physical scars but he had been deeply affected by the horrors of three years in the trenches. He resumed his job as the Neskainlith band chief but he couldn't put the war behind him. In 1921, the sight of a seaplane flying over his field caused him to have a flashback that was followed by a complete mental and physical breakdown that ended with his death a few weeks later.[12]

William Pierrish had lost an arm in the fighting in France, but his experiences turned him into a political activist. He took over as band chief after François' death and he turned Neskainlith into a political outpost for the recently formed Allied Tribes of British Columbia.

The Allied Tribes was made up of sixteen tribal groups that were preoccupied by the so-called "BC land question." Unlike Ontario, the Maritimes and the Prairie Provinces, where colonial authorities signed treaties with the First Nations, the BC authorities had not made formal arrangements for extinguishing aboriginal title.

The Allied Tribes enjoyed widespread support from grass-roots Indian communities. In Neskainlith, Chief William Pierrish arranged to have a horn sounded to call the people from the hills when one of the organizers visited the community. Today's elders remember that when the call came, everyone, young and old, streamed down the hillside to the community hall near the river to attend the meeting. [13]

By all accounts, they were lively affairs, especially when the Squamish leader, Andy Paull, was present. Along with being a key organizer for the Allied Tribes, Paull was a sports reporter for *The Vancouver Sun* and a boxing and lacrosse coach. In Vancouver, he had a reputation as a flamboyant dresser, which complemented his flamboyant personality. But when he was on the stump for the Allied Tribes, he dressed in country clothes and relied on his considerable skill as an orator, in both Chinook and English, to entertain the people by verbally shadow-boxing with the white authorities, poking fun at their pretensions and jabbing at their stubborn refusal to obey their own laws of land ownership when it came to the First Nations' lands.

The Allied Tribes' main strategy at the time was to put the BC Indians' case for aboriginal title before the Privy Council in London. The organization appeared to be on the right track in 1921 when the Privy Council ruled that a Nigerian tribal group did, indeed, retain aboriginal title to their land because the colonial authorities had never signed a treaty with them.

In 1926, Chief William Pierrish travelled to London with two other BC chiefs to deliver a petition to the King demanding the restoration of their land and sovereignty under the same conditions that the Nigerians had won. The petition stated that "We Indians want our native titles to our native lands, and all our land contains as we are the original people of Canada. We Indians want our consent before laws are made upon our possessions."

As a war veteran, Chief William Pierrish was also concerned about a government plan to automatically enfranchise (remove the Indian status from) all the Indians who had served in the war. So the concluding paragraph of the petition stated: "We do not want enfranchisement, we want to be Indians to the end of the world."[14]

The delegation was intercepted in London by the head of the Canadian High Commission who promised to deliver the documents to the King. He then persuaded Chief Pierrish and the others to return to Canada and take up the matter with the Dominion government.

There is no evidence that the High Commissioner delivered the petition to the Crown or the Foreign Office, but shortly after William Pierrish and the others returned to Canada, a meeting was arranged between the federal government and the leaders of the Allied Tribes.

By the time the Allied Tribes delegation reached Ottawa in the spring of 1927, however, the deck had already been stacked against it. British Columbia had a large contingent of MPs ready to pounce on the Indian leaders at every turn, and when the meeting began, Duncan Campbell Scott stood up to dismiss the case of Indian land ownership out of hand, even before the Indians were allowed to speak.[15]

Not surprisingly, the land claim was turned down by the committee because, as Duncan Campbell Scott later explained to Andy Paull, "if Indians were to get the kind of decision to which you are entitled – you would smash Confederation."[16]

Ottawa then moved quickly to ensure that the First Nations would never again be a threat to confederation by enacting a law that made it illegal for anyone, Indian or white, to solicit funds from Indians for the purpose of pursuing land claims. For the Allied Tribes and similar organizations that depended on grass-roots funding, it was a death knell. Indian resistance had been made all but illegal in Canada, and it would remain so for the next quarter century.

At the same time, the Department of Indian Affairs was putting into place a systematic campaign to contain any expansion of First Nations' social and economic rights.

During the mid- and late 1920s, Parliament enacted a web of new restrictions on everything from the right of Indians to assemble, and to sell their farm produce off the reserve to the right to spend more than two hours a day in a pool hall. One of the most harmful results of these measures was to transform the local Indian agent from an irritation to a kind of overlord who controlled the minutiae of the peoples' daily lives.

By 1930, the post-First World War Indian movement was in tatters. Until the early 1950s, when the proscription on Indian organizing was lifted, the movement would remain in a kind of legislated *grand moirceur*, while successive federal governments continued to chip away at the native land base and historic rights.

George Manuel remembered feeling this sense of growing encirclement by outside forces while he was growing up. In 1930, when he was nine years old, he and his grandfather were travelling by wagon to visit a neighbouring Shuswap village and they were stopped by two uniformed men, either RCMP or local forestry officers, who were looking for fish or game taken illegally. The men rifled through their belongings and dumped some of the bundles on the wet ground, then roughly ordered them to proceed.

After they had repacked the wagon, Dick Andrew was silent for a long time. Then he spoke: "You can't hunt deer except when the towns-folk are in the bush, during what they decide is the right time to hunt. You can't bring down a bird to feed yourself when you're trapping. You can only fish four days a week, and they choose the days. Now they show us better ways to use nets and then say we can't use them. . . . Now they only want us to eat what we buy in their stores or grow with their tools."[17]

The words were spoken with weariness, but somehow Dick Andrew held out a hope that the Shuswap people would one day win back their nationhood. He made this point to George and his cousin Mary one evening when he took them by their hands and, in an almost storybook fashion, recited a "weird chant" and told them that one day they would have to fight for their people.[18]

Years later, when George Manuel was faced with a choice that amounted to his family or his political work, Mary reminded him of his grandfather's words; she believes this helped him carry on with his political struggle.[19]

For the nine-year-old George Manuel, the personal struggle with the outside world began a few months later when a cattle truck pulled up to the reserve and the Indian Agent called out the list of names of the children who were to be shipped off to the Kamloops residential school. George's name was on the list. He was about to be thrown into what he later called "the laboratory and the production line of the colonial system."[20]

» «

The arrival of the truck was a traumatic moment for the whole community. A Shuswap woman who attended the school around the same time as George Manuel recalled that many of the younger children viewed their forced departure as a punishment for something they had done wrong. On her first day, "[the kids] they're all bawling . . . and Mums crying, and I can remember [saying] 'What'd I ever do to you? Why are you sending me away?'"[21]

For some of the older children, the truck was greeted by a different set of emotions. After spending eleven months a year at the school for up to ten years, they had become more accustomed to residential school life than to life in their own community. For many, the English language was replacing Shuswap as the first language that came to their lips. As George Manuel later observed, after "learning to see and hear only what the priests and brothers wanted you to see and hear, even the people we loved came to look ugly."[22]

For the schools, the students who turned their backs on their parents and grandparents were the success stories. This showed that the policy of "aggressive civilization" was working, and once the children's pride in their Indianness was stamped out, it was an easy task to undermine their traditional culture and values.

The Kamloops school was run by the Catholic Oblate order, who were assisted on the girls' side by the Sisters of Saint Anne. Their monopoly over the Shuswap young would last until the 1960s and it was, as George Manuel saw it, "the greatest gift the Dominion of Canada made to the Church." In later years, he would suggest that native people should launch a class-action lawsuit against the Vatican for the abuse generations of Indian children suffered at the hands of the priests, Christian Brothers and nuns.[23]

That abuse included poor diet, a proscription on the Indian language, forced labour and a military-style discipline that was enforced by beatings.

One student of the Kamloops school recalls that the whole purpose of the institution seemed to be to crush their pride in themselves as Indians. During the daily religious services the priests would "hammer it into our heads that we were not to think or act or speak like an Indian. And that we would go to hell and burn for eternity if we did not listen to their way of teaching."[24]

This assault on his people was particularly confusing for George Manuel, who was brought up in the strong moral atmosphere of his grandfather's teachings where "purity was a state of being within yourself."[25]

The teachers at the school portrayed men like Dick Andrew, who refused to embrace the Church, in demonic terms. Mary Thomas, who went to the school at the same time as George, but who lived on the segregated girls' side, remembers that after many years at the school, she began to see her grandfather through the eyes of her teachers. During her visits home, when she heard her grandfather chanting or singing the old Shuswap songs, she imagined that it was the devil himself who was speaking.

At the same time, the students were given very little in the way of useful academic instruction. After their morning allotment of fire and brimstone, most of the day on the boys' side was taken up in hard labour on the school farm while the girls were given cooking and sewing classes. George Manuel recalled that there was so little time spent in actual learning that after two years at the school he could barely write his own name.

What he and most other students remember most clearly and painfully about the school was not the hard work, which was at times spurred on by beatings, but the hunger. After eating only a ladle of porridge for breakfast and a ladle of watery stew and a piece of bread for lunch, supper was another ladle of stew and another piece of bread.

As George Manuel put it, "hunger is both the first and last thing I can remember about that school. . . . Not just me. Every Indian student smelled of hunger."[26]

As a result, the students were forced to steal food, pick berries and wild vegetables and in some cases even eat cattle feed to survive.

The hard work and poor food also contributed to the high incidence of illness, but medical care was almost non-existent. During his first year at the school, George Manuel developed mastoiditis, a painful infection of the inner ear. The condition usually requires surgery, but for the young Shuswap boy, the priests didn't even bother to call a doctor. Instead, he was laid out on a table while the priest operated on him with a kitchen knife, and without anaesthetic.[27]

It was a more serious illness, however, that allowed George Manuel to escape the full brunt of the priests' and the Christian Brothers' teachings and what he always described as the darkest years of his life. It began during his second summer at home when a bad-tempered reserve dog bit a chunk out of his hip. When he climbed onto the cattle truck at the end of the vacation, the wound had swollen into a hard lump. Throughout that autumn, he felt a continuing soreness in his hip; then he developed a slight fever and began to lose weight.

Finally, one winter morning, he could not raise himself from his cot and a doctor was called in to confirm what most of the Brothers suspected. The Shuswap kid had contracted the white plague: tuberculosis. In his case, it was tuberculosis of the hip, or osteomyelitis. At the age of twelve, he began an almost decade-long battle for his life, fighting a disease that was becoming the scourge of his people.

## CHAPTER THREE

# White Plague, Red Victims
## 1932-1954

If the Indian race is a degenerated race, I am afraid that the whole effort is wasted. It may or may not be that a remnant of the race can be saved; I am not convinced one way or another.

> Agnes Macphail
> House of Commons Debates, 31 Mar. 1930

When George Manuel was officially diagnosed as having tuberculosis, he was shipped off to the Coqualeetza Preventoria in southern BC. At the time, Coqualeetza, which means "meadowlark" in the local Sto:lo language, was staffed by Protestant missionaries and financed by an Indian Affairs grant of ten cents a day per patient.

Despite its poetic name, Coqualeetza had a ghoulish reputation among the interior Indians as a place from which few returned. Government statistics show that the Indian death rate was twenty times higher than that of whites. In sheer numbers, TB killed almost as many Indians in British Columbia in the twentieth century as smallpox had killed in the nineteenth. In extreme cases, whole families were dying from the disease; the worst hit community was the Kootenay Arrow Lake band, where only one band member survived into the 1940s. [1]

Each year, the mounting number of cases was discussed in the House of Commons as part of the debate over the Indian Affairs budget. Yet despite the havoc TB was wreaking on the native people, virtually nothing was done to slow its progress. As in the case of the smallpox epidemic, Canadian authorities spoke in vague terms of Indians being "naturally subject to the disease"[2] and seemed prepared to let nature take its course.

The real reason for the severity of the epidemic among Indians as compared to whites was as simple as the difference in the living conditions and care given to the two groups. By the 1930s, most whites were inoculated against the disease, and in high-risk areas x-rays were taken annually. Those who did contract TB were sent to sanatoria where they received the best care available at the time.

Native people, on the other hand, were denied the vaccine and few were x-rayed. When a full-blown case was detected, they were not sent to the modern sanatoria because Indian Affairs refused to pay the price. Instead, they were sent to church-run "preventoria," which were little more than isolation hostels where care consisted of Our Fathers and bed rest.

The causes of the steep Indian death rate were known as early as 1932, when the president of the Saskatchewan Anti-Tuberculosis League began an experimental program at the Fort Qu'Appelle Indian Hospital. He gave regular x-rays to the local Indian children and administered the BCG vaccination that was available to whites. Not surprisingly, the infection and death rates dropped dramatically, but it was to be more than a decade before the government would spend the small amount of money to extend the program to Indians across the country. This negligence resulted in the death of thousands of people, with children accounting for two-thirds of the fatalities.

Yet despite the pain and the gravity of the disease, George Manuel would come to look on it as his salvation because it allowed him to escape from the soul-destroying residential school. At Coqualeetza, he was spared the Christian Brothers' unrelenting attacks on his Indianness. The food was more varied and plentiful and he was able to meet Indian children his own age from all corners of the province, from Protestant as well as Catholic communities. He also met individual whites who, unlike the Christian Brothers, treated him and his people with respect. He remembered with fondness the "hundreds of simple acts of kindness" of the nurses and the fact that they taught him how to read, brought him books and games and taught him to use his enforced quiet to his own advantage.[3]

It was during these years that much of George Manuel's future character was set. The pain of his illness, the inactivity and the long periods of reflection forced him to develop an inner life and a degree of self-knowledge that few people who have not survived a long illness ever achieve. These lessons came at a high physical price, however, as the bacteria's assault on his body left him with a badly twisted hip and a severe life-long limp.

George had his first chance to test his hip when he was fifteen years old and was allowed to return to Neskainlith for a visit. It had been more than five years since the cattle truck had taken him away to the residential school, but the initial pleasure of his return was marred by the changes he saw in the community. The combination of hard economic times, increasing restrictions on hunting and fishing, and a young generation that had been deculturalized by the years at the residential school had begun to break the circle that kept families and the community together.

He noticed that people were drinking on the reserve, something that had been rare only six years earlier. Since Indians were forbidden to drink legal alcohol, they drank overproofed home brew, known locally as Chilcotin mickeys, that quickly led to stone-drunkenness and all too often to outbursts of violence.

During the 1930s, the young people who had passed through the residential school also began to spend more and more time in Chase, but they soon found that the town held little promise for them. The poor quality of their education and the racism in Canadian society made employment in the white world almost impossible, even for the school's graduates. They were, George Manuel said, "equally unfit to live in an Indian world or a European world."[4] The young people had learned contempt for their own community and families, and yet when they went into Chase they were expected to sit in the back rows of the movie theatre. Afterwards, if they wanted to buy a soft drink before heading back to the reserve, there was only one restaurant, the most run-down greasy spoon in town, that would serve them. If Indians tried to go to one of the better restaurants they were either asked to leave or were simply left unserved until they gave up and slipped away.

This unofficial Jim Crow was not limited to Chase or to British Columbia. The same unwritten rules were in effect across Canada, with most restaurants, almost all hotels and, of course, all beer parlours strictly off limits to native people.

George Manuel noted, "You did not have to have an advanced political consciousness to realize how wretched and despised our people were in the eyes of the white men who held the power in the area. . . . For a long time this seemed to me just a part of the way things were, like the distance to town or the rain that soaked you on the way home."[5]

George Manuel spent the rest of the 1930s moving back and forth between Neskainlith and Coqualeetza. He was back in Ncskainlith in 1939 when the Second World War broke out and, like most young Canadian men, he reported to the local recruitment office where he was quickly turned away because of his twisted hip.

The war did open up an opportunity for him to get his first job, however. With another generation of young men heading overseas, George Manuel's doctor was able to arrange for him to be hired as a busboy at the white sanatorium at Tranquille, across the river from Kamloops. His status was little different from the other ambulatory patients, except he paid for his care with a few hours of work each day in the cafeteria.

He was at the hospital in 1941 when Dick Andrew died at the age of 101. The old man had reportedly spent his last day walking several kilometres to visit his daughter, Maria, then coming back home where he had dinner and died that night in his sleep.

The death was a major loss to the whole community. He was, as Mary Thomas had said, "everybody's grandfather." Dick Andrew provided the people with a living link to the time when the Shuswap were masters of their own lives and their own lands. For George Manuel, the old man's death was also the death of his father and teacher. For the rest of his life, he used the memory of his grandfather as a kind of beacon to guide him through the often rough personal and political waters he traversed.

» «

George Manuel did not have to face these personal challenges alone, however. At Coqualeetza, he had developed a close friendship with Marceline Paul, a Kootenay from the Cranbrook area who worked in the hospital kitchen. Like him, she had a limp. In her case it was caused by a dislocated hip in infancy that was left untreated because medical care was not available to her people.

George had first spotted her from his hospital window at Coqualeetza. When he found out her name, he began to shout

"Marceline!" whenever he saw her. Initially, Marceline was too shy to respond, but George persisted until she went to visit him in the ward. Marceline had also been raised by her grandparents and was strongly influenced by traditional values. She had suffered through the abuses of residential schools, including sexual abuse, and despite the horrors of that experience, had retained a deep sense of compassion for others. She and George immediately became soul mates in the dreary setting of Coqualeetza.

Even after George went to Kamloops they stayed in close contact and made plans to get married. That event was hastened when Marceline discovered her parents were arranging for her to marry a Kootenay man. Her response was to hop on a bus and go to live with George in Kamloops. They were married soon after.

Their first child, Annie, was born in April 1945, but the happiness over the event was dampened a few weeks later when George was laid off from his job at the sanatorium and he found himself out in the street with a bad leg, a grade-two education and a young family to support.

At the time, fruit growers were one of the few large-scale employers of Indians in southern BC and the northwestern United States; so that spring, George bought a battered old car and headed south, with Marceline and Annie, in search of work in the orchards of Washington State.

While he was busy working on that fall's harvest, tragedy struck the young family when Annie died suddenly of crib death. George and Marceline wanted to bury her in Neskainlith, rather than in a foreign land, so they brought her coffin home in the trunk of the car and laid her to rest on the hills above the community, before making a sad return to the orchards in the south.

A year later, when Marceline became pregnant a second time, they returned to Neskainlith. Louis Manuel and Maria had moved to Kamloops several years before, so George settled on the family land and built a makeshift one-room house which, like the one Rainbow Manuel had built thirty years earlier, lacked indoor plumbing, running water and electricity.

Once again, George Manuel was faced with the prospect of finding work. But this time, he turned his attention across the river to the lumber mill that was running full tilt in the post-war boom.

Until then, few Indians had been hired to full-time positions at the mill, although a number were employed as seasonal workers hauling and rafting logs. But George Manuel limped in and announced that he wanted a job as boom man, one of the best jobs on the river. And one of the toughest.

The boom man was responsible for keeping the logs moving into the mill pond and up the jack ladder, a sort of spiked conveyor belt that hoisted the logs into the mill. Boom men, it was said, had to learn to "walk on water" by leaping from slippery log to slippery log to reach the jams. Despite the fact that it required a great deal of agility and was generally reserved for whites, George Manuel was determined to get the job.

He felt that he had proved himself as worker in Washington, where he had been promoted to crew foreman, and thought he deserved a shot at a job on the river. It is a testament to the forcefulness of the young Shuswap man's personality that he convinced the mill foreman to give him a chance, despite his crippled leg and the company's preference for hiring whites.

The foreman would not regret his decision. Men who worked with George Manuel remember that he was a tireless worker who became the local expert at jam busting. If he wasn't around when the logs twisted into a Chinese puzzle at the river mouth, someone would be sent to get him because he was often the only one who could figure out how to untangle the mess.

Manuel's work days were long and demanding, but after his shift he would head back across the river to work his father's land. It had not been tilled in years and he had to struggle to break the ground, seed the hay field and repair the damaged fences.

At the same time, he and Marceline were also busy raising their family. Their second child, Bob, was born in 1947, followed by Arnold, a year later.

Arnold was never very healthy, however, and he died suddenly when he was two months old, thus compounding George and Marceline's grief over Annie. It was a difficult time for both of them and during this period the household was a sombre one. The sadness was gradually lifted in 1948 when their second daughter, Vera, was born and she was followed by Arthur in 1950, Doreen in 1951 and Arlene in 1953.

As his family grew, George built a couple of additions to the back of his house and his friends began to joke that if he had any more children, his house would reach all the way to Skunk Hollow. Eventually, they bought a strip of reserve land on the town side of the river where he built a larger house. This one had electricity, but it still lacked running water.

The Manuel children remember that life was tough in those early years and that their father was strict. George had worked hard during his own childhood and he expected the kids to pitch in and help around the house in the same way. Bob Manuel remembers that when he was still quite young he and Vera were given small buckets to fetch water, and as they grew older, the buckets got bigger and they were expected to trot off down to the river, past the large round hole of Dick Andrew's *kekuli*, to get water for the family.

They were all preoccupied with making ends meet. To earn some extra money in the late fall, George, Marceline and the children went up into the bush behind the house and cut Christmas trees. During freeze-up, when things were slow at the mill, George travelled 500 miles north to Athelmere, where he cut Christmas trees for a contractor. While he was gone, Marceline would bundle up the kids, grab the double-edged saw and cut the trees herself; the children helped to haul them out of the bush.

In fact, life for the family was not much easier than it had been when George and Marceline Manuel were growing up in the 1920s. In many ways it had become worse. While the Canadian economy was going through a rapid post-war expansion, Indian people were still excluded from the political and economic mainstream and their small reserves made it impossible for them to achieve a viable economic base for their communities.

The economic crisis drove many more Indians into the slums of the city, while at the community level, the cumulative effect was a permeating sense of defeatism and despair. It was a time when Colonel Jones's Indian agents ruled at the reserve level and the band councillors and even chiefs were expected to stand hat in hand outside the Agent's office waiting for an audience. When the people went to town, they walked with their eyes downcast to avoid making eye contact with whites, not so much because they feared an attack (although this certainly happened on occasion) but simply to avoid the insulting glance they would get in return.

George Manuel experienced this political malaise in Neskainlith first hand when he began to concern himself with the fifteen km irrigation system that the community had built with picks and shovels in the 1920s to link Neskainlith Lake and Adams Lake. The system required a great deal of upkeep but, as with many other community initiatives, people no longer bothered to take care of it. When George Manuel called a meeting on the subject, no one even showed up.

It was, Manuel remembered, the worst of times, with his people reduced to "a condition of . . . servitude, and dependence."[7] But this growing despair he saw in his Shuswap nation was also slowly drawing him toward his political vocation. In the meantime, the burden of leadership was still being carried on the shoulders of Andy Paull.

» «

A few years after the imposition of restrictions on Indian fund-raising and the collapse of the Allied Tribes, Andy Paull was back in business with a new organization, the Progressive Native Tribes of British Columbia. He travelled regularly to Ottawa to speak on behalf of BC Indians, addressing such issues as civil rights and the growing hunger in Indian communities caused by the Depression. In the late 1930s, he forged a short-lived alliance with the more conservative Native Brotherhood in an attempt to bring together the interior and coastal peoples.

The Native Brotherhood had been founded in 1931 to represent the coastal Indians who, unlike the Catholic interior Indians, had been influenced by the Protestant missionaries. When Paull's association with the Native Brotherhood failed, he formed two new organizations, the Confederacy of the Interior Tribes of British Columbia and the North American Indian Brotherhood (NAIB), with representatives from Quebec, Ontario, Saskatchewan and BC.

Both Paull's NAIB and the Native Brotherhood were trying to take advantage of the movement for post-war reform. This spirit could be seen in an article published in *The Canadian Forum*, that cited parallels between Canada's Indian policy and the racial policy of the European Fascists. Canada's attitude towards the Indian nations, it was suggested, traditionally fell into two categories. The first and most blatantly racist went something like:

"Treat your Indian like your dog, kindly but firmly. You must sometime give him the whip, but if you're kind, he'll be faithful."

The second view was a paternalistic one that suggested that Indians be raised "into a civil and industrious people, by introducing the English language among them; and thereby instilling into their minds and hearts, with a more lasting impression, the principles of virtue and piety."

Both versions, the article stated, bespoke the "complacent racial superiority which we dislike so much in other people that we're willing to fight a war with them about it."[8]

Similar articles began to appear in *Saturday Night* magazine and the major dailies. In the late 1940s, the government responded by setting up a special Joint Committee of the Senate and House of Commons to review the Indian Act. In a precedent-setting move, the Joint Committee invited Indian organizations from across the country to make submissions.

The federal government was also putting pressure on the BC legislature to lift the prohibition on voting in provincial and municipal elections for Canadians of Chinese, Japanese and Indo-Pakistan descent. BC responded by enfranchising not only the immigrant communities, but by giving the vote to the Indians. The Native Brotherhood welcomed the move. In the 1949 provincial election, one of its leaders, Frank Calder, presented himself as the CCF candidate in a BC riding with an Indian majority and won a seat in the legislature.

Andy Paull, on the other hand, vigorously opposed Indian participation in any Canadian elections. By doing so, he feared, they risked losing their special status within Confederation.

The division between Paull and the Native Brotherhood was one that went much further than the voting issue and reflected two very different positions on native rights. Along with many other Indian leaders of the day, the Native Brotherhood's leadership saw the Indian struggle largely as a civil rights issue and focused on winning native people equal rights with whites.

While Paull never missed a chance to fight for civil rights, he saw the issue as only a part of a larger native struggle. It was not enough that Indians win equal individual rights to whites, they must also have their aboriginal rights recognized. When Indians met whites on what would become known as a "nation-to-nation" basis, only then could they negotiate fair land settlements and ensure the survival of their people.

Understandably, the government was much more amenable to the civil rights arguments. The 1951 Amendments to the Indian Act contained measures like the lifting of restrictions on Indian organizing and on potlatch ceremonies. It also gave Indians the right to consume alcohol in beer parlours, but continued to forbid them the right to drink at home on the reserves or in private clubs like the Legion.

At the same time that it offered these minor reforms, the new Act also contained limitations on band council powers and opened up, for the first time, the possibility of non-Indians purchasing Indian lands.

Paull was immediately on the attack. He dismissed the new Act as a sham and charged that "White people have not yet paid for this country. They must treat us in a decent way, not wield dictatorial powers over us." [9]

Andy Paull still had the intellectual fire to lead the battle against the new Indian Act, but his health was beginning to fail. He continued to be a factor on the BC Indian scene for the next several years but his energies were ebbing and this was creating an opening in BC Indian politics for a new leader to emerge.

George Manuel, at home in Neskainlith and becoming increasingly frustrated by the condition of his people, was beginning to look around for a solution to their problems. Mary Thomas remembers that when their two families got together, the discussion around the kitchen table often turned to the plight of their people. She remembers the bitterness in George's voice when he observed that the only Shuswap accepted in the white man's world were the Indian girls who were forced into prostitution on the streets of Vancouver. They wondered how they could fight the white man, who had all of the power, education and wealth. The only solution they found was to use their own kind of strength, the kind they had inherited from their grandfather, but neither of them knew quite how to begin. [10]

For George Manuel, however, the call was clearly there. His grandfather had told him he would be a leader some day and that prophesy was reinforced in the mid-1950s when Michel Anthony, a respected Shuswap elder, summoned George to his bedside where he was holding a "death court." George hurried over with his son Bob, who recalls feeling frightened at the sight of the dying man and by the sound of his raspy breathing. The eeriness of the moment only increased when he heard the old man tell the small group at the bedside that George Manuel was going to be a great leader some day so he should be treated with respect. [11]

Michel Anthony's prophesy had come at an opportune time. In 1955,

George Manuel was thirty-four years old. He had built a life for himself and his family. He had proved himself in the often uncompromising world of working-class whites and he felt he was ready to step forward and assume the mantle of leadership.

George Manuel's entry into the political fray began a few months later, when his son Arthur had been sent to hospital for a tonsillectomy. After Arthur returned home, George Manuel was surprised to see the family doctor, James Treloar, drive up to the house.

Dr. Treloar showed him a letter from the Department of Indian Affairs stating that it would no longer pay the medical costs of gainfully employed Indians. At first, George thought the doctor was suggesting he was a dead-beat and insisted he would pay the bill. But that was not why Treloar had come. He knew George, with his boom man job, could afford to pay. But Treloar was concerned that if he did, the government would try to force the rest of the band to do the same, including those who were unemployed or only seasonally employed.

The doctor's warning drew George Manuel up short. After Treloar left he discussed the matter with Marceline. She took Treloar's warning seriously and was concerned about what the new policy would mean to her people. After all, she was going through life with a limp because medical care had been denied her and she was determined that the same injustice would not be visited on another generation.

George agreed and sat down to write a letter to the one man he knew could offer him guidance: Andy Paull.

Although Paull was in poor health, he responded quickly. "If you pay, you will be fighting me on this issue because I have already taken the government up on it."[12] George Manuel would never have considered fighting Andy Paull on any issue so he decided he would refuse to pay the bill. When others in the community heard of Manuel's decision, they began to show up at his house with their own medical bills and George realized that the doctor had been right. He found that "the poorest people, who had not had a cash-paying job in years, came around with bills in their hand and the most worried looks on their faces."[13]

To each of them, George Manuel relayed Andy Paull's blunt message: "Don't pay."

With those two words the South Thompson River boom man had taken his first political stand. He would never stand down.

## CHAPTER FOUR

# Local Agitator to Provincial Leader
## 1955-1960

British Columbia for British Columbians – White Man Go Home!

Banner at 1959 NAIB Convention

Word of George Manuel's defiance quickly reached the office of Fred Clark, the Indian agent in Kamloops. Clark had already arranged with the local chiefs to let the new regulations pass without public debate, and George Manuel's refusal was a stick in his spokes. To prevent the issue from getting away from him, Clark called a snap meeting on the Adams Lake reserve, the Shuswap community adjacent to Neskainlith, to get quick public approval for the rule change.

George Manuel heard about the meeting after he had arrived in Athelmere to cut Christmas trees and he jumped back into his car and drove all night to attend. He was surprised to see that the hall was packed, and for the first time he understood just how important the issue was for his people. He also learned a number of other valuable lessons that night. When he walked into the hall, Fred Clark was sitting at a table at the front. He was about to bring the meeting to order when he spotted George Manuel in the crowd. He paused, then announced that there was someone from another reserve who didn't belong there and he asked the band council to order him out.

Everyone knew Clark was referring to George Manuel, and there was a moment of silence. But for George Manuel it was a moment of clarity. He remembered the village meetings of his youth when the people gathered together on their own to decide issues by consensus. Now a white bureaucrat sat in front of them like a stern schoolmaster deciding who would speak and even who could stay in the room and listen. George Manuel was tired from the all-night drive, but when he stepped forward he let loose a lifetime of frustration.

"Mr. Clark," he began, "you're a gutless son of a bitch."

Then he launched into a long rambling speech, the first he'd made in his life, in which he offered a litany of complaints, threatened to organize all the Indians in British Columbia and told Clark that he had been chosen to act as spokesman at the meeting.[1]

Clark understood the importance of the last statement. The spokesman was traditionally one of the most trusted and widely respected men in the community because it was to him that the people turned to negotiate with outsiders.

Clark apparently suspected that Manuel was bluffing because he asked around the room if it was true. After a moment of hesitation, one of the chiefs spoke up and said yes, George Manuel was their spokesman.

Rather than standing up to Manuel and arguing the medical bill issue, Clark brought the meeting to a close. According to some observers, George Manuel was the first interior Indian to challenge the Indian agent's authority directly and around the Agency it sparked rumours that he was a "Marxist," a serious charge in the Cold War paranoia of the 1950s.[2]

For George Manuel, though, the confrontation with Clark was a step toward his political vocation. He discovered that if the people stood together they could make the white man back down. He also discovered that he could be a spokesman, a leader in his peoples' struggles, and he decided to put his new-found talent to work.

His initial task, he decided, would be to overcome the decades of frustration that had led to a profound sense of apathy that weighed on his peoples' public and private lives. He would have to rekindle the sense of community he had known when he was growing up in the 1920s, so he set out to organize as many community events as he could think of.

He began with sporting events. He started a fund-raising drive for the local baseball team and then launched a local hockey team, the

Shuswap Maple Leafs, where he served as manager, coach and even, on occasion, the back-up goalie.

One of the Indian players George Manuel recruited was his half-brother Joe Manuel (son of Maria and Louis), who had worked as a rodeo rider on the northwestern United States professional circuit before returning to Neskainlith. Joe Manuel was a natural athlete and he was a welcome addition to the hockey team that became a fan favourite among the interior Indians.[3]

Along with sporting events, George Manuel also brought Indian musicians into the community. His favourite band was one that featured Chief Dan George playing bass fiddle with his two sons on guitar. George Manuel and Chief Dan George, who later went on to international acclaim as an actor, developed a close friendship, and during the late 1950s and early 1960s, George acted as his booking agent in the interior.[4]

He also became a member and later the president of the local chapter of the Legion of Mary, a Catholic lay society, because, in his words, he "hoped that the outreach . . . would provide [entry] into every corner of the community,"[5] and that the respectability of the church-sponsored society would give him more credibility in his organizing work.

These outside activities still had to be fitted around his shift at the mill, where he had also managed to get his half-brother Joe hired on. Joe Manuel remembers that booming was a tough job, even for a young man like him, and he was duly impressed by his older brother's stamina and by the respect shown to him by the white workers George Manuel over-saw on the jam-busting jobs. One of his favourite memories of his brother is as a stocky brush-cutted boom man standing on the shore shouting to the white workers to "pull out that log . . . now the one in the middle . . . and the one to the left," and then, miraculously, the jammed logs would suddenly break free.[6]

After their arduous shift on the river, most of the workers would head over to the hotel for a couple of beers, but George Manuel headed home, had a quick supper and then went to his room where he would work on his new-found political vocation, often until well after midnight.

Along with organizing community events he had begun writing letters to federal and provincial departments about the day-to-day concerns of his people – like the need for better irrigation equipment, repairs to the bridge between the reserve and Chase and support for the local widows.

These exchanges turned out to be valuable in the long run as they gave him an idea of the various government departments and how they worked. But the experience also showed him that he lacked some of the basic tools for the leadership task he had set himself. Typically, he didn't try to hide his weaknesses, but confronted them and went to look for someone who could help him overcome them.

For help with his writing skills, he went to the pool hall owner, Paul Paulsen, a Danish immigrant who had married a local girl and moved to Chase a few months earlier. Paulsen had an easy-going nature and none of the anti-Indian prejudice that infected the local population, and he agreed to lend a hand.

George Manuel's first letters were little more than handwritten scrawls. Paulsen showed him the proper way to set up a letter and after cleaning up the grammar, typed it out for him. Eventually, George Manuel bought his own second-hand Underwood and became a proficient two-finger typist. His children remember that most nights they fell asleep to the persistent clackety-clack of the typewriter.

In later years, George Manuel greatly improved his writing skills by going back to night school; he also worked on his speaking ability by enrolling in the local Toastmaster's Club. As the members of the Joint Parliamentary Committee were soon to find out, George Manuel was a natural public speaker and he later won a province-wide speaking competition.

In one of the stranger twists during this period, George Manuel also found himself as a member of the Chase Board of Trade and the local Elks Club. He was invited to join these organizations by Paulsen, and in the end he was able to take something useful from both. His membership in the Board of Trade gave him his first real look at how a formal organization was set up, and through the Elks Club he made connections that he later used for renting the local Elks Hall for public meetings.

Perhaps even more important, the forays into the world of the local businessmen allowed George Manuel to test himself. A few years earlier, he and Mary Thomas had looked at the white elite as a closed society armoured with money, influence and education. But he quickly discovered he and his people were giving them far too much credit. With his grade-two education, he found he could more than hold his own with the local hotel owner, the realtor and the newspaper publisher. (In later years, he would make the same discovery about cabinet ministers and even world leaders whom he met in his travels).

During 1956, George Manuel also began to visit neighbouring reserves to consult with the local leadership or attend local North American Indian Brotherhood meetings. The brakes were gone in his car so he either hitchhiked, spending the night on the road or sleeping in haystacks, or he had his friend, Jacob Kruger, drive him. Soon, the local trips expanded to the point where he and Jacob were driving all over the province. At night they would sleep in churches or in Jacob's car.

While he was exploring the political terrain in BC, George Manuel was also learning about the national Indian struggle from one the greatest experts in the country: Andy Paull. To help the Shuswap boom man in the medical bill issue, Paull contacted the deputy minister of Indian Affairs and told him that the issue was "a matter of grave concern to the Indians of this province as well as on a national scale,"[7] and insisted that the care of Indian health remain the sole responsibility of the Canadian government.

When Andy Paull was in the interior, he also began stopping by to visit George Manuel in Chase. Paull's main concern at the time was the new head of the Indian Affairs Department, Jack Pickersgill, who had shocked the Indian world by announcing that he wanted to abolish the Indian Act, clear out all special legislation concerning aboriginal rights and make Indian people Canadian citizens like everyone else.

Pickersgill's aims were alarmingly similar to D.C. Scott's a generation earlier. As Pickersgill saw it, Canadians should "not be fully satisfied with our Indian policy until the day comes when all the Indians from coast to coast . . . have been integrated with the rest of the population and the Indian Affairs Branch and the office I now hold become merely a part of our history."[8]

On the face of it, the program appealed to small "l" liberals because it spoke of individual equality. But by abolishing the Indian Act and making Indians citizens "like everyone else," the government would be removing the distinct status assigned to Indian lands. Reserves could then be divided up among their members and could be bought and sold on the real estate market where they could fall, piece by piece, to lumber companies, mining companies or neighbouring municipalities.

Some of the older Indian leaders, like the former president of the Native Brotherhood Alfred Scow, predicted that the First Nations would eventually disappear in Canada if the policy was implemented. He asked only that the government lift fishing and hunting restrictions to make life more bearable for the present generation. But Andy Paull reacted with uncontrolled fury. As he told a *Vancouver Sun* reporter, Indians were not interested in following Pickersgill's assimilation program because whites were "the lowest form of animals."[9]

In his discussions with George Manuel, Paull brought him up to date on what was happening in Ottawa and stressed that regardless of whether the government couched its assimilationist ideas in flowery post-war liberal rhetoric or in the domineering language of the past, it had to be resisted at all costs because assimilation meant the annihilation of Indian nations.

George Manuel's discussions with Paull were both invigorating and inspiring, and later he credited Andy Paull as "the spark and the catalyst" who inspired his national vision for the First Nations movement.[10]

For his part, Andy Paull was also impressed with George Manuel's leadership potential and he soon began to invite him along on his tours of the interior. He introduced the South Thompson River boom man to his other NAIB contacts, Jimmy Scotchman and Victor Adolph in Lillooett, Bill and Forrest Walkem in Spence's Bridge, Gus Gottfriedson in Kamloops and Genevieve Mussell in Chilliwack. In the future, they would form the core of George Manuel's political support in the interior as they transferred their allegiance from Paull to him.

One of the more interesting introductions Paull made for George Manuel was to arrange for him to meet Jay Silverheels, the native actor who played Tonto on the Lone Ranger show, when he was visiting Vancouver on a publicity tour. It was the first time Manuel had ever been in the big city and at the time he didn't even own a suit, so he showed up at the Vancouver airport with his friend, Chief Dan George, wearing his work clothes.

The two of them were so naive, George Manuel recalled, that they expected to see not Silverheels, but Tonto himself, wearing moccasins and buckskins and with a feather in his hair. When the Indian actor passed by in a suit, George Manuel and Chief Dan George didn't recognize him. After the plane had emptied, they were told by a customs official that Tonto had already passed through. They caught up to him as he was climbing into a limousine and had to drag him back into the airport so they could properly welcome him with the drumming ceremony they had planned.[11]

Another of Paull's introductions was to bring George Manuel together with the NAIB's young lawyer, Henry Castilliou, Jr., who had been born into the struggle for Indian rights in British Columbia. His father, Judge Henry Castilliou, had been a Native Brotherhood lawyer who had worked with Andy Paull before going on to the provincial bench. Henry Jr. followed in his father's footsteps by going to law school. After a stint in the lumber business, he opened a law office in Vancouver, and called on Andy Paull to offer his legal services, which Paull accepted "as long as they were free."[12]

The meeting between George Manuel and Castilliou took place in Kamloops in 1957. Castilliou remembers that even at that early date, George Manuel was already being tagged as "Andy's man" in the interior. Castilliou's impression of George Manuel was as someone who was very bright, a quick learner, but still rough around the edges."[13]

Castilliou suggests that Andy Paull served as George Manuel's "guru," but it seems that the respect that developed between Paull and Manuel was mutual, because in the fall of 1957, when the NAIB organized a separate Interior Branch, George Manuel emerged as the first president of the region that had always been at the heart of Paull's political base.

Castilliou also began to find a place for George Manuel in his legal work. In his years working with the NAIB, Castilliou never received a salary. Instead, his reputation as a fighter for Indian rights allowed him to make his living defending Indians in criminal trials, which were paid for by the government, while he did his political work for free.

In researching his criminal cases, Castilliou often found it necessary to get a native liaison from the area, but he soon found that he could contract George Manuel to serve as an interpreter and researcher around the province. He recalls that "George could get along anywhere with anyone." Even on the coast, where the people were usually suspicious of the interior Indians, George Manuel "could walk into a beer parlour, sit down and strike up a conversation, and before you knew it, he'd be collecting evidence" that Castilliou says he could not have gotten otherwise.[14]

More often than not they found that the culprit was a batch

of overproof Chilcotin mickeys. Castilliou and others had long argued (as it turned out, correctly) that the murder rate in Indian communities would drop dramatically if the safer government liquor was made available. But the government's refusal to lift the restrictions on selling liquor to Indians outside the beer parlours led to the uncontrolled drunkenness and outbursts of violence that the high-test concoctions caused.

The booze restrictions had a silly as well as tragic side. In his NAIB work, George Manuel often met with both Castillious at the Plaza Hotel where they stayed when they were in Kamloops. They would be having a few beers and when George came in Henry Sr., then a BC court judge, would have to go through the motion of saying, "The beer's in the bathtub, George. I can't offer you one, but we won't see anything, either." [15]

George Manuel had a great respect for the judge. He liked the older man's tough style and no-nonsense approach to politics. He also learned something about guff (don't take it from anyone) when, after a late-night session at the Plaza Hotel, George decided to stay overnight but was refused a room. He was going to let it pass and rent a room at a local flophouse when Judge Castilliou intervened. He raised hell with the manager and got George Manuel a room and a formal apology. After that incident, Manuel never again remained silent when he came across so much as a hint of racism in his daily life.

In his travels with Henry Castilliou, Jr., he was also gaining valuable insights into the inner workings of the legal system. When he started with Castilliou he assumed, as most do, that if you were charged with an offense, you were guilty. From Castilliou, he learned the subtleties of the law and the ways it could be used to free as well as convict the accused. These legal lessons with Castilliou would serve Manuel well in his later work, when he was locked in a series of legal battles with the federal and BC governments.

The travels with Castilliou were also used for a little NAIB politicking and at times they ran into trouble from the rival Native Brotherhood. Castilliou remembers that in Skeena, a rare Catholic community affiliated with the NB, their presence caused such concern that both the NB president, Robert Clifton, and one of its leading spokesmen, Guy Williams, were rushed into town to see what Manuel and Castilliou were up to on their turf. [16]

The NAIB-NB rivalry was not one that George Manuel welcomed. From the moment he made his promise to the Indian agent to organize all of the Indians of British Columbia, he had been concerned by the split between the Protestant Native Brotherhood and the Catholic NAIB. To George Manuel, that split seemed even more spurious in light of the new developments on the national scene.

Pickersgill and the federal Liberals were swept from power by the Diefenbaker Conservatives in 1967. The new regime promised to reinvigorate a country that had grown stale after a quarter century of one-party rule. On native issues, the Conservatives promised to repeal restrictions on liquor and to give native people the vote without taking away their Indian status. Diefenbaker also kept a promise to put the first Indian into the Senate by appointing James Gladstone, a former president of the Indian Association of Alberta, to the Upper Chamber.

More important, the new government set up the Joint Parliamentary Committee of the Senate and the House of Commons with a mandate to refashion the Indian Act.

In BC, the regional director of Indian Affairs called a conference in Vancouver in April 1958, to discuss the new measures and George Manuel was sent as the NAIB delegate from the interior.

Paull's health was failing at the time, and the Vancouver conference marks George Manuel's first move out of his mentor's shadow. Andy Paull's organizations had generally served as vehicles for his own meteoric personality. But George Manuel had come to see the need for a more broadly based organization to represent BC Indians, and he quietly struck out on his own to try to promote province-wide unity.

In Vancouver, he discussed the possibility of the BC Indians getting together to file a common brief to the upcoming Parliamentary Committee hearings in Ottawa. Most of the Native Brotherhood delegates, however, were reluctant to cooperate with the NAIB. The exception was Oscar Peters, a NB vice-president and coastal Salish leader who shared George Manuel's belief in Indian unity.

In the summer and fall of 1959, George Manuel's interior NAIB branch and some of Peters's backers on the coast held a series of meetings to discuss the idea of a common brief to the Parliamentary Committee. At a meeting in Hope, the NAIB branch and a handful of NB representatives agreed to set up the Aboriginal Native Rights Committee as an umbrella organization to draw up the brief. In the interest of attracting more NB support, Oscar Peters was elected to chair the committee with two Manuel colleagues, Bill Walkem and Genevieve Mussell, as vice-chairs.

Although most of the committee members were affiliated with the NAIB, the new Committee was to take an approach to organizing that was radically different from Andy Paull's. Instead of sending a single emissary to Ottawa "on behalf of the Indians of Canada," they decided to embark on an exhaustive consultation by visiting all the interior bands to find out the concerns of the people. Once that survey was complete, they would draw up a comprehensive brief and then return to the communities to have it ratified.

Considering that there were close to 117 bands in a territory that stretched from the Yukon border to the US border and from the Fraser Valley to the Alberta border, it would be a formidable task. The Aboriginal Native Rights Committee had no paid staff and the only funding was a $10,000 grant the government made available for the preparation of briefs. That amount would pay for only a fraction of their travel expenses and the members of the committee would have to take the rest out of their own pockets.

To carry out the work, George Manuel took a leave of absence from the mill and hit the road in the Indian organizing style of the 1950s and early 1960s. He travelled with Jimmy Scotchman, Gus Gottfriedson, Len Marchand and a couple of other members of the committee crammed into his Chevy. On most nights, they were billeted in the communities they visited. On others, they spent the entire night driving, usually with the young Len Marchand behind the wheel. Occasionally they took a cheap hotel room where they would crowd in for a quick supper of bologna and bread before flipping a coin to see who got the bed. The others camped out on the floor and tried to catch a few hours sleep before heading back onto the road.

The local organizers in each community set up the public meetings where George Manuel would outline the committee's goals and try to provoke a discussion with crowds that sometimes swelled to three or four hundred people. Invariably, the first issue that arose was land, as the growing Indian population continued to put impossible strains on the land base of the reserves. More and more people were being forced to survive on outside jobs, but their residential school educations made employment difficult to secure.

As Len Marchand had discovered, even higher education wasn't enough to allow Indians to break into the mainstream. Marchand had recently graduated from the University of British Columbia with a B.Sc. degree at a time when a university degree was supposed to be a ticket to success, but he found it impossible to get a job and ended up on the road with the NAIB. In his stump speeches, George Manuel would often point to Len Marchand as an example of how the system was stacked against all Indians, rural or urban, man or woman, formally educated or not.[17]

In their travels, the committee members were again and again struck by the calamity that had befallen their people. They met with widows with TB living in shacks with only a few dollars a month in government assistance to keep them alive. They met with teenagers whose teeth were rotted from a poor diet and who had no access to dental care. They saw men who, in another time, would have been hunters and providers, lost in a perennial alcoholic fog. The majority of families were struggling year after year just to survive, and each year they were finding themselves slipping further and further behind. For George Manuel, the plight of his people added to the pain he had felt when he returned to the reserve as a teenager, but it also gave him the impetus he needed to stay on the road and complete the exhausting travels through the province.

While the consultations were going on, he was also following up on his other initiative: bringing BC Indians together in a province-wide organization. He began by getting in touch with Frank Calder, the CCF MLA and leader of the Nishga Tribal Council, to discuss a merger of their two organizations with the larger and more economically self-sufficient Native Brotherhood. Calder was interested in the idea and George Manuel offered to arrange a NAIB convention in Kamloops to which the Nishgas and the Native Brotherhood would be invited.

The meeting was held in Kamloops in April 1959, with 130 chiefs from the three organizations taking part. As Paul Tennant, who has written extensively on BC native politics, observed, "it was the most substantial and representative Indian gathering yet held in the province, having as its only predecessors one or two assemblies of the Allied Tribes."[18]

It was also one of the most colourful, mixing Indian tradition with a bit of 1950s' small-town flash. On the day the delegates arrived, George Manuel arranged for an outdoor parade with Indian Brownies and a local Indian school band led by an Indian war veteran, his chest covered with medals, who saluted the chiefs during a march past. To house and feed the conference, George Manuel used his Elks Club connections to secure the Elks Hall, and he arranged for the native women's Homemakers' Club to prepare a banquet. After the meal, the chiefs were entertained by Indian singers and dancers.

The festive atmosphere seemed to be working on the NB leadership. Guy Williams proclaimed the Kamloops convention "one of the finest conventions ever attended by the Brotherhood" and Maisie Hurley, a white woman who was a strong backer of the NB and the editor of their newspaper, thanked George for his organizing work and echoed his call for province-wide unity.[19]

The event even seemed to soften the Brotherhood's attitude toward Andy Paull. The NB president, Robert Clifton, expressed regret that ill health had kept Paull away from the meeting and read a message from the NAIB leader that thanked George Manuel for organizing the conference and urged all BC Indians to work together as they had in the days of the Allied Tribes.

With the preliminaries out of the way, the delegates got down to business under a banner that read: *British Columbia for British Columbians: White Man Go Home!*

As the banner suggested, the main issue would be the land issue and Guy Williams addressed the question with one of his toughest speeches ever, to the point where the local paper found the whole meeting "disturbing."[20]

To Manuel and Calder's disappointment, however, the NB leadership was still reluctant to take the final step toward unity. George Manuel and Frank Calder had hoped that the NB would "revise its own goals and structure to transform itself into a truly province-wide organization."[21] But the Brotherhood's leaders refused.

Even worse, George Manuel and Frank Calder discovered that despite the fine words from the podium, the Brotherhood leaders were not planning to lead a renewed fight on the BC land question.

In the end, the conference failed to bring the rival BC organizations together, but it did confirm that the organizer of the conference, George Manuel, had emerged as one of the most influential Indian leaders in the province. This fact was underlined after Andy Paull succumbed to his long illness in August 1959, and George Manuel was elected to succeed him as the president of the North American Indian Brotherhood.

At the time, the Aboriginal Rights Committee was still writing its brief to the Joint Committee for its May 1960 submission. With Paull's death and the failure to work a merger with the Native Brotherhood, there no longer seemed any reason to continue with what had become a largely artificial distinction between the NAIB and the Aboriginal Native Rights Committee. At a November NAIB convention in Kamloops, the Aboriginal Native Rights Committee dissolved into a new North American Indian Brotherhood under George Manuel's leadership.

When George Manuel appeared at the May 1960 hearings in Ottawa he kept the Aboriginal Native Rights Committee name because that was the group that had been scheduled to testify. His performance in the two-day session reflected how far he had come as a leader and how his vision was expanding with his political experience. In many ways, it marked the end of the beginning of his political career. In five years, he had emerged from a local activist organizing sporting events on his home reserve to an influential provincial and even national spokesman for native rights.

In his organizing philosophy, he combined the traditional vision of his grandfather with the leadership skills of Andy Paull. But he also had something to offer that Paull didn't. As George Manuel later observed, the death of Paull had been "the end of an era of the one-man show."[22] What was needed was a leader who could bring people together into an organization that could take on the government with a united front of Indian nations. Andy Paull had been unable to accomplish that, but within the next decade, George Manuel and his generation of leaders would.

By 1960, in fact, the movement had reached a cusp, with the scattered Indian organizations from across the country beginning to come together and meet each other for the first time. While the Quiet Revolution was taking place in Quebec, an even quieter revolution, the First Nations revolution, was moving through the country at large, and the consequences would reshape Canada's political landscape.

George Manuel would be an integral part of that revolution, but on a personal level the struggle was coming at a high personal cost. His relentless travel and the loss of income from months off work were making life all but impossible for Marceline and his family at home in Neskainlith.

Marceline had been left to raise the children alone with almost no money to support them. To earn money for groceries, Marceline would work far into the night making moccasins – tanning the hide and sewing and beading them herself – to sell to tourists passing through Chase. While she struggled to feed her children, she also tried to help her husband by raising funds for the NAIB through the local chapter of the Homemakers' Club. For a number of years, she even served as the treasurer of the interior branch of the NAIB and, in her own way, she was as committed to the cause as he was.

But by 1960, she was near the end of her rope. Keeping hearth and home together while George was away was becoming too much, and the kids remember that things started to sour between their parents. When their father was home there were disputes over his frequent absences and the money he was spending on his political work that should have gone to the family.

According to some of George Manuel's friends, Marceline also suspected that George was not totally faithful to her during his travels, and these suspicions complicated the tensions over the time and money he spent on the road. The womanizing issue would arise again. Friends remember that George Manuel's passion and wit, his crooked grin and rousing speeches made him an attractive figure for some of the local women he met in his travels, and his friends were not sure that he always – or even often – turned his admirers away.

George's disputes with Marceline during this period did not always end with words. Vera Manuel remembers that both her parents began to drink a great deal and their fights often became frighteningly violent, with Marceline leaving him for short periods.

Looking back, Vera Manuel, now a Vancouver poet and playwright, sees in the deterioration of her parents' marriage the deep imprint of the residential school experience that scarred the souls of generations of native people in Canada. It was there that her parents had been introduced into the culture of violence and abuse, which would take them half of their lives to overcome. "Both of them worked hard to give us some kind of life," Vera recalls, "but neither of them had a lot to work with in terms of normal family experience. They were part of the general community breakdown."

Some have suggested that, as the atmosphere at home became increasingly bitter, George simply found more reasons to stay away. But Mary Thomas believes that the deteriorating situation at home was something George was trying to solve, not escape. She also worked at raising money for the NAIB, and remembers that when George stopped by to chat and discuss new fund-raising schemes, he would often wrestle with the question of how to keep his family together while continuing with his political work. On a number of occasions he even told her he was considering giving up politics altogether.

It was a dilemma that would stay with him for the next five years, but as George Manuel once told Henry Castilliou, "politics is like buckin' horses. Once it gets into your blood, you're hooked for life."[23] And by 1960, George Manuel had it in his blood.

## CHAPTER FIVE

# A Future for Your Children
# 1960-1963

You're not abandoning your children. You are building their future.

Mary Thomas to George Manuel

For Canada's First Nations, the 1960s was a decade of consultations that began with the Joint Parliamentary Committee hearings and continued with an almost unbroken string of national and regional soundings on everything from renaming the Indian Act to abolishing it altogether.

During this period, the scattered Indian organizations were also struggling to build a national organization that would allow them to take their fight directly to Canada's political leadership in Ottawa. From the beginning, George Manuel was deeply involved in both the consultation and the organizing processes.

The first attempt at a national organization was the National Indian Council (NIC), which grew out of a series of government-sponsored annual meetings of Manitoba Indians in the late 1950s. The meetings offered the Manitoba Indians an important forum to air their concerns and exchange information and soon attracted Indians from other provinces. By 1960, national participation had reached the point where native leaders like BC's Frank Calder were suggesting that they use the annual meetings as a base for launching a national Indian organization.

As the leader of the North American Indian Brotherhood, George

Manuel was invited to the National Indian Council's founding meeting in Regina in August 1961. At the time, the shape of the new organization was still uncertain. The delegates decided that "Indian" would mean anyone of Indian origin, including Métis and non-status Indians; but there was no decision as to what relationship the NIC should have with existing Indian organizations, or precisely what role it would play in the overall Indian movement. In fact, the only real decision taken was to adopt "red, buckskin and sky blue" as the official NIC colours because of their "relationship with the past and their deep significance for the people of Indian descent."[1]

When it came time to elect a six-person executive that would draw up the NIC constitution, George Manuel was among them. More typical than Manuel in the NIC leadership, however, was the chair of the committee, William Wuttunee. Like most of the NIC members, Wuttunee was an urbanite, a Saskatchewan Cree lawyer who had worked for the Department of Indian Affairs in the past and who had appeared at the Joint Parliamentary Committee to advocate the privatization of the reserves.

It was not a position that George Manuel shared. In fact, at the 1960 hearings he had warned that Indian people "would not willingly surrender" their reserves and said that if they were privatized the only result would be to drive Indian people "to Vancouver's skid row."[2]

But George Manuel was in a minority on the National Indian Council. The agenda was controlled by urban professionals with little experience in the grass-roots movement. This was confirmed at the second meeting in Toronto in August 1962, when William Wuttunee was elected chief of the Council and the three Councillors (or sachem, as they were called) were an Ojibwa high school teacher living in Toronto, a Toronto real estate broker of Chippewa origin and George Manuel, the only community-based activist on the executive.

George Manuel had come to the meeting armed with five resolutions from the NAIB that he hoped would steer the NIC toward a more aggressive agenda. He wanted the NIC to endorse a call for a separate Indian Affairs Department with its own staff and cabinet minister,[3] a "dynamic" standing committee on Indians Affairs, a more equitable social welfare system and government grants to native associations.

The NIC was reluctant to take any firm positions, however, and instead settled for a hazy definition of its role. Its charter dedicated it to "serving all existing Indian organizations" and to "promoting the culture of the Indian people."[4]

The lack of a clear-cut mandate led to the NIC spending its time on issues such as an emblem to go with the organization's colours, Indian dance recitals and an annual "Indian Princess pageant," instead of addressing the more difficult political and economic problems confronting the First Nations.

The only serious policy that had anything to do with fundamental Indian rights was a resolution adopted with George Manuel's backing that urged the government to set up an Indian land claims commission to deal with unsettled claims. There was little follow through on the issue, however, and the NIC would remain largely a social and cultural organization.

As a result, George Manuel devoted most of his energy during this period to his political work in BC. In January 1961, he was elected as the Neskainlith band chief. He had run for the position two years earlier against chief Anthony August, because he felt August wasn't keeping in close enough touch with the people. During that first campaign he had gone to the local MP, Davie Fulton, and asked for advice. Fulton told him to shower the people with promises and he would get elected. George Manuel did so and was soundly defeated. It was the last time that he ever campaigned "in the white man's way" and it was the last time he ever lost an election in the rest of his thirty-year political career.

In his 1961 bid for band chief, George Manuel ran what would become his usual quiet but thorough campaign that involved building support from key community leaders, then listening to what the people had to say and trying to respond to their needs in practical ways.

His election as band chief, a post his great-uncles François and William Pierrish had held for most of the first half of the century, was a source of personal satisfaction, but it also added to his already considerable workload. Along with his band chief duties, he was still working his eight-hour shifts at the mill and serving as an NIC sachem and NAIB president, a job that still had him on the road for much of his free time.

In his NAIB work, his highest priority continued to be building a united BC Indian organization with the Nishga Tribal Council and the Native Brotherhood. He spent most of the summer and early fall of 1961 organizing a province-wide powwow in Lillooet. The theme of the gathering was the shared heritage of BC Indians, and he arranged for Indian dancers in their traditional costumes to perform for the visitors.

Like the 1959 Kamloops meeting, the Lillooet powwow had a province-wide impact. As *The Native Voice*, the NB's newspaper, saw it, the powwow made them feel "once again, that the great Indian cultural tradition is by no means something that belongs to the past, soon to be forgotten.

"This proud tradition, which is as old as the mountains and valleys of this beautiful country and which has stood like a rock and weathered all storms, is very much alive!"[5]

George Manuel expanded on the theme in his speech where he noted that the "culture of the white people was forced upon us by people who did not understand Indians and who did not give us the time to adjust to an entirely new environment.

"This is the first time in our history," he said, "that our children get the same education as white children and from now on our people will gradually . . . begin to take the place in society that is rightfully theirs."[6]

But along with stirring cultural pride, Manuel also used the powwow for a little shrewd politicking by awarding Maisie Hurley, the editor of *The Native Voice*, an honorary life membership in the North American Indian Brotherhood.

The powwow and George Manuel's discreet political courtship of Maisie Hurley marked another step toward closing the gap between the NAIB and the NB, with George Manuel's speeches and activities gaining an increasingly prominent place in *The Native Voice*.

A speech he made to the BC Nurses' Association, for example, was printed as a three-part article which highlighted George Manuel's unity platform and outlined his current thoughts on the role of the modern Indian movement. At the time of European contact, he observed, "Indians of one language group felt no sense of brotherhood with other Indians. In British Columbia, for example, the Shuswap were quite often at war with the Chilcotin Indians, or the Kootenays invaded the hunting grounds of the Blackfeet east of the Rocky Mountains.

"All this has changed entirely . . . For the first time in all known North American history there exists now an Indian sense of identity and common interest with other Indians, from the icy shores of the Arctic to the burning deserts in the Southwest and beyond."

The new sense of Indianness was rooted in common traditions and a common sense of the land. But it was not at all a backward-looking movement. Respecting the old ways did not mean Indians had to "go hunting with bow and arrow if we own a rifle or that we go on horseback if we can afford a car or a bus ticket. . . .

"It means, on the contrary a positive, constructive approach. In the first place we wish to preserve our great Indian cultural heritage and we wish to revive the interest in this heritage, because we, as a free people in a free country, have a right to possess it . . . it is our property that has been handed down for thousands of years. . . ."[7]

George Manuel's speeches around the province and the coverage of his activities in *The Native Voice,* brought him to the attention of the BC Indian Advisory Council, a group of five Indians and four whites who were appointed by the provincial government to advise on Indian matters. The chairman was Chief William Scow, the past president of the Native Brotherhood, and he invited George Manuel to take the seat at the table that was long denied Andy Paull because of his differences with the NB.

The Council's position on native issues tended to be modelled on the more conservative Native Brotherhood policies, but George Manuel's participation turned out to be a useful practice round for what he would encounter as the chair of a national advisory body set up by the Department of Indian Affairs a few years later.

While things were moving forward on a political level, however, George Manuel's family situation continued to deteriorate. After years of frustration, Marceline walked out and left him with the job of single parenthood that she had been stuck with while he was on the road with his political work.

This gave George Manuel the opportunity to display his mediocre parenting skills as he continued to put his political work above all else. His youngest son, Arthur, remembers being on the road with his father and finding himself let out on the side of the highway outside of Lillooet because his father had an evening meeting to attend and Arthur had school the next day.

Neskainlith was a couple of hundred kilometres away, but his father told him to hitchhike home. Only twelve years old at the time, Arthur remembers being surprised as his father pulled away, leaving him alone on the highway without a nickel in his pocket.[8] Arthur made it home, but it was the type of incident that reflected his father's "the hard way is the best way" philosophy and led to a sense of estrangement between George and his children that took many years to overcome.

The family situation became even more complicated when Marceline returned home. Her travels had taken her to Calgary where she lived with a non-native man for a time. When she returned to Neskainlith after a year's absence, she brought home a child. The arrival of the child raised a few eyebrows in Neskainlith, but it is a testament to George Manuel's traditional sensibility – that looked at every child as a gift – that he formally adopted the boy, named Richard, and treated him as his own son.

The gulf between George and Marceline could not be so easily crossed, however. Marceline moved back into the house, but they slept in different rooms and George turned his bedroom into an office and spent most of his time there after working his shift at the mill. The marriage was, for all intents and purposes, over.

It was a case of staying together for the sake of the children. And even here there were problems. Their oldest son, Bob, was going through a rebellious stage, which had been aggravated by the years of turmoil in the family. His grades in school plummeted and to get out of the house he took a job as a night watchman at a shingle mill and moved into the watchman's shack on the site.

When Bob quit school, George told him to either return to school or come to work with him at the mill. As sons are wont to do, Bob Manuel flatly refused both alternatives. "I'm not going to work for you," he told his father "and I'm not going back to school." Instead, he took off to the Kootenays and went to stay with his maternal grandparents.[9]

Realizing that things were reaching an end, Marceline asked George one more time to give up politics and to put his energies into patching things up at home. It was either that or leave her and the kids so they could make a life on their own.

George Manuel stopped by to visit Mary Thomas on a rainy night in the early 1960s, just after his wife's ultimatum. Mary knew something was wrong as soon as she opened the door. "He looked so pained," she recalled, "as if the weight of the world was on his shoulders."

She noticed, too, that he had been drinking but he explained it away as "drowning his sorrows" and told her about Marceline's warning. He was most upset about what would happen to the kids, who ranged in age from ten to sixteen.

But quitting politics? He hadn't fulfilled his promise of uniting all the Indians in BC, and now things were starting to move on the national level. And yet the pressures for assimilation, the poverty, the despair, were still there at the community level. How could he quit now? And how could he not? The kids were still young and they needed a father.

Mary Thomas remembers that he seemed "half dead inside" and when he finished speaking, she had no ready answer. She was raising her children alone and she knew how hard it had been on Marceline. Yet George was like a brother and she reminded him of their grandfather and the strength that he had given them to face whatever needed to be faced. She believed that George had a calling and she told him, "You're not abandoning your children. You are building their future."[10]

By the time he left Mary's that evening, his mind was made up. And so, apparently, was Marceline's. She didn't wait for George to move out. She took the kids aside and asked them who they wanted to live with. Her or their father? They all chose to stay with her.

Bob Manuel remembered the scene. His grandparents had convinced him to take the train back home and when he got to the station, he was surprised to see his mother and his brothers and sisters gathered on the platform. Marceline had a blanket stuffed with food and a few belongings tied around her shoulders and all the kids had their bags packed. The image of his mother's lonely courage on the railway platform would stay with him all his life.

He recalled, "I guess we had two or three minutes, and she didn't even know where she was going. They just got on the train and they were gone."

Bob Manuel walked back to the house where his father had been left alone. At the time, he felt resentment toward the man and an abiding distaste for his father's political passions, which he believed were responsible for breaking up the family. He stayed in the house with his father and out of necessity went to work with George at the mill. It was there that he began to have a glimmer of understanding of his father.

The work was tough and his father was a skilled and respected worker, and it is probably a feature of father-son relationships that the Neskainlith band chief, president of the North American Indian Brotherhood, sachem of the National Indian Council, member of the BC Indian Advisory Council and member of the Chase Board of Trade finally impressed his son with his ability to leap from log to log, bust a jam and pike the logs onto the jackladder.

It would be quite a few years, though, before George Manuel and his oldest son would reach the point where they would become friends and political allies. Bob worked with his father in the mill for a year and then hit the road. It was several years before he and his father crossed paths again.

Marceline ended up in Chilliwack where she spent a year working as a domestic to support the family. In later years, after her return to Neskainlith, she became active in the community and built a reputation as a woman of spirit, intelligence and compassion in trying to heal the wounds of her people. But during the mid-1960s, both she and George were fighting to regain their personal and familial equilibrium. In George Manuel's case, the turmoil of the family would be reflected in some odd twists and turns in his political life.

The first came in 1963 when he declined to stand for re-election as the Neskainlith band chief. Instead, he ran and was elected to the much less demanding position of band councillor. In April he was also re-elected as president of the NAIB in a convention that was attended by the National Indian Council chief, William Wuttunee, the Native Brotherhood president, Guy Williams, and the head of the Nishga Tribal Council, Frank Calder.

Not surprisingly, the main theme of the convention was Indian unity and Manuel once again proposed a new province-wide organization. As *The Native Voice* reported: ". . . delegates pointed out that there are now numerous Indian organizations and that it is essential that a united front be developed in petitioning for various reforms and advances for Indians.

"As a result, they called for establishment of a British Columbia Indian Federation with elected representatives to provide a clearing house for concerted action for resolutions and other endeavours."[11]

The clearing house idea was designed to allow the existing organizations, the NB, the NAIB and the Nishga Tribal Council, to continue with their internal structures, while also taking part in a federated superstructure. In a sense, what George Manuel was proposing was a provincial version of the National Indian Council, (which probably explains Wuttunee's presence) but even this approach received only a lukewarm response from Guy Williams and the Native Brotherhood.

The continued failure to build a unified front of BC Indians, and the growing turmoil at home, caught up with George Manuel during the fall of 1963 when he made a sudden and still not fully explained change of course. Without consulting anyone, he resigned as the president of the NAIB and joined the Native Brotherhood.

The idea of the greatly respected interior leader joining the coastal Indians' organization sent shock waves through Indian country and from his resignation letter it seems that that was one of George Manuel's aims. He had decided that if the NB refused a formal merger with the interior organization and the Nishgas, then he would become a sort of Trojan Horse who would lead an invasion from the inside.

In his letter of resignation published in *The Native Voice*, he stated that ". . . provincial unity for the Indian people is the answer to the unsolved problems which we are facing. Without such unity, there is little we can accomplish.

"In the past," he wrote, "we have been led to believe that Coast Indians and Interior of BC Indians had very little in common; that we were 'different' from each other; and it was concluded that the separate groups would have to solve their problems separately, independently from each other.

"I, like other responsible Indian leaders in British Columbia and beyond, feel that the need for unity on a provincial level has become so urgent now that steps in that direction must be taken without unnecessary delay." He admitted that the decision to quit the NAIB had been a painful one on a personal level, but he concluded by urging "all Interior Indians to follow me on the road to a better future for all of us" and to "help one another in a brotherly way, just as our ancestors did in the past."[12]

In a later letter to *The Native Voice* he hinted at another reason for his resignation from the NAIB. He was replying to a circular his NAIB successor, Ben Paul, had sent around the province to counter George Manuel's suggestion that there were forces within the NAIB that opposed his unity program.

Ben Paul stated that the NAIB had always shown "a perfect willingness to deal with other BC organizations in respect to unity." Manuel agreed; after all, that had been his policy all the time he was president. But then he went on to point a finger:

"The Brotherhood's legal advisor conveyed a message to me where he maintained that Indian unity was not desirable and that it would be better if Indians were split up in different organizations."

The legal advisor was George Manuel's friend and former part-time employer, Henry Castilliou, Jr., but George Manuel stated frankly that Indian organizations should not take direction from their non-native advisors.

As he put it: "I am a North American Indian and have obligations only to my Indian people, and to Canada. I maintain that no non-Indian has a moral or legal right to interfere with the efforts for Indian unity, which every one of us desires."[13]

Almost thirty years later, Castilliou doesn't recall a serious dispute with George Manuel over unity or any other matter. But Arthur Manuel remembers that his father and Henry had a stormy argument in the house before George Manuel left the NAIB and Henry Castilliou never set foot through the door again.

Whatever the reason for George Manuel's resignation, either as a strategy to bring the NAIB and the NB together, or as a result of a dispute with Henry Castilliou, the move did not have an energetic follow-up. Instead of seizing the day and trying to push NAIB-NB to unity from inside the coastal peoples' organization, or attacking the roadblocks to unity from the outside, George Manuel disappeared from public view.

Throughout most of 1964, he remained at home in Neskainlith and limited his political activity to local matters. His only major initiative was to start a Shuswap cultural society with his former rival in the band chief election, Anthony August.

It was a period for George Manuel to lick his wounds from his family break-up and his near decade of political battles. For the first time in years, he seriously started to work his farm and tried, among other things, to market green beans.

While George Manuel was sitting back and tending his own political and literal garden, things were once again moving on the national scene, as the public began to take a new interest in Indian issues.

The spark had come from the civil rights movement in the United States. Many non-native Canadians (and some Indian leaders) tended to see the Indian struggle as a local equivalent of the American black movement. This led, however, to Canadian liberals adopting the vocabulary and the solutions of the U.S. civil rights movement and trying to apply them to the native issue in Canada.

A typical example is a feature article in *Maclean's* in July 1963, where Canada's quintessential liberal journalist, Peter Gzowski, went looking for "Our Alabama." He found it in Saskatchewan where a "white woman" told him that she had been called "Indian lover" in the same tone of voice Southerners use for "Nigger lover."[14]

The recognition by mainstream Canadians of the very real discrimination that Canadian Indians faced in their own land was long overdue. But the fact that it was being seen in the same light as the American civil rights movement meant that the solutions would also be borrowed from a poorly fitting foreign model. Instead of looking at the basic issue of a fair land-base and self-government for the Indian nations, liberals like Gzowski trumpeted the civil rights movement's panacea of "integration."

The word was also increasingly becoming part of the Department of Indian Affairs vocabulary with its official newspaper, *Indian News*, churning out articles on the theme of Indian and white kids "Learning and Playing Together" in integrated schools. Putting brown and white kids together in the same classrooms in provincial schools was as far as the department went, however. There was no attempt to answer the repeated calls for Indian-controlled school boards or to alter the distorted European-based curriculum that was being taught.

Still, there was a new wind blowing through the cracks of the DIA fortress in Ottawa. At the top, Colonel Jones was pensioned off and a departmental stalwart, Robert F. Battle, took over the director's job. In a precedent setting move, George Manuel's friend and colleague, Len Marchand, was appointed as the special assistant to the minister of Indian Affairs. Marchand had been recommended for the post by Henry Castilliou (who had close connections to the Liberal Party); he was the first Indian to hold such a high post in the department. As it turned out, Marchand would end up being "the first of everything," the first Indian MP in 1968 and the first Indian cabinet minister in the mid-1970s.

Another important change in the department came among the lower officials where a few mavericks, like Walter Rudnicki, breached the military-bureaucratic complex.

Rudnicki, who would later become a close friend of George Manuel's, had drifted into the Arctic Affairs Department in the mid-1950s. He was assigned to the Eskimo Affairs desk with a staff comprising an old Hudson Bay man and a native woman, but he had no idea exactly what he was supposed to do. While Rudnicki was still trying to define a job for himself, he was appalled by the callousness and racism of the bureaucrats working around him. Many Inuit people during this period were suffering from famine and a shockingly high number were starving to death, but the Arctic Affairs Department officials were suggesting, in all seriousness, that the Inuit didn't need much food "because they had small stomachs."[15]

After six or seven years at Arctic Affairs, Rudnicki transferred to the Department of Indian Affairs. "At the time," he recalled, "there was a certain bureaucratic terrorism against the Indian people with the department controlling every minute of their lives." But there was also a narrow opening for change within the department because, as Rudnicki put it, the DIA was trying "to pull itself into the 18th century."[16]

Rudnicki himself would play an important role in pushing it along with two new programs that would have a great effect on George Manuel's life.

The first was a community development program for Indian communities that fit with the broad range of new initiatives of the Pearson era. Rudnicki remembers that "the department went along with it because it seemed fashionable." The plan was to train thirty non-native community development officers and thirty Indian community development workers a year, for three years. The officers were to have an academic background and be paired, as George Manuel put it, "Lone Ranger style" with Indian community development workers.

The second major initiative was a national Indian Advisory Board that the department would consult before making major alterations to the Indian Act or other matters affecting Indian people. Unlike advisory boards in the past, which consisted of "mucky-mucks" like "Gordon Robertson . . . two or three Oblates, the Bishop of the Arctic" getting together to "cluck their tongues and discuss the terrible problem of drinking in Frobisher Bay,"[17] the National Indian Advisory Board would consist almost entirely of Indian leaders.

Later in the decade, George Manuel would emerge as the Indian chair of the National Board, but in 1964 what caught his attention was the community development program. He first heard about it at the November 16 meeting of the provincial Advisory Council in New

Westminster, when a UBC professor gave a talk on the "Community Development Approach to Indian Problems." The Native Brotherhood president, Guy Williams, attended the meeting and enthusiastically backed the proposal. George Manuel shared Williams's enthusiasm. Community development, he decided, would allow him to work closely with the people and he would have the resources to get things done in the vital areas of housing, health care and education that had improved little in his years of political organizing.

It would also get him away from home, where he hoped he could put his family difficulties behind him, although, as it turned out, that would not be easy.

Just before his interview for the C.D. job, Marceline went into the hospital in Coqualeetza to have an operation on her hip. She sent the kids back to Neskainlith for George to take care of and he was forced once again to take over the responsibilities of single parenthood. It was not a role he welcomed, and before long he would be slipping the bonds of full-time fatherhood as he headed off to carry on the struggle at a new level.

# PART TWO

# Building the National Movement

For the first time in all known North American history there exists now an Indian sense of identity and common interest with other Indians, from the icy waters of the Arctic to the burning deserts in the Southwest and beyond.

George Manuel
1963

## CHAPTER SIX

# Community Development and the Arthur Laing Gang 1965-1967

The main goal was that they wouldn't be captured by the system and in that way we screwed them up pretty good. Then we let them go and all hell broke loose. . . .

Walter Rudnicki on the community development training program.

For the applicants, the first indication that the community development program was not standard DIA fare came during the interview. The questions were set up by Farrel Toombs, a Toronto academic who had been brought in to train the C.D. workers, and the interview was designed to weed out the type of "bureaucratic terrorists" who had staffed the Department in the past.

One example was the nice Mountie question. Applicants were asked their response to an RCMP officer coming onto the reserve and taking them aside for a friendly chat. The officer explains that an illegal still is operating in the community and causing all sorts of problems, and he asks the C.D. worker to help him locate it. Aware that they were dealing with a government agency, most of the applicants solemnly promised they would help the RCMP uphold the law. These applicants were thanked for their time and their applications tossed into the waste bin. The C.D. program would have no room for bureaucratic snitches.

George Manuel had no trouble passing the interview, but he was too late for the first class of thirty C.D. trainees in January 1965, and had to wait a year for the second session. He did not wait idly, however. His brief political sabbatical ended in the spring of 1965, when he was caught up in the second major DIA initiative of the period, the National Indian Advisory Board. The Advisory Board was set up in 1965 with both a regional and national structure. The BC-Yukon regional council had nine members, with six elected from various geographical zones and three seats reserved for representatives of the NB and NAIB and the Homemakers' Association. The purpose of the councils and the national board was to advise the department on Indian issues and to study revisions to the Indian Act.

The elections for the Regional Council were held on 31 May 1965. George Manuel was chosen to represent the interior Indians, James Gosnel the Nishgas, Ken Harris the coast, Chief Richard Malloway the south, Clara Tiyza the Yukon and Phillip Paul Vancouver Island.

Although only in his mid-twenties, Phillip Paul was already a friend of George Manuel's. They first met in 1960 when Manuel was head of the NAIB. Paul's South Saanich Reserve had backed the NAIB since the days of Andy Paull and Andy had been a friend of Phillip Paul's family. In his youth, when he was a boxer in the Buckskin Gloves boxing tournaments in Vancouver, Phillip stayed at Andy Paull's house and he developed a great respect for him as a man and as a leader. In later years he came to have the same sort of respect for George Manuel, whom he compared to Nelson Mandela and Julius Nyerere for the leadership he gave his people on both the national and international scene.

Phillip Paul began his own political career in early 1965 when he was elected to head the newly formed NAIB affiliate, the South Vancouver Island Tribal Federation. He remembered that George Manuel had urged him to run for a place on the Regional Advisory Council, and then, according to Paul, "politically engineered" his election.[1]

With Phillip Paul's support, along with that of his own political allies in the NB and the Nishga Tribal Council, George Manuel was elected to chair the Regional Council and was guaranteed a position on the National Advisory Board.

By the time the first meeting of the National Indian Advisory Board was called, however, Manuel was off to Quebec City's Laval University for his community development training. Before he left, he had to decide what to do with the kids, so he went down to Coqualeetza to visit Marceline. It was a poignant moment for both of them. Coqualeetza was where the two of them had met; now it was where they would decide what to do with their children during their permanent separation.

Amy August, an old friend of George Manuel's family, was in the hospital at the time and she remembers that the meeting between George and Marceline was a surprisingly warm one. When George came in he was full of enthusiasm about the community development job and Marceline seemed genuinely happy for him. She agreed that he should take the course and suggested that while she was still in hospital, they place the younger children in the Kamloops residential school. George left Coqualeetza grateful for Marceline's understanding and pleased that after the bitter years leading up to their separation, there was a hope that he and Marceline could become friends again.

When George Manuel arrived in Quebec City, he expected he would be confronted by a bucketful of sociological jargon and a lesson in official form-filling, but he and the other Indian trainees were in for a surprise. Farrel Toombs's course was imbued with the spirit of 1960s radicalism. It was designed so the trainees wouldn't "be captured by the system." Instead, their role would be to go into the communities and help the people in "liberating their minds, their souls, their spirits," which had been trampled by almost a century of overbearing Indian agents and the priests who had "beaten and cowed" them into submission.[2]

The methods for training the C.D. workers were as unconventional as its goals. Instead of preparing lectures, Farrel Toombs came into the class and asked the students what they wanted to talk about. For days, nothing was accomplished, and the trainees began to get restless. They wanted to be lectured, to take notes, to be taught. But as community development workers, they would have to learn how to motivate groups into action. Toombs had simply recreated the situation they would face in the field. The frustration level reached the point where George Manuel himself wrote home to Anthony August and told him he was considering quitting because the whole thing appeared to be a waste of time.

Then something happened. The students broke down and began to talk about their own experiences in dealing with the system. Academics and seasoned civil servants "began to tell of the frustration that had built up in them when nobody had laid down a clear-cut agenda for them to follow."

"Learning, for all of us," George Manuel later wrote, "had become a strict set of rules, a curriculum laid down by people who had never met the class, a teacher whose orders were to wade through the course outline

. . . and a class filled with students who dutifully made notes, read the texts, counted the footnotes and were prepared to respond with the correct references whenever asked."[3]

From the community development point of view, this sort of teaching created "people who saw life, and work, and their place in the community in pretty much the same terms that had been set down for them in the classroom." Toombs described the system as one of "unilateral dependence." His three-month course was designed to break down that unilateral, authoritarian dependence and to replace it with mutual dependence.

In George Manuel's case, the community development method made him rethink his past organizing strategies. He began to feel that while his political activities had demonstrated his concern for the needs of the people, "there had been a tendency for political leadership to become a matter of a few friends developing a platform and selling it to potential supporters."

After the community development course, George Manuel became "more concerned with trying to find the unspoken focus of the community and the person best suited to articulate that concern."[4]

While absorbing some valuable lessons from the C.D. course, George Manuel also noted a few of its limitations. In the field, he noticed that some of the C.D. officers took their passive role too seriously and, in George's words, would "sit around and not do a damn thing."[5]

He also discovered that the progressive attitude of Toombs and the Department did not extend to paycheques. When George Manuel was sent to Cowichan on Vancouver Island, he discovered that his non-native partner, Tony Karch, was being paid eight hundred dollars a month while he was receiving three hundred dollars. It was a revelation that surprised Karch as well. George Manuel was, after all, an older man with a province-wide reputation, so the pay-cheque injustice was an embarrassment for both men.

It did not prevent them from developing a close working relationship, however. Karch says he found Manuel's wisdom and dedication "inspiring," and today attributes their community development accomplishments to George Manuel's drive and political savvy.

Cowichan was not, after all, an easy posting. It is actually made up of five separate communities, all within an eight-kilometre radius of the city of Duncan. The region is prosperous, with the local economy based on agriculture, fishing and logging the coastal rain forests. More recently, the mild climate (*cowichan* means "land warmed by the sun") has attracted retirees who have settled in the town and on the nearby Gulf Islands.

But for more than a century, the prosperity of the area had been denied its original inhabitants. A BC social worker described the conditions he found on the reserve in the mid-1960s.

"The houses are overcrowded and . . . there is no electricity in at least 35% of the homes and the majority of the homes are with no running water and indoor plumbing. There is a high infant mortality on the reserve and out of every 1,000 live Indian births, 74.7 (against 27.2 for the whole of Canada) will not survive."[6]

According to the social worker, the lack of minimum housing standards, indoor plumbing and electricity, meant that the Indian children's start on life was so far behind their white neighbours that it was nearly impossible for them to catch up.

Because of his political reputation, George Manuel couldn't slip into the community unnoticed. *The Victoria Colonist* reported his arrival in Duncan in an article that compared him to Sitting Bull, Pontiac and Geronimo. But Manuel knew that even with his province-wide reputation as a fighter for Indian rights, he would have to win acceptance from the local community.

As he put it, "the major defence of any small community against invasion by outsiders is to isolate them." From his experience with coastal peoples he also knew that "the advantage of my being an Indian could almost be offset by the fact that I was from the interior. Coastal Indian people have traditionally taken such a pride in their own culture that they tend to look down on interior Indians, whose way of life is a good deal less elaborate."[7]

The most serious disadvantage, however, was the fact that he was an employee of the Department of Indian Affairs. If he was to be allowed to share in the life of the community, he would quickly have to show that he was an Indian first, and a DIA employee only by circumstance.

After he moved into a house in Duncan, he and Tony Karch spent a couple of weeks wandering around the reserve to get their bearings.

Manuel's C.D. training had instructed him to continue to wait until he was approached by someone in the community for help, but he was not the type to sit back and do nothing. So he and Karch drew up a questionnaire about the community's social and economic life and went to the chief and council for permission to go house-to-house to gather the information.

When permission was granted, they set out systematically to visit every home and virtually all of the 1,400 residents of the community to have the questionnaire filled out and to simply chat with them about their day-to-day concerns.

Wes Modeste, then in his mid-twenties, remembers that George Manuel had the knack of relating to the people in a very direct and forthright manner. Despite the fact he was an outsider and nominally a DIA employee, he "inspired a kind of immediate trust."[8]

Through this round of informal discussions and their own direct observations, Manuel and Karch concluded that the one issue that could unite and spark the people to action was the same one that had shocked the social worker: the need for decent housing.

There had been attempts by the community to address the problem in the past, with a number of meetings held by the band council's housing committee. But as one Cowichan resident recalled, they turned out to be little more than "bitching sessions" with no follow-up. To ensure that the discussions led to action, George Manuel looked around for someone who could lead the fight.

He settled on Abraham Joe, a member of the council who had worked as a fruit-picker and logger and who had a reputation as a first-rate scrapper. Joe was also the only member of the council who "would tell the agent where to file his ideas of what was good for the community. He was quite capable of elevating words and principles into action."[9]

Abraham Joe was, in many ways, typical of the men and women George Manuel would recruit to the cause over the next two decades. If he had a choice between someone with academic credentials but little life or practical experience, and someone with a willingness to learn and a large dose of life experience, he preferred the latter.

All Abraham Joe needed, George Manuel believed, was a push to get him started and a bit of guidance along the way. The push came in the form of an off-hand suggestion that Joe look into the housing issue, because that was what the people themselves seemed most interested in. Then he waited. A few days later, Abraham Joe invited George Manuel to go saltwater fishing with him.

They spent the entire afternoon on the boat discussing the housing issue, the problems surrounding it and the possible solutions. Abraham Joe expressed one main concern. He was worried that if he set out on his own, he would be seen as usurping the authority of the chief and the council's housing committee. George Manuel told him to gather around him a small number of friends who shared his housing concerns so he would not find himself isolated in any public forum. But as Abraham Joe feared, the chief got wind of his activities and saw the extra-council organizing as a threat to his leadership. To head off the challenge, the chief called a meeting to censure the young logger publicly.

When George Manuel heard the news, he told Abraham Joe that he would have to pull an end-run on the chief by calling his own public meeting to sell the idea directly to the people. To pack them in, he was to go around and tell everyone that if they showed up at the meeting, they would get their houses.

Not surprisingly, it became the largest public meeting ever held in Cowichan. But it got off to a rocky start when the chief stood up and said that this was the wrong forum for the issue; that the band council already had a housing committee and that was where the problem had to be addressed.

Someone had to swing the meeting away from procedure and back to the housing issue, so George Manuel stood up and announced that he knew where band members could get money to build their own homes. "The money is there," he told them. "All you have to do is to tap it. But only you can get it."[10]

George Manuel later admitted it was a risky move. The chief could have had him thrown out because he was not a member of the band, but there was something about his forceful personality, and perhaps, too, about his reputation as a provincial leader, that prevented anyone from questioning his right to speak. By the time he sat down, the meeting was back on track. The people wanted houses, George Manuel had said the money was there, and they were going to make sure they got hold of it.

Afterward, an eight-member grievance committee was set up, and with Manuel's help it developed a strategy to get the DIA's attention and have it fulfil its housing obligations. With the knowledge that the one thing that drove the Department to action was public embarrassment, the committee decided to invite the press to view the housing conditions. They prepared a press release and sent it to the Victoria and Vancouver dailies, which sent reporters to the reserve to see the promised Third World conditions.

The members of the press were shown extended families crammed into small one-room shacks, a community elder who was forced to live in a dirt-floored smokehouse, and women trying to care for infants and older children in houses without running water or electricity. In the mid-1960s, such glimpses into the living conditions on reserves were rare in Canada; the Cowichan housing conditions came as a surprise to the journalists. When the story was picked up by the CP wire and sent across Canada, the glimpse into life on the reserve shocked the whole country.

Because of the publicity, the Cowichan band council was able to get the new DIA minister, Arthur Laing, to visit the reserve. They took him on the same tour as they had taken the press, and Laing was sufficiently shamed to promise that the people of Cowichan would get "all the houses they needed."

That was an obvious exaggeration, but the Department did launch a major housing construction program on the reserve. In the first five years, DIA built one hundred new houses with electricity and water services. Over the next ten years, a further 250 houses were added. A member of the housing committee recalled that even after the fifteen-year building program was complete, Cowichan was still short one hundred new houses, but the 350 new units were a major physical and psychological boost to the community.[11] The people gained not only homes, but a new self-confidence and assertiveness.

To put this assertiveness to good use, George Manuel began leading the members of the committee, and anyone else who was interested, on field trips to Victoria. He would introduce them to MLAs and explain how they could use the politicians to publicize their struggle. Modeste recalls that George Manuel even went so far as to physically walk them through the various government departments in a sort of ambulatory civics lesson, while he explained how each department was set up and what services it delivered.

Another important program he pushed during this period was adult education. He had been critical of what he saw as the DIA orthodoxy that was expressed by one official with the comment that "Any of those Indians over thirty years old, we may as well forget about them" and "Let the present generation die off, then we'll see the results of our policies. . . ."

George Manuel saw this approach as not only bloody-minded, but also bad policy. From his own experience, he knew "the education process must last as long as active human life itself. Children don't change society, adults do."[12]

Adult education, whether it be academic or vocational, gave immediate benefits not only to the community but to the home environment. This new attitude was of immeasurable importance in reinforcing any positive influences the young received at school. In Cowichan, George Manuel put these theories into practice by helping to set up an adult education committee that would target literacy and basic academic skills. Typically, he told the committee that with his grade-two education he had no right to be running the program; so he enrolled in the course himself to upgrade his own skills.

An offshoot of the adult education committee was the community workshops, which George Manuel believed were necessary to improve the community's skills in coping with social problems. He enlisted a cross-section of people and had them meet once a week to discuss and analyze the past, present and future of the community. Out of this simple process, he hoped people would discover their local problems and the means by which they could be solved.

While he was working on local issues with his C.D. work, George Manuel was also active on the national scene with the National Indian Advisory Board. The first meeting of the Board had taken place in January 1966, when George Manuel was still at Laval.

As the government set it up, the Board had Indian and non-Indian co-chairs. The non-Indian was the assistant deputy minister, Robert Battle, and the Indian representative was to be chosen by the Board. At that first meeting, Chief Wilfred Bellegarde of Saskatchewan was elected to the post and George Manuel was chosen as vice-chair. When Bellegarde lost his band election shortly after the meeting, George Manuel automatically became Battle's co-chair. He did not want to inherit the job by default, however, so he insisted on having his chairmanship put to a vote by the Indian advisors. They did, and he won unanimous support.

The Advisory Board chair position made George Manuel one of the best-known Indian leaders in Canada and allowed him to refine his talents as a spokesperson and strategist of the movement. But his first challenge was to steer the Board toward the Indians', rather than the Department's, agenda.

In this, he worked closely with Phillip Paul, who had also been elected to the Board. In private meetings before the hearings, he and Paul recognized that they were likely to "become subjected to the government and controlled by the government" in the official forum. But they also saw that the Advisory Board provided "the first time that Indian people had got together nationally in the history of Canada" and they felt that they could use the government money as a springboard to forming a national organization that was truly representative of the First Nations. The most useful meetings, they believed, would take place in the hotel rooms before and after the public wrangling with Robert Battle and the DIA crew. [13]

George Manuel and Phillip Paul's suspicions about the Department trying to keep a tight rein on the meetings were confirmed when Arthur Laing, who had been described by Rudnicki as "a hardware merchant . . . a typical western red neck," opened the first session.

He began by suggesting that he was "too old to grow a forked tongue" and explained that his role was to "raise the stature and morale of the employees, who are your servants." The role of the Indian advisors, he said, was to "raise your people, preserve and revive their culture and reconstruct that fine pride and self-direction that had made such a contribution to what we all enjoy in Canada." [14]

Before the Indian advisors had a chance to offer any advice, they were subjected to a long-winded discourse from Robert Battle, titled "Yesterday, Today and Tomorrow," which had as its theme how much the Department had done for the First Nations in the past, how much it was doing in the present and how much it would do in the future. [15]

When the speech was finished, the Department's agenda for the meeting was introduced and it was so pre-packaged that the Maritime representative, Wallace Labillois, complained that the Indian advisors were in the position of an "ant charging an elephant." [16]

What the Department had in mind for the advisors was not a wide-ranging discussion on the conduct of Indian Affairs in Canada, but a very narrow focus on the Indian Act, with the advisors limiting their input to a clause-by-clause, line-by-line review of the legislation.

Still, by working closely with Phillip Paul, George Manuel managed to find a space in the official agenda of that first meeting for two motions that would broaden the scope of the National Board. The first called for the minutes of the National Board to be sent to the Regional Councils. The second asked for travel money for the Regional Councils (of which all the National Board members were part), to allow them to consult the people at the grass-roots level.

Behind those two bland-sounding propositions was George Manuel's and Phillip Paul's strategy to make the advisors responsible to the people and to get government funds to continue their organizing activities, both regionally and nationally. Manuel and Paul were planning a meeting in Musqueam, BC in March 1966, to launch the Confederation of Native Indians of British Columbia (CNIBC) as an umbrella organization that would allow the existing native organizations to work together on specific issues.

In Ottawa, they were also using the hotel-room meetings with the other leaders to discuss replacing the NIC with a more dynamic and representative organization.

At the time, the NIC was foundering. Its only real successes had been in the cultural area, but even here, it ran into trouble when the Mohawk fashion model and political activist, Kahn-Tineta Horn, was crowned "Indian Princess" in 1964. Horn immediately became embroiled in a very public dispute with William Wuttunee that ended with her accusing him of misusing NIC funds.

When Wuttunee had the executive strip her of her title a few months later, she crashed the NIC dinner in Toronto. As *The Native Voice* reported, Kahn-Tineta arrived "robed in a simple, straw coloured piece of cotton, caught over the left shoulder and falling to her ankles. She looked exquisite . . . but most of the two hundred guests, wearing plastic feather headpieces, seemed unconcerned by Miss Horn's arrival or the controversy."[17]

After her appearance, Horn was expelled from the NIC, but the organization quickly found itself in trouble again when Wuttunee accepted

$9,000 from the federal government to hold a conference on the government's widely discredited Claims Commission bill, which had called for a government-appointed panel to unilaterally decide on native land claims. At the conference, the NIC contradicted most of the Indian organizations in Canada by praising the bill as "holding tremendous promise for the Indian people of Canada."[18]

As a result, even some opposition members in the House of Commons began to suggest that Wuttunee was working with the Liberals and by the end of the year, interest in the NIC and its work among Indian leaders had fallen to the point where the organization was temporarily forced to close up shop. It never regained even the small amount of credibility it had at its launching.

What was needed, the Indian leaders agreed, was a new start in building a status-Indian organization with the leadership coming from the Indian communities. Government travel funds for the National Indian Advisory Board members to organize at the local level were seen as an important first step in launching the new organization.

At the Advisory Board meetings, George Manuel and Phillip Paul pushed hard on the issue. But the DIA representative, Robert Battle, pushed back. He not only repeatedly turned down the requests, he stated flatly that the role of the board members was to offer advice as individual advisors, and therefore, no consultation with the people back home was necessary.

While Battle was stonewalling the Board on the issue, the members continued building valuable contacts among themselves. One of the most important figures to emerge during this period was Walter Dieter, who took over from Wilfred Bellegarde as the Saskatchewan delegate to the Board. Dieter lived in Regina where he had become a successful businessman, but he kept in close contact with his own community and he combined an unflagging dedication to the cause with the type of amiability and humility that made him an important consensus-builder.

Another important figure who came in contact with the board members was Harold Cardinal, then twenty years old and studying at St. Patrick's College in Ottawa. Cardinal approached the Board in late 1966 to ask them to endorse his plan for a Canadian Indian Youth Council.

He had already met privately with Arthur Laing with the proposal and a request for $40,000 in funding. Len Marchand, then Laing's ministerial aide, remembers that his boss "really liked Cardinal's spunk," but

Laing offered Cardinal only a few thousand dollars to "buy an old car or something," so he could travel around and organize the Council on his own.[19]

Harold Cardinal found Laing's offer and attitude patronizing and the following morning he went to the press to denounce the minister. That afternoon, he appeared before the Advisory Board to ask for backing for his Youth Council proposal.

Cardinal explained that the Youth Council wanted "the support and advice from the older people" and described his meeting with the minister. After going over a few of the details of his proposed budget, he explained that he was not willing to accept anything less than his $25,000 administration budget and concluded by announcing that "the Council would attempt to get money from any source, including foreign governments."[20]

After a brief debate among the board members, Phillip Paul moved that they endorse the Youth Council's request for the full $40,000 and the motion passed by a wide margin. But like almost all of the Advisory Board's advice, the funding resolution for the Youth Council was ignored by Laing and the Department. Harold Cardinal, however, would soon emerge as an important figure in the movement and would play a key role in George Manuel's ascension to the national leadership.

The most immediate goal of the advisors remained the issue of funding for the Regional Councils and when the Advisory Board was back in session, George Manuel got together with Phillip Paul, Walter Dieter and Quebec's Chief Max Gros-Louis for one last-ditch attempt to have the DIA foot the bill.

Their strategy called for George Manuel to begin the session by attacking the Regional Councils as more of a hindrance than a help without the requested consultation funding, thus putting Robert Battle on the defensive.

"The Indians of British Columbia," Manuel explained, "had been trying to organize on a tribal basis or along union lines, but this process had been upset when the Regional Advisory Councils were introduced."[21]

He went on to suggest that he would like to take the whole issue of the role of the councils back to the regional level and have them decide on the framework they wanted to set up. Paul then pointed out that "the Advisory Board was responsible to the Regional Councils, since the board members were elected from the Regional Councils" and he would like to see "the issues concerning the role of the Regional Advisory Councils and the Board reviewed by the Regional Councils themselves."[22]

At this point there was a surprising breach of solidarity, and it came from an Ontario representative. Wilmer Nadjiwon suggested that the advisors should speak on their own, as individual leaders, and not worry "or be influenced by their people." This was precisely the point that Battle and the DIA were using to deny consultation funding and George Manuel moved quickly to cut Nadjiwon down. He glared at him from the chair and said that such "dictatorial attitudes kill the grass-roots initiative for the Indian people themselves."[23]

It was an uncomfortable moment for the whole Board. In the past, George Manuel had used his power as the Indian chair to guide the meetings toward the issues he and his colleagues had agreed on in the private strategy sessions. The public attack on Nadjiwon, a fellow Indian leader, was a serious breach of etiquette and a worse threat to the unity of the Board than Nadjiwon's remark had been.

Realizing this, George Manuel quietly backtracked. He explained "that he had seen so many Indian leaders lose touch with the Indian community at the grass-roots level and said he felt guilty himself that he had lost such contact with his people." He then apologized to Nadjiwon "for the way his statement had sounded."[24]

By this time, however, feelings were getting even more strained on the other side of the table. The continuing criticism from the Board and the persistent demands for consultation funds were taking a toll on Arthur Laing, and his public statements became more and more aggressive. He began to hint at dark motives behind the Indian leaders' criticisms of his Department, suggesting that "a very large part of the problems we face today are psychological. An aggrieved people sometimes prefer their complaint to a solution."[25]

In February 1967, Laing flew out to a Native Brotherhood convention in Vancouver and he asked the Indian leaders "to turn away from brooding on the past." He pleaded with them to join him "in a forward movement with all the help I can muster on your behalf," and promised that "together we can make you free of the bonds of dependency." At the same time, Laing was prone to political panics whenever Indians showed a willingness to free themselves from that dependency. In 1967, what was most deeply troubling the minister was the Indians of Canada Pavilion at Expo.[26]

George Manuel had been appointed as one of the advisors overseeing the pavilion's storyline, which was written on the pavilion's walls to accompany the murals and exhibits. An Expo Indian Pavilion Advisory Board had originally been set up by the Department under the leadership of the Mohawk engineer, Dr. Gilbert Monture. The members of the committee immediately revolted, however, and demanded the right to pick their own chair. In the dispute that followed, in which George Manuel denounced Monture as "a Westmount Indian," Monture was forced to resign.

The spectacle was an embarrassment for the government. So Laing appointed Chief Andrew Delisle of Kahnawake as the Commissioner-General of the pavilion and allowed input into the pavilion's storyline from the National Indian Advisory Board, the National Indian Council and from a series of hearings that were held in native communities across the country.

As it turned out, the Indians of Canada Pavilion became one of the most popular at Expo and it still serves as an eloquent testimony of a people, their collective memories, and their hopes and fears for the future. Visitors were welcomed with the simple message:

"In the beginning, there was the land – the forest, the rivers and the lakes, the mountains and the plains, and all the creatures that walked on the land, flew in the air, and swam in the waters.

"And there were The People. Within their horizons they were the total of mankind – all were created by the Great Spirit and the spirit was in all living things. . . ."

The only mildly contentious part came near the end, where the storyline questioned the validity of the treaties.

"For the Indians, treaties were less a legal instrument than an act of trust. Few could read English or French and the Indian had no written language of his own. He understood how to pledge his honour but he could not sign his name. He was certainly not in a position to judge whether these contracts were equitable, either for himself or his posterity."

The storyline went on to offer the same sort of mild rebuke to the Churches for their attempts to wipe out native culture and to the Department of Indian Affairs where "the welfare of the Indian was regarded as proper work for retired soldiers" who treated the Indian people "like amiable backward children."[27]

When Laing saw the results in a special preview, one DIA official remembers, "he just about shit," and said he was going to shut the place down.[28] Laing was persuaded that closing down the pavilion would cause a political scandal, but when he toured it on Indian Day at Expo on 4 August 1967, he described it as "the anguished cry of the frustrated" and suggested that "we must break through this frustration and go on to the better life which lies ahead."[29]

Laing and the stalwarts in his Department could not comprehend that the Indian movement was moving beyond the "we" stage, meaning Indians co-operating with the Department. The day when the Indian leadership was willing to look to the DIA for answers to their problems or even "guidance" was long gone.

George Manuel and Phillip Paul felt the DIA's suffocating embrace on Indian Day when they toured the Pavilion with Laing and the other invited guests. Among them was a Soviet representative who was interested in meeting with Canadian Indians and struck up a conversation with George Manuel. Immediately, a DIA official was at their side. George Manuel moved on with the Russian and the DIA official sidled back up to them.

In exasperation, Manuel signalled to Phillip Paul to follow him into the washroom, where he explained the situation and asked Paul to "come along and come in between me and the Indian Affairs guy and just block him. And I'll take off with the guy from the Russian Pavilion because he wants to talk to me privately."

They pulled it off and Paul recalled that the Indian Affairs official was "about ready to have himself."[30]

The manoeuvre was typical of George Manuel's attitude toward the Department during this period. He saw the DIA as an obstruction and a hinderance whose power only came from its control of the purse strings. His goal was to have Indians controlling their own funds, as a necessary first step toward setting their own agenda. As one of his favourite sayings during the period went, "Just give us the gas, we'll do the driving."[31]

By this time, the ultimate destination George Manuel had in mind was sovereignty for the First Nations. While attending a conference at the University of Victoria, he announced that Indians were now "seeking economic and political equality, freedom of occupation, land ownership, speech and employment" and he called for "self-determination in a revamped reserve system."[32] In 1968, he went further and spoke the forbidden word in Canada by calling for "independence" for the First Nations with the DIA budget being turned over to the various communities to administer as they saw fit.[33]

Such pronouncements by George Manuel, who as a C.D. worker was an employee of the Department, were viewed as scandalous by the regional director and his bosses back in Ottawa. But George Manuel was not alone in attracting the Department's ire. The whole community development staff were increasingly seen by the upper bureaucrats as untrustworthy boat rockers who were part of the 1960s radical opposition to the existing order.

Seeing his universe wobble, Laing began to attack his own program publicly, by announcing that "it is not the role of community development programs to create dissension in the Indian communities." More forcefully – and more insultingly to Indian people – he claimed that community development was not "a process of agitation and revolt," but a means to "arouse the people from sloth and apathy."[34]

For George Manuel, the change of heart in the Department led to increasing friction with the local DIA officials who not only frowned on his radicalism, but began to question his travel while he was organizing for the CNIBC.

The final straw came in 1967 when Phillip Paul, with the support of George Manuel and the South Vancouver Island Tribal Federation, fired off a brief to the Department accusing the DIA "of racial prejudice, broken promises and insufficient social welfare."[35]

On 2 January 1968, Laing pronounced: "This self depreciation and self pity has to stop. Living in this world is first of all a personal challenge and the individual who demands attention and then accuses his benefactor of a patronizing attitude is not going to go very far."

Laing then described Canada's Indians as "potentially the wealthiest of Canadians" and cited their land holdings in the reserves. What he didn't mention was, that in calculating Indian "wealth," the Department looked at the reserves as real estate, rather than as homelands. Laing concluded by stating that, "If the Indian had been a little greedier in the past, he would be better off today."[36]

For George Manuel and the other C.D. workers in the field, the pressures from the local superintendents and the return of the Indian

Affairs Minister and his bureaucrats to the mind set of Colonel Jones led to a growing frustration. In Cowichan it had reached the point where the DIA came to investigate the local band elections after a group of radicals were elected to the council. That enquiry was blocked by the people's refusal to speak to the government-appointed investigator in anything but their own Cowichan language, which he didn't understand. But it was obvious that the Department was determined to crack down on the spirit of rebellion that the C.D. program was engendering. After two years at the job, George Manuel decided that if he was to remain "loyal and committed to the principles of community development" he would be forced to resign from the Department of Indian Affairs program.

But where was he to go? He had heard that there was an opening for another job with the Department in Ottawa, but he had had it with the Arthur Laing gang. Yet he couldn't devote much time to working for the movement if he had to go back to eight-hour shifts on the South Thompson River.

The solution to the problem came in a phone call from the brash young Cree, Harold Cardinal, who had recently won the election to the presidency of the Indian Association of Alberta. Cardinal told George Manuel he had wrested funds to start up an IAA-run community development program in Alberta and he wanted George to come to Edmonton to train the Indian field workers. There would be no "Lone Ranger" style pairing of Indian and white workers in Alberta. In Harold Cardinal's plan, Tonto would be running the show.

## CHAPTER SEVEN

# Down the Garden Path:
# Chrétien/Andras Consultations
# 1968–1969

Some reserve communities will not produce enough to give all the families who stay a satisfactory standard of living. The government cannot
be expected to support such communities indefinitely . . .

From *Choosing a Path*
Spring 1968

In the months before Harold Cardinal's call, there had been a significant
change in George Manuel's personal life. It began during one his visits
back home to Chase. He was staying with his half-brother Joe and his
wife Minnie and the three of them had gone for a few drinks at the local
tavern. When they came home, they put on a couple of Ernie Tubbs
records and sat down at the kitchen table with a bottle of whisky until
well after midnight.

Later, finding it difficult to sleep, George got up and went into the
kitchen to pour himself a nightcap. He was walking down the hall in the
buff when he was startled to see a young woman he vaguely recognized
looking up at him from the basement stairs. He wheeled around and
headed back to his bedroom.

The woman was Anthony August's niece, Marlene August; she had
been babysitting Joe's kids in the room downstairs and she had decided
to stay the night. Marlene, a quiet, shy woman, remembers that afterward she had laughed about her surprise meeting with George, because
she had always been a bit in awe of him. After all, George Manuel was
not only the former band chief, he was one of the best-known Indian

leaders in Canada through his work in the NAIB and on the National Indian Advisory Board. Seeing him in Joe's hall "buck naked with a bottle of Canadian Club" had given her a much different view of the renowned Indian leader.

The incident led to a great deal of kidding during the weekend and it wasn't long before George Manuel and Marlene August became friends. In the summer of 1968, Marlene went to live with him in Duncan. She was with him when Harold Cardinal's job offer came and she remembers that George was intrigued by the idea of working in Edmonton for the young Cree leader.

Since George had first met Harold Cardinal at the Advisory Board meeting, Cardinal had emerged as the rising star of the Canadian Indian movement. In 1968, at the age of twenty-three, he was elected as the president of the Indian Association of Alberta (IAA), and a year later he published *The Unjust Society*, a sweeping indictment of Canada's Indian policy. The book, which began by charging that generations of Canadian Indians had grown up behind "a buckskin curtain of indifference, ignorance and, all too often, plain bigotry," catapulted Cardinal into instant media fame.[1] *Maclean's* ran a major profile describing him on the one hand as "the most persuasive Indian spokesman since Cochise" and on the other as "an educated, vindictive treaty Indian whose ancestors were pushed around, slaughtered and swindled, and who now is out to get what he can for his people."[2]

Cardinal was most effective when he was taking on the dinosaurs at the DIA. And Arthur Laing was one of his favourite targets. Cardinal described him as "the most notoriously artful minister in the history of Canadian Confederation" for the way he managed to use DIA funding statistics to excuse the shameful neglect of the real problems of Indian people.

According to Cardinal, Laing's ignorance of the Indians of Canada "was exceeded only by his arrogance. He had his foot in his mouth so often he surely must have learned to love shoe leather. His idea of a thoughtful solution was to tell Indians to get out and pull themselves up by their bootstraps," but he "never bothered to make sure they had bootstraps."[3]

In articulating the anger and frustration of a generation of young native people, Cardinal was performing a useful service. But he also made valuable contributions to the strategic development of the movement, and one of his soundest moves was to bring George Manuel to Alberta to head the new Indian-run community development program.

George Manuel had proven his leadership ability in British Columbia and on the National Indian Advisory Board, but Cardinal also saw in him a man who had "a very deep sense of pride in his heritage as an Indian . . . what made him unique for a man of his generation and background was that the State had not succeeded in invalidating his Indian culture."[4] It was this pride in his heritage, and his forthright manner, Cardinal believed, that made Manuel so approachable and why he was held in such high esteem among the other national leaders.

After he began working with Manuel in Edmonton, Cardinal was also impressed by the older man's intellectual depth. He remembers that George "was constantly weighing his experiences and if there were some new thoughts or new approaches being made, he would try to put them together in his own mind to see how they would work and what the consequences would be. He was what I would call a strategic thinker."[5]

As much as for the C.D. program, Cardinal needed George Manuel's personal and intellectual resources in confronting one of his own domestic problems. At the time, Alberta's two major Indian nations, the Cree in the north and the Blackfoot in the south, had a relationship that was similar to that of the coastal and interior peoples in BC, with the relatively urbanized Blackfoot tending to look down on the isolated northern Cree. Cardinal himself was often met with suspicion by the Blackfoot people. With George Manuel working with the IAA, he had a respected national leader who didn't carry any of the baggage of the old Cree-Blackfoot rivalry. So along with setting up the C.D. program, George Manuel was given the job of reconciling the two native communities.

When he arrived in Edmonton, the $50,000 government grant for the C.D. program had not yet come through, so George Manuel spent some time travelling the province with Cardinal to get acquainted with the chiefs and the local people. He was impressed with Cardinal's approach. The young Cree leader "went out and listened to the people," he later told Michael Posluns, "he paid attention to their concerns."

When the government funding finally came through, George Manuel began screening applicants for the C.D. program and he tried to bring in those who had street-smarts as well as intelligence and commitment to the cause. He then set up regional workshops where he expounded the main principles of community development and warned the trainees about the forces of resistance they would face. As he put it, a real reformer had to demand changes "which may prove unpopular in certain quarters. Organizations for change will almost inevitably generate conflict; hopefully, in a country such as ours, this should not necessitate violence."

He later added that "if the powers that be are not listening and remain too attached to the structures they have created, then sometimes the emerging groups find no other recourse."[6]

Much of his training work involved pep talks that urged his workers never to give up the struggle. "You have a right to control your future," he told them, "you must gain a voice in politics, in the economic field and the social field of your communities. You will run into a lot of jealousy, a lot of opposition; but don't give up. And if ever you should fail, don't worry. It's not a real failure, because you still will have learned. So just try again."[7]

The idea of using every failure, as well as every success, as a learning experience, had become a feature of George Manuel's way of looking at things. He knew that the struggle would be a long one and that one of the main enemies would be the sense of defeatism caused by the lost battles. To inoculate himself and others against this reaction, he refused to acknowledge defeat. Everything was merely "a learning experience" on the road to the ultimate triumph of the Indian struggle.

During this period, George Manuel was also looking more closely at the self-image problems of his people. In Alberta, just as in Cowichan and Neskainlith, he found that one of the most insidious effects of the decades of oppression was to make many people ashamed of their own Indianness. In his own family, he had discovered the extent of the problem years earlier when he had taken his children for a rare visit to his mother's place in Kamloops and Maria had powdered the kids' faces to make them look whiter.[8] He hadn't said much at the time, but by the late 1960s, it came to symbolize in his own mind the need to restore to the people their pride in themselves.

At the time, another oppressed minority in North America – the blacks in the United States – were undertaking their own experiments in self-esteem building. Manuel and Cardinal decided to head south to see what they could learn. They travelled to the black ghettos in Chicago where they met with local activists and studied the black pride programs.

On the same trip, they went further south to visit Navaho reservations to examine their pioneering Indian education system; they wrapped up their tour in New York where they looked at special minority training programs and visited various offices of the United Nations.

At the UN they met with people from UNESCO, the World Health Organization and the Food and Agriculture Organization. Both George Manuel and Harold Cardinal were impressed by how similar the goals were of the North American Indian struggle and the anti-colonial struggle elsewhere in the world. Manuel filed the information for future reference.

While they were in the US, however, rumours began to circulate back in Canada that Cardinal and George Manuel were meeting with Black Panther leaders. Ottawa was already receiving RCMP reports of links between the *Front de libération du Québec* terrorist group and the Panthers, and there were concerns at the DIA that the Indian movement would merge with other self-styled revolutionary movements in North America and take up arms to address their grievances.

In those turbulent times, the idea of an Indian uprising was beginning to get serious attention across Canada. Ross Thatcher, the premier of Saskatchewan, was warning that a time bomb was ticking among the Indians of his province and Don Mazankowski warned the government in the House of Commons about a plot to train Canadian Indians in "riot techniques."[9]

Cardinal himself had done nothing to dispel these suspicions. In *The Unjust Society* he stated that current organizing "represents the final attempt by Indians to try to solve their problems within the context of the political system of our country. If it fails, and particularly if it is destroyed by the federal government, then the future holds very little hope for the Indian unless he attempts to solve his problems by taking the dangerous and explosive path travelled by the black militants of the United States."[10]

The attempt at organizing that Cardinal was referring to was a move to build a new national Indian organization. In late 1967, the leaders of the NIC had gotten together with many of the National Indian Advisory

Board members and agreed to disband their group to pave the way for a new organizing effort that would result in the emergence of two new organizations: one for status and one for non-status Indians.

The non-status Indians formed the Métis Council of Canada (forerunner of the Native Council of Canada). The status Indians launched the National Indian Brotherhood (NIB). The founding meeting of the NIB took place in Ottawa in early December, 1967. George Manuel was still in Edmonton but he was kept closely informed on the developments by Harold Cardinal and the large BC contingent, which included Guy Williams, Gus Gottfriedson, Victor Adolph and, most significantly, Phillip Paul.

In all, twenty-eight Indian leaders from across the country attended the meeting and Harold Cardinal recalls that there was a feeling of history in the making. It was, he suggests, "the first time since colonization that Indian people came together, not organized by outsiders. "[11]

Walter Dieter, the amiable Saskatchewan Cree, was elected to chair the meeting. The NIB's first priority was to avoid the mistakes of the NIC, which had its mandate diluted by an amorphous structure that included individual as well as organizational memberships. Unlike the NIC, which had concentrated on basic human rights issues, the National Indian Brotherhood would put its focus on the collective struggle based on an alliance of the existing provincial and territorial organizations, which in NIB jargon became known as PTOs.

This alliance structure was most strongly backed by the leaders of the highly developed prairie organizations. Harold Cardinal in Alberta, Walter Dieter in Saskatchewan and Dave Courchene of the Manitoba Indian Brotherhood all felt that "the people with the primary responsibilities were the leaders at the local level and the provincial organizations . . . because of the amount of work they had done in building their organizations."[12]

In other words, basing the NIB on the provincial and territorial organizations was first and foremost a simple recognition of the reality of the time. The NIB had no intention of usurping the local organizations that had been painfully developing their own structures for decades and were closer to the people and their immediate needs.

With the broad strokes of the organization drawn, a nine-member executive were selected to draft the NIB constitution. Walter Dieter was chosen as the provisional president with Dave Courchene as his vice-president. The remaining executive positions were filled by Harold Cardinal, Guy Williams, Phillip Paul, Gus Gottfriedson, Bob Charlie (Yukon), Harold Sappier (New Brunswick) and Omer Peters (Ontario).

After the elation of the founding meeting, however, came the realization that the NIB existed only on paper, and that it would remain in that flimsy state without a funding source. The government had supplied a small amount of money in early November to help pay for travel expenses to the founding meeting, but they would need much more to get the organization off the ground with office space and a staff. The executive had decided to go after core funding from the government, the way Harold Cardinal had done for Alberta's C.D. program, but in the meantime, Dieter was forced to return to Saskatchewan and take out a second mortgage on his house to provide the NIB with $55,000 in start-up funds.

With his own money backing the organization, Dieter moved to Ottawa with a vague mandate to get things started. He rented an office-apartment and tried to attract young people to the cause. He found fertile ground in Ottawa, where the DIA had recently instituted a program to hire Indian university students. In the summer of 1968, dozens of Indian students were working in various jobs for the department. Christine Deom, one of the students, remembers that Dieter would stop by to see the Indian students at the Traviata Tavern where they hung out, or visit them at their apartments and sit on the floor and speak to them about the national struggle. At the time, she remembers Dieter was "running the NIB out of his suit pocket. Literally. He would start checking his pockets and say, 'I have a letter somewhere here from Indian Affairs that says. . . .'"[13] As a result of Dieter's efforts, a number of those students were drawn into the movement and stayed in Ottawa to help build the organization.

George Manuel was following the launching of the NIB from Edmonton, where he was busy giving his C.D. course and engaging in political work in the south. His personal life was also full. He began his second family in January 1970, when Marlene gave birth to a daughter, Martha. The couple was also joined in Edmonton by Arthur, who like his older brother Bob, was still resentful of what he saw as his father's abandonment of his mother and the rest of the family.

Like Bob, Arthur had lived through a turbulent adolescence. He had been placed in the Kamloops residential school during his mother's hospitalization, and he and some friends went AWOL with a vague idea of hopping a freight to Toronto. Unfortunately, they were asleep when the train pulled into Calgary. They were caught by the CN police and ended up in the city jail. Even though Arthur was only fifteen years old, he was given twenty-five days in jail or a twenty-five dollar fine; because he was broke he had to serve the time.

He called his father from the jail and George said something to the effect of "You got yourself into this, you get yourself out of it."[14]

It was, Arthur recalls, another instance of his father's "the hard way was the best way" child-rearing philosophy. In this case, though, George waited until Arthur had some time to think things over, then sent the money for the fine and a bus ticket to Duncan on the condition that Arthur return to school.

By the time Arthur joined his father in Edmonton, he was eighteen years old. Unlike his brother Bob, who had sworn off politics in his younger years, Arthur's revenge was to embrace the most radical strain of politics. He immersed himself in the writings of Malcolm X, the Black Panthers, Cuban revolutionaries and members of the Red Power movement in the U.S.

With this type of ideological intake, he began to look on his father as a hopeless "establishment" figure and frequent political arguments were added to the day-to-day family disputes.

Arthur Manuel did have a glimpse of the softer side of his father during this period, though. In June 1970, word came from home that George's mother, Maria, had been hit by a car in Kamloops and had died from her injuries. George and Arthur drove to Kamloops together for the funeral and Arthur remembers that a few miles out of Edmonton, his father asked him to take over the wheel while he climbed into the back, where he sat without saying a word as he stared out of the window at the late spring rains and contemplated his often painful memories of his mother.

Maria, George knew, had not had a happy life. After she left Neskainlith and settled in Kamloops her confidence and sense of herself and her people began to ebb and she began to drink heavily. George had seen his mother only a few times over the previous decade and he had never really overcome the estrangement from her that he felt as a child.

Her sudden death ended any hope he might have had that they could reconcile their differences.

Shortly after his mother's funeral, George began to look at his own record as a parent and to realize some of his shortcomings. It was perhaps inevitable that he would have difficulty in his family relations. Over his forty-eight years, he had survived the rejection by his mother, two years in a residential school, a long painful battle for his life against T.B., a dozen years booming on the river and a dozen years on the road as a political organizer and leader. And he had done it all by sheer grit: the hard way is the best way.

His children with Marceline recall that while they were growing up, their father seemed to have a protective shell around him that none of them was able to pierce. After Maria's death, he was still committed body and soul to the cause and he was still the sociable guy who would get up and play his banjo and sing a song at a party, but he also began to put some effort into raising his second family with Marlene and in trying to patch up things with the children he had with Marceline. George Manuel would never be a model husband or father, but he did, at least, become more open and accessible to the people closest to him.

» «

In early 1968, the founders of the National Indian Brotherhood had envisioned a slow and measured drive to build the organization. But while the first halting steps toward launching the NIB were being taken, they found themselves with a new slate of opponents in Ottawa and a new set of challenges to face.

In April 1968, when the NIB was just a few months old, the federal Liberal Party elected Pierre Trudeau as its leader and, by extension, as the new Prime Minister of the country. Trudeau called an election for June 25 and the Liberals won a majority government. The Trudeau era, which would stretch well into the 1980s (with only a brief Conservative interregnum in 1979) had begun. This period would offer the Indian movement some of its greatest gains along with a few of its most painful setbacks.

For the first six years of the Trudeau reign, the government point man in the battle with the Indian movement was Jean Chrétien, who was named the new Minister of Indian Affairs and Northern Development shortly after the June election.

Indian Affairs hadn't been Chrétien's first choice. He had been working with Mitchell Sharp at Finance and he hoped he would be appointed
Canada's first French-Canadian Finance Minister. He recalled that during the 1968 campaign someone in British Columbia had asked him,
"what will the policies of the Trudeau government be for the Indians
of Canada?"

"Do you want a frank answer?" Chrétien replied, "I don't know a
damn thing about it." Everyone laughed. Three weeks later Trudeau
invited him to become Minister of Indian Affairs.

Chrétien mentioned those remarks to Trudeau when the Indian
Affairs cabinet post was offered, but Trudeau, the Outremont aristocrat,
replied that Chrétien represented a "similar background. You're from a
minority group, you don't speak much English, you've known poverty.
You might become a minister who understands the Indians."[15]

The 1968 election also saw Len Marchand elected to the House of
Commons as the first status Indian M.P. Marchand's replacement as the
special assistant to the Indian Affairs minister, Bill Mussell, was also a
familiar face to George Manuel. Genevieve Mussell's son Bill had graduated from the UBC school of social work in 1957 and had worked with
the NAIB and as the director of the Vancouver Indian Centre. Henry
Castilliou, still acting as the Liberal Party talent scout, had recommended him as Len Marchand's replacement at Indian Affairs.

The other important new figure in the Department during this
period was Robert Andras, who was attached to the DIA as minister
without portfolio in charge of new initiatives. In this case, the new initiatives were the round of cross-country consultations that Arthur Laing
had introduced in late 1967 as a way of going over the heads of what he
saw as his unruly Indian advisors.

At the time, Laing promised that the consultations would lead to a
new Indian Act that would "provide for the emancipation of Canada's
reserve Indians."[16] He then sent to every reserve in the country a booklet
called *Choosing a Path* that asked thirty-four questions about the course
the government should take in its future Indian policy.

*Choosing a Path* soon became known as "Down the Garden Path" in
Indian country because it seemed to point toward gutting the entire
reserve system. Among other things, the booklet suggested that "some
reserve communities will not produce enough to give all the families
who stay a satisfactory standard of living. The government cannot be

expected to support such communities indefinitely." It then went on to suggest that many Indians would have to leave the reserve and "choose between the conveniences and demands of modern life and some of their own traditional attitudes."[17]

As Cardinal pointed out, "Indian leaders shuddered at the thought of a dialogue with the Honourable Mr. Laing," but in the short term, his replacements weren't much better.[18]

Chrétien and Andras carried out Laing's *Choosing the Path* consultations with a vengeance. While the native leaders were still trying to draw up a constitution for the National Indian Brotherhood, they found themselves in the middle of a consultation blitz that began with Andras visiting Yellowknife in July 1968, and moving at a hectic pace to Toronto, Fort William and Sudbury on what was purported to be a cross-country sounding of Indian opinion.

In those first weeks, Andras received a decidedly mixed reception. In some places, Indians were curious about the new process but in other areas, such as in the far north, he was greeted with a pint of beer poured over his head and the suggestion that Indians would choose their own path without DIA interference.

Andras's most difficult reception came in Edmonton, where Harold Cardinal refused to meet with the minister until he had consulted with his people, and in British Columbia, where George Manuel returned for the consultations to serve notice that the BC Indians would not be railroaded into any new DIA scheme.

Both Manuel and Cardinal were concerned that the hurried pace of the consultations and their narrow focus on the thirty-four questions of *Choosing a Path* were masking a hidden DIA agenda. They feared that if Indian people didn't have time to reach a common position on the main issues, any discord would be used by the DIA to justify whatever course of action they had already privately decided on.

But George Manuel's greatest fear, which he discussed with Phillip Paul, was that Chrétien wanted to declare Indians "equal" to other Canadians and abolish the reserve lands, which had been the official Liberal policy from Pickersgill in the 1950s to Laing in the mid-1960s.

These suspicions were given more weight on September 28, when Chrétien announced a major reorganization of the Department of Indian Affairs without consulting a single Indian organization. The fact that the minister would make such a move when his government had pledged to work closely with the Indian people suggested that the DIA was moving along its business-as-usual track.

As expected, Indian leaders denounced Chrétien for the move, but to his surprise, he also came under fire from Robert Andras. On September 29, Andras publicly criticized Chrétien and the Department's unilateral reorganization in a nationally televised interview.

After opposition MPs began joking about a "tribal war" in the DIA between "the minister and the real minister,"[19] Andras was forced to back down. The impression this left with most Indian leaders was that they were facing a good cop/bad cop strategy, with Andras playing the former and Chrétien the latter.

George Manuel confronted the good cop, Andras, when he returned to BC to chair a consultation meeting in Nanaimo. Before the DIA team arrived, he and Phillip Paul hatched a plan to seize the initiative from the Department and return the consultation to the people. Their first move was to meet with the delegates who would be at the hearing and to draw up a brief that outlined a common position on the Indian Act. When the government consultation began, they would submit the brief, then use the rest of the meeting to discuss aboriginal rights. If the DIA officials objected, they would walk out of the meeting.

As it turned out, Andras didn't arrive until the second day of the consultation. The meetings began with the regional superintendent, Jeffery Boys, announcing that he would be the chair for the moment and asking the delegates to introduce themselves. Before the introductions began, Phillip Paul was on his feet insisting that the election of the chair be the first item on the agenda.

When Boys tried to side-step the issue, Paul announced that the delegates had agreed to hold a meeting *in camera* which would take the rest of the morning. The delegates then filed out and left the DIA people cooling their heels for the next three-and-a-half hours.

When they came back to the hall, George Manuel had been elected chair, and not co-chair as Boys had proposed, and he announced to Boys that a brief had been adopted by the delegates. After it was read into the record, Boys found his Department under attack from the floor for its failure to uphold its fiduciary responsibilities toward Indian lands and Indian hunting and fishing rights. Boys replied with an odd speech about Indians being "free to sue and be sued, free to go where they wished as citizens of Canada" and denied that there was any guardian-ship relationship expressed in the Indian Act.

Phillip Paul suggested that the whole meeting was a waste of time without Andras present and called for an adjournment. George Manuel proclaimed the session closed and announced a private meeting among the Indian delegates for that evening.

The next day, Boys made an effort to bring the meeting back to the Indian Act, but once again Phillip Paul stood up to call for an *in camera* meeting. When the delegates returned, George Manuel announced that they had decided "to terminate discussions on the Indian Act" because they believed their brief covered the main points on the proposed changes.

Clearly flustered, Boys decided to wait until Andras arrived before making any further attempts to push the DIA's agenda. When Andras showed up, Boys told him how the consultation was slipping out of control and the minister wisely decided not to try to force the issue. He acknowledged George Manuel as the legitimate chair of the meeting and accepted the delegate's brief as the official word on the Indian Act. When he responded to it, he did so diplomatically.

The brief was, he said, "the best I've seen in the sense that it's very easy to follow," but there were some things that "other Indian people in other parts of the country might not agree with." The main problem was the point that called for removing the section in the Indian Act that stripped a native woman of her status if she married a non-native. Andras said that he personally agreed with the idea of taking out the discriminatory clause, but he thought other Indian groups might disagree.

What Andras had most trouble with, however, was what he called "the price tag" on settling the BC land question. When dealing with the cost he said, "I want to come before you quite honestly. I know my colleagues would say, it's a very large price tag and we may have to face this over many, many years, quite a few years if it's huge."[20]

The Indian leaders had not, in fact, expected much more in the way of concrete results from the meeting. What they wanted to do was to use the consultation to send a message to the government: if the Department wanted to consult with the Indian leadership, it would have to do so from the floor rather than from the podium.

If there was any doubt in the matter, it was dispelled during the final national consultation meeting that was held in Ottawa from 28 April to 5 May 1969. The meeting had originally been scheduled for the early spring, but the Indian leaders had convinced Chrétien to put it off so they would have time to prepare a common position.

Working behind the scenes, Harold Cardinal, George Manuel and the NIB leadership came together and agreed to reject the government's agenda for studying the Indian Act. Instead, as George Manuel had done in Nanaimo, they would use the conference to attack the paternalism of the Department of Indian Affairs and then steer the discussion toward the land issue.

It is a measure of George Manuel's stature in the Indian community that when the five-day national conference opened on the morning of April 28, the forty Indian delegates from across Canada chose him, and not the provisional NIB president Walter Dieter, as their chair.

As soon as George Manuel gavelled the session open, it quickly became apparent that the politicians were in for another rough ride. Harold Cardinal stood to challenge the Department's organization of the conference and the delegate distribution. Then he announced that "the Alberta people had given a clear instruction to the Alberta delegation that the Indian Act was not the issue and that they should talk only of their rights – rights that had been denied to them for over a hundred years."

He went on to state that the Indian Act was only "a symptom of larger problems that existed – namely paternalism" and that the delegates from Alberta "had not come to suggest things that the government wanted to hear, but to tell the government and the people of Canada what the Indian people of Alberta wanted."[21]

For the next four days, the conference oscillated between a forum to hold Chrétien's feet to the fire and a kind of informal National Indian Brotherhood meeting where the presence of the DIA officials was more or less ignored.

The most important accomplishment during the meeting was the establishment of a new body that the main figures in the NIB had designed in evening sessions in their hotel rooms. The new organization was called the National Committee on Indian Rights and Treaties (NCIRT). It would begin a major research project on Indian aboriginal and treaty rights and, eventually, act as a negotiating body with the government on behalf of the First Nations.

At first the NCIRT was to be set up as a separate organization, but when Jean Chrétien pointed out that it would be difficult to answer funding requests from both the NIB and the NCIRT, the delegates agreed to establish it as an ad hoc committee of the NIB. They then presented Chrétien with a bill for over a half a million dollars to fund the Committee's country-wide research. Chrétien greeted the request with raised eyebrows and agreed only to study the matter.

Andrew Delisle, who had founded the Indian Association of Quebec in February 1968, was elected to head the new National Committee; it would be his job to pry funding from the department. After the May 1969 consultation meeting in Ottawa, however, he had little success getting to see the minister. At the time, Jean Chrétien was busy putting the final touches on his White Paper, which would set a new Indian policy for his government. The Paper was to be tabled in the House of Commons in June, on the first anniversary of Trudeau's election victory, and it promised to blaze a completely new trail in Canadian-First Nations relations.

When it was released, however, it read as if it had been secretly put together by Arthur Laing as an act of revenge on the leaders of the National Indian Advisory Board for making his political life so uncomfortable. Or going back further, it contained echoes of D.C. Scott's objective of working for the day when "there is not a single Indian in Canada that has not been absorbed into the body politic and there is no Indian question, and no Indian Department."

Among the First Nations, the White Paper caused such a shock that it instantly united them in opposition to it and lifted George Manuel into the leadership of the National Indian Brotherhood as the one man Indian leaders thought capable of blocking the Trudeau-Chrétien assault on their historic rights.

Ironically, Chrétien would later claim that one of his greatest accomplishments in the Indian Affairs portfolio was the promotion of Indian unity. But George Manuel later remarked that Chrétien's claim as the father of Indian unity could be compared to "Dwight Eisenhower and John Foster Dulles claiming credit for the success of the Peoples' Republic of China."[22]

## CHAPTER EIGHT

# From White Paper to Red Paper
## 1969-1970

We couldn't believe it. He was transferring everything to the provinces
and washing his hands of the Indians. And he said he had consulted
with us. That was bullshit.

Dave Courchene on the Chrétien White Paper

As George Manuel and Harold Cardinal had feared, Jean Chrétien
already had his own agenda before the consultations were under way.

As early as 20 September 1968, Chrétien had told an Indian-Eskimo
Association audience: "it is possible that the Indian people will decide
that there should not be an Indian Act at all. They might decide that
they do not want special legislation. There would then be required some
transitional legislation which would transfer federal responsibility for
the land to the Bands and individuals. On completion of the process, the
Act would pass out of existence."[1]

What Jean Chrétien had hinted at in September 1968 was exactly
what he delivered to the House of Commons in June 1969. To a visitors'
gallery packed with Indian representatives, and to the 200 other Indian
leaders in the capital awaiting the new policy, Chrétien announced that
the government had decided to relinquish its trust position toward
Indian lands, turn the services for Indian communities over to the provinces and disband the Indian Affairs department over a five-year period.

As compensation, the government would appoint a claims commissioner and launch a five-year $50 million economic development
program for the poorer reserves.

The White Paper would, however, effectively end Indians' special status in Canada. Their national territories would be reduced to real estate and the federal government would rid itself of its obligations to the people of the First Nations.

Dave Courchene's reaction – that Chrétien's consultations had been a fraud – was shared by Indian leaders from across Canada. Walter Dieter issued a press release from the National Indian Brotherhood that charged that the result of the government proposal would be "the destruction of a nation of people by legislation and cultural genocide."[2] Over the next week, telegrams from Indian bands and associations poured into Indian Affairs blasting the government for its unprecedented attack on their aboriginal rights.

Harold Cardinal, who had refused to go to Ottawa to hear the speech, compared the policy to the physical genocide of earlier generations. "The Americans to the south of us used to have a saying: 'The only good Indian is a dead Indian . . .'," but Chrétien had amended this to read "The only good Indian is a non-Indian."[3]

George Manuel didn't even have to look at Canada's neighbours for historical precedents. He compared it to the "Mackenzie King policy, which said, in effect, 'Indian or Canadian, and never the two shall meet'."[4]

Manuel's observation was reinforced in the aftermath of the White Paper when the Prime Minister suggested that the Indians of Canada had enjoyed a "special status" in the past, but they were now at a crossroads and it was time to "decide whether the Indians will be a race apart in Canada or Canadians of full status."[5]

While rejecting the idea of aboriginal rights, Trudeau admitted that the government would have to honour treaty rights, but only for the time being. The treaties, he said "shouldn't go on forever," because it was "inconceivable . . . that in a given society one section of the society have a treaty with the other section of the society."[6]

The idea that the government planned to eventually abrogate its Indian treaties was fuel for the White Paper fire, uniting and mobilizing the First Nations in a way that had never happened before.

Jean Chrétien, however, greatly underestimated the forces that were ranging against him. His first tactic was to send his bureaucrats across the country to find individual Indian leaders who agreed with his position. Then he would defend his policies by claiming that the Indians themselves were not united on the issue and suggest that his White Paper policies were the only way out of the deadlock.

It was an old DIA ploy and it had often worked in the past, but this time it failed miserably. On reserve after reserve, in province after province, the DIA officials not only were unable to enlist support for their new policies, but often found that local leaders refused to meet with them. In Alberta, Harold Cardinal went as far as to direct the people to "if necessary forcibly exclude federal officials from Indian lands."[7]

By mid-July, the only Indian leader in Canada who had spoken out in favour of the new Chrétien policy was his fellow Liberal MP, Len Marchand.

Marchand had backed the main principles in the proposal in March, when he told the House that "there should not be special status in Canada for any group of people. There should not have to be special laws saying that I am an Indian. We are all Canadians."[8]

In a major Parliamentary debate on the White Paper, Marchand echoed this stand by stating that "a lot of these things that are embraced in the policy are things for which the Indian people have been asking. We have been asking ourselves, are we going to be treated as children for the rest of our lives or are we going to take on the responsibilities of adults?"

As the extent of the opposition to the White Paper became clear, however, even Marchand began to backtrack. In the House, he spoke of the fears of the Indian people that the new policy would lead "to a constitutional change which will turn over the responsibility for Indians to the provinces . . . I plead with the minister to look at this matter very carefully, and clarify it so that it will be clearly understood."[9]

Chrétien took Marchand's advice and began a clarification offensive. In the fall of 1969, he explained that "at root of much of the reaction of Indian spokesmen to the proposals is distrust of government and serious misunderstandings as to what the proposals mean."

To enlighten the Indian leaders, he began a series of speeches explaining what the proposals were "not." Chrétien announced that "the statement is NOT a final policy decision to be implemented regardless of what anyone else says.

"The Statement does NOT propose or suggest that Indian reserves should be abolished.

"The Statement does NOT propose that the provincial government should take over responsibility for Indian land.

"The Statement does NOT propose to disregard treaties and end them unilaterally."[10]

While the minister droned on about the NOTs, he must have been aware, or certainly should have been, that his own department was acting in direct contradiction to its central thesis, that the White Paper was not a firm policy decision.

Two *Winnipeg Free Press* reporters who studied the period discovered that in August 1969, Chrétien's assistant deputy minister, John Mac-Donald, circulated a letter to his staff which stated that the White Paper contained, along with proposals that were subject to modification, "certain principles, which are incontrovertible. . . ."[11]

The DIA had also enlisted seven public relations firms from Halifax to Vancouver to sell the proposals and hired William Wuttunee, the former head of the National Indian Council, for $200 a day to lobby reserve Indians on the government's behalf.

Wuttunee's ideas had never been far from official DIA policies. As early as 1959, he backed Diefenbaker's Indian citizenship bill because "in the age of rocketry and sputniks . . . It is incumbent upon us to look to the new and forget the old." According to Wuttunee the lucky Indians were those who had "rubbed shoulders with white civilization," and he believed that assimilation and the abolition of Indian reserves would solve the Indian problem.[12]

Ten years later, his ideas hadn't changed. But those of the Indian people had. When Wuttenee tried to spread his good news in his home province of Saskatchewan, he was promptly disowned by the chiefs of ten bands in the Battleford area and he was refused entry to reserves across the country.

Wuttunee did not take this rejection lightly. He sat down to write *Ruffled Feathers*, a stinging condemnation of the Indian leadership at both the national and provincial levels. But by the time the book was published, Wuttunee was largely a forgotten figure and his attacks on his fellow Indians were ignored by both Indians and non-Indians.

In fact, all of the energies of Canada's Indian leaders were dedicated to building the National Indian Brotherhood up to a position where it could lead a nation-wide fight against the White Paper.

This strategy was in evidence during the 17-19 July NIB meeting at the Fort Garry Hotel in Winnipeg. The *Indian News* reporter described the meeting as "one of the most crucial meetings of Indian leaders in Canada,"[13] and it was an indication of things to come that once again George Manuel, and not Walter Dieter, was chosen to chair it.

The reporter was Dave Monture, the nephew of Gilbert Monture. He recalled that at the outset some of the Indian leaders wanted to have him ejected from the room because *Indian News* was a DIA publication and they didn't want anyone remotely connected to the government present. But George Manuel intervened and told him, "go ahead and report. It's better for the government to know how people feel."[14]

Monture wrote that he was impressed with the "able chairmanship" and "rallying power" of George Manuel, although at that meeting very little prodding was needed to move the delegates. The room was permeated by a feeling of crisis as the delegates pondered the disastrous effects the White Paper could have on their lives, their children's lives and the future of their nations.

They decided that one strategy to block the White Paper's implementation would be to build an alliance with the provincial premiers, who would have to accept the new costs entailed in the federal transfer of jurisdiction over Indian social services to the provinces. The NIB already had one provincial ally in the NDP premier of Manitoba, Ed Schreyer, who met with the delegates in Winnipeg and promised not to accept the new responsibilities without the approval of the Indian people.

The two largest provinces, Ontario and Québec, had publicly supported the White Paper transfers, but there was hope that they would change their positions. The main targets, however, were the western premiers, who were reportedly worried about the cost of delivering provincial services to their large Indian populations.

After agreeing to lobby the premiers, the delegates decided they would collectively refuse to speak to "any government task-force member on any new policy until the Indian people made their own studies and drew up a set of concrete policy proposals of their own."[15]

The delegates then turned their attention to internal matters, specifically to the NIB's constitution. They agreed that the role of the organization would be to act as a "national spokesman for the PTOs [provincial and territorial organizations] throughout Canada" and to ensure "the enforcement and fulfilment of all Indian treaties and of the aboriginal rights of Indians."[16] The new definition of "national spokesman" was an important expansion of the NIB's original mandate to act as coordinator of provincial and territorial bodies. The change reflected the realization that only a national organization with real powers could hope to derail Chrétien's White Paper Express.

Even in its infancy, the NIB wasn't free from internal politicking, however. Dieter's leadership was being quietly questioned because it was believed he was too easygoing to lead the White Paper battle effectively. At the Winnipeg meeting there was an open challenge to his leadership from the National Committee on Indian Rights and Treaties (NCIRT) chairman, Andrew Delisle. But Delisle had some cumbersome political baggage of his own.

There were rumours that he had links to the federal Liberal Party and fears that he would be out of control if he added the NIB presidency to his NCIRT chairmanship. The suspicions about Delisle intensified when the government awarded him and the NCIRT $300,000 to carry out land claims research. Delisle was able to use the money to open a large office in Ottawa and hire a staff of experts. More important, he was responsible for disbursing land claim research funds to the provincial organizations and this could give him incalculable political clout.

Walter Dieter responded to Delisle's surprise leadership challenge in Winnipeg with an odd speech that began by reminding his friends that all he had started out with was $61 and "and a resolution to organize the Indians of Canada," and he said that he had "tried to find money for Indian people with no strings attached.

"The money I gave to them, telling them all I wanted was their receipts. I told them I don't want the bills or anything, this money is your business – if you gather together and all get drunk, at least there's one thing you'll have done – you'll have gotten together."[17]

Dieter's appeal to the more prosaic instincts of the executive was probably not necessary, however. Most of them, like Dave Courchene were worried that in Delisle's NCIRT they had already "created a monster."[18] The fear was that the NCIRT would rise up and swallow the NIB whole so they reluctantly backed Dieter at the Winnipeg meeting – just to keep Delisle at bay.

As soon as the meeting was over, however, the provincial leaders again began to look for a more acceptable replacement for Dieter. While they searched, the NIB remained in a precarious financial state. The organization had received only $20,000 in government grants to pay for travel expenses and rent halls for conferences. There was no core funding to open and staff an office and the NIB was forced to use a donated corner of the Manitoba Indian Brotherhood office in Winnipeg as its official home.

At the time, even the non-native Indian and Eskimo Association was getting more funding than the NIB and there was a sense that the Department was trying to isolate the politically orientated NIB, while it used the NCIRT as a negotiating partner in carrying out the provisions of the White Paper. This fear increased when the Department responded to the NIB boycott of government talks by appointing Lloyd Barber, the vice-president of the University of Saskatchewan, as the claims commissioner to horse trade with Delisle on the land issue. The NIB was being frozen out.

Without funds, and with the leadership issue up in the air, the organization was left in limbo. So George Manuel turned his attention to British Columbia, where he and Phillip Paul were taking advantage of the White Paper crisis to realize their long-standing goal of bringing BC Indians together into one organization.

The two men had recognized the possibility of using the White Paper as an organizing tool as soon as it was released. As a member of the NIB executive, Paul was in Ottawa at the time and he shared in the shock of Indian leaders across Canada at its contents. He remembers that he and another BC activist, Don Moses, saw the document as "the ultimate in assimilation," and they sat up all night in their hotel room trying to decide what they should do about it.[19]

They decided they would call an all-chiefs conference, but when they returned home, they found that George Manuel had already beaten them to the punch. He had called Chief Denis Alfonse of the Cowichan reserve and had urged him to send a letter to the BC chiefs announcing an all-chiefs meeting in Kamloops in October to discuss setting up a province-wide organization to fight the White Paper proposals.

Alfonse's letter got a very good response, and Phillip Paul and Don Moses joined with him to promote the October meeting. Paul and Moses spent the entire summer on the road visiting nearly every Indian community in BC to speak about the urgency of a united BC organization to fight the White Paper proposal. They found very little urging was needed. In British Columbia, as elsewhere in the country, fears about the

White Paper ran deep within the grass roots, as well as among the leaders, and for the first time since the Allied Tribes was founded fifty years earlier, there was a willingness among BC Indians, both coastal and interior, to work together.

George Manuel's hand in organizing the October meeting was reflected by the fact that it was held on his home turf, at the residential school in Kamloops. One hundred and seventy chiefs answered the call. George Manuel was elected to chair the conference with Phillip Paul assuming the unofficial leadership from the floor. Paul began with a sombre warning. "The history of disunity in this province gave birth to this conference . . . and depending on the outcome of this conference is the future of your children and mine."[20]

Before the three-day meeting was over, the chiefs had voted unanimously to found a province-wide organization called the Union of BC Indian Chiefs. The Union would have a three-tiered structure. At the top would be a three-person executive that was responsible to a regional council of chiefs. The regional council was in turn responsible to the annual assembly of chiefs.

The first executive was made up of Victor Adolph, Herbert Maitland and Phillip Paul, although Paul was recognized as the organization's unofficial leader.[21]

The creation of the province-wide organization was a dream come true for George Manuel. Early in the new year he had been approached by Don Moses and others and asked to return to BC to "give some direction" to the Union, and he had tentatively agreed to do so; but first he headed off to Ottawa with the Alberta delegation for a special meeting of the NIB to give a national endorsement to Alberta's Red Paper.

The Red Paper was Alberta's formal response to the White Paper. It had grown out of the same sort of painstaking process of consultation at the community level that George Manuel had used for his Aboriginal Native Rights brief in 1960.

The hundred-page paper was officially titled *Citizens Plus* from a quote in a DIA report which stated that "Indians should be regarded as 'Citizens Plus'; in addition to the normal rights and duties of citizenship, Indians possess certain additional rights as charter members of the Canadian community."[22]

Most of the Red Paper was devoted to a clause-by-clause refutation of the White Paper, but the Alberta chiefs also included a scathing indictment of the general direction of the government's policies, which offered a future where the Indian people "would be left with no land and consequently the future generation would be condemned to the despair and ugly spectre of urban poverty in ghettos."

The White Paper, the document stated, had been an insult to the Indian people and the consultations that preceded it had been a cruel joke with no one in the Department listening to what the people had said. "Even if we just talked about the weather," the Red Paper charged, the minister "would turn around and tell Parliament and the Canadian public that we accepted his White Paper."[23]

The Alberta counter-proposal called for an immediate halt to the implementation of the White Paper until the Indian people were consulted about their ideas on changes to the Indian Act. The Alberta Indians also demanded a transfer of funds to the Indian people so they could run their own education system, and a formal recognition by the government of aboriginal as well as treaty rights.

Soon after the Red Paper was released, the NIB adopted it as the official national position and arranged to have it presented to the Prime Minister and the entire cabinet in a formal ceremony on Parliament Hill.

The fact that Prime Minister Trudeau and the Cabinet had agreed to meet with the Indian leadership was a reflection of how well their anti-White Paper campaign was working. It was also an important historic milestone. As Harold Cardinal observed, "In the 1940s our leaders had to be content with meetings with Indian agents at the local level. In the 1950s, they had upgraded the level of contact to what they used to call regional superintendents of Indian affairs. In the sixties, they had been brought, as a result of the advisory committees, to the level of the director of Indian affairs and, occasionally, the minister. "In the late 1960s, that had been upgraded to more contact with the two ministers as opposed to relying on bureaucratic channels."

The presentation of the Red Paper "represented the first time that Indians could sit down and have substantive discussions with the Prime Minister and his cabinet. Diefenbaker and Pearson only met with Indians as photo-ops, when they put the feathered headdress on."[24]

The 200 Indian leaders who gathered in Ottawa had their own appreciation of the usefulness of photo-ops and a large portion of the NIB's 2-3 June meetings were devoted to planning how to give the presentation its greatest impact.

As usual, George Manuel was elected to chair the meeting, and after the provincial delegations formally adopted the Red Paper as joint IAA–NIB policy, discussion was directed toward the ceremony. It was planned to the smallest detail; the Indian leaders even held a rehearsal the night before to make sure there were no slip-ups.

As George Manuel recalled, "it was a life-and-death situation. The whole future depended so much on how the government was going to react to it."[25]

As it turned out, the ceremony went off without a hitch and had an even greater impact than the organizers had hoped. The meeting began with Prime Minister Trudeau introducing the members of his Cabinet and Walter Dieter introducing the Indian representatives. Then the NIB launched its *coup de théâtre*.

After a brief prayer by a Blood Indian elder, two prairie chiefs in ceremonial dress stood up and approached the cabinet table. One handed a copy of the Red Paper to Prime Minister Trudeau, the other handed a copy of the White Paper back to Jean Chrétien, because "We have our own set of ideas as to what the Indians should be doing for themselves and we have come up with a proposal. We do not need this any longer. Our people do not need the Indian policy paper."[26]

Then it was Dave Courchene's turn. He explained that "this past year, like the past hundred years, has been most difficult for our people. But unlike the past hundred years, this year is not ending in frustration and anger. We have, for the first time in our history, joined together as one. . . . The government of Canada has had one hundred years to prepare its White Paper. We have had but one year to prepare our views. We now have but one hour to meet with you. This hour is one hundred years . . . We hope that this will not be our last hour."[27]

The presentation seemed to move the Prime Minister and his cabinet (with the possible exception of Jean Chrétien who was being invited to eat crow) and the discussions that followed took on a respectful tone on both sides. Harold Cardinal was applauded by the delegates, observers and even some of the reporters when he spoke of the historic importance of the meeting, and the Prime Minister was cheered when he admitted that after all the work on the White Paper, "the Indian people have looked at this and they have said, it's not good."

Trudeau then went on to share the blame with his Indian Affairs minister by admitting that "We had perhaps the prejudices of small 'l' liberals and white men who thought that equality meant the same law for everybody, and that's why as a result of this we said, 'well let's abolish the Indian Act and make Indians citizens of Canada like everyone else. And let's let Indians dispose of their lands like every other Canadian. And let's make sure that Indians can get their rights, education, health and so on, from the governments like every other Canadian'. But we have learnt in the process that perhaps we were a bit too theoretical, we were a bit too abstract, we were not as Mr. Cardinal suggests, perhaps pragmatic enough or understanding enough, and that's fine. We are here to discuss this."

Trudeau then made an emotional plea:

"You can say that the government doesn't understand, that it's dumb, that it is stupid or ignorant. Perhaps all these things are true, at least in part, but don't say we're dishonest and that we're trying to mislead you because we're not. We're trying to find the solution to a very difficult problem that has been created for one or two hundred years."

The Prime Minister reflected on his recent tour of Southeast Asia and Eurasia, where he claimed that he found Maoris in New Zealand doing well without any special legislative protection and the Malays in Malaysia with a great deal of protection doing poorly in comparison with the ethnic Chinese settlers. He then hinted that the White Paper was finished and said his government was "not looking for any particular solution."

But he warned that "the ultimate arbitration body is not going to be some court or some commissioner, or some committee of the Senate and the House of Commons. It is going to be the Canadian people. And these are the people you've got to convince."[28]

The meeting broke up with a promise of future meetings and a sense on all sides that a new era in Canadian government – First Nations understanding was now possible. But George Manuel was still sceptical. After the presentation he told Dave Monture that he had mixed feelings about the whole thing. Despite the government's fine words, he feared that the Department of Indian Affairs would still try to "move full speed ahead" on implementing the discredited policies.

Later, Cardinal agreed that the elation most of the Indian leaders felt after the presentation was misplaced. He compared the public humiliation of Chrétien to bringing down a grizzly bear, but they had failed to finish him off. In a very short time, the grizzly revived and came after them, "madder and wiser."[29]

Harold Cardinal and the other Western leaders still believed that the NIB under Dieter was not up to the challenge of battling the wounded Chrétien. So only days after the Red Paper presentation they met secretly in Drumheller, Alberta, to choose Dieter's replacement.

At the meeting were Harold Cardinal from the IAA, Dave Courchene from the Manitoba Indian Brotherhood, Dave Ahenikew from the Federation of Saskatchewan Indians and George Manuel. For the Western leaders, the sole item on the agenda was to convince George Manuel to run against Walter Dieter at the NIB's August meeting in Vancouver.

George Manuel initially refused and explained that he had already made up his mind to return to BC and work with Phillip Paul in building the Union of BC Indian Chiefs.

But Cardinal and the others persisted. George Manuel, they believed, had the tact and toughness, the sharp political instincts and the respect of Indian leaders across the country that would enable him to spearhead the fight against Chrétien.

"Because of his lifelong involvement with the Indian movement," Cardinal and the others felt, George Manuel "was familiar with the issues that were important to people with aboriginal rights. Because of the time he spent with us in Alberta, he had also developed an understanding of the issues important to treaty people. And so with that kind of complete background he was the best man for the position."[30]

Equally important, though, was George Manuel's ability to relate to the people at the reserve level, an ability that many of the urban Indian leaders lacked. If the White Paper was to be stopped, it would take the involvement and commitment of the grass roots and no one could better stir the people into action than a genuine man of the people like George Manuel.

During the meeting, the Shuswap leader continued to plead his commitments to the Union of BC Indian Chiefs, but as Cardinal put it, "We asked him, and we coaxed him to run and kept at him until he agreed."

Even though George Manuel was uncomfortable with the idea that to open up the NIB leadership, they would first have to find a way to dump Walter Dieter, he finally relented and agreed to run. They all knew that "Indian politics was the hardest kind of politics,"[31] because it so often involved competition between friends and at times, even family. Dieter was a friend, but the fight against the White Paper was more important than friendship. If Dieter had to be cast aside for the good of the movement, so be it.

After the meeting, George Manuel decided it would be good idea to disappear for a time while the western leaders engineered Dieter's ouster. He headed south for a short vacation in Mexico where he could recharge his batteries and ponder the direction he would take the National Indian Brotherhood.

On his way down, he stopped off to see his son Bob who was working in the orchards in Washington. Bob was going through a difficult time. He had been picked up for a driving offence in BC a few months earlier and faced a thirty-day jail sentence or a $250 fine. He was young and broke, so he skipped out and headed south where he found a job in the orchards similar to the one his father had had twenty years earlier.

They discussed Bob's legal problem and his father advised him to return to BC and see Phillip Paul, who was then running the native studies course at Camosun College on Vancouver Island. They also talked about the family and George Manuel tried, for the first time, to set things straight between him and his oldest son.

The meeting went a long way to repairing old wounds and before he left, George gave his son a copy of Harold Cardinal's book, *The Unjust Society*.

Bob Manuel read it after George left and for the first time in his life he began to see the Indian movement not for the personal toll it had taken on his family's life, but in the way his father saw it, as the struggle for the liberation of their people.

When he finished the book, he packed his bag and headed up to see Phillip Paul. Paul convinced him to enrol at Camosun and promised to help him with his legal troubles. Paul called a friend at the John Howard Society who went to the prosecutor and explained the situation. Taking into account that Bob Manuel was still in his early twenties, that he had turned himself in, and that he was enrolled in college, the prosecutor agreed to suspend the charges.

Phillip Paul then took Bob Manuel under his political wing and the younger Manuel became an eager student. He started to hitchhike to meetings around the island and sit in on Paul's strategy sessions. Like his father fifteen years earlier, Bob Manuel had been bitten by the political bug and would gradually find a prominent place for himself among the new generation of Indian leaders.

On his return from his Mexican vacation, his father, George Manuel, was ready to lead the national fight against Chrétien's White Paper. When he met with Harold Cardinal in Edmonton, he was told that the western leaders had arranged what has been described as "a constitutional coup" to remove Dieter and open up the president's job for Manuel.

The former South Thompson River boom man was about to become the leader of the First Nations of the country, and he would need all his log-rolling and jam busting skills to hold the young movement together and move it forward toward its goals of recapturing political and economic independence for the First Nations.

## CHAPTER NINE

# The National Chief

## 1970-1971

If Indian people have access to different departments of government, they can start playing one branch against the other . . . The Indians can come up better for that.

Doug Sanders
NIB legal advisor, 1971

The device the Western leaders used to force a leadership vote for the NIB's assembly of 21-23 August 1970 focused on a delay in the filing of the organization's incorporation papers. Walter Dieter had been elected for a two-year term at the Winnipeg meeting in July 1969, but the NIB by-laws hadn't been ratified or the official papers filed until a special 26-27 March 1970 meeting in Montreal. Dieter's 1969 election had thus taken place before the NIB was legally in existence and the Western leaders used that loophole to force a new vote.

At the time, the NIB was structured so that each PTO received one vote for every five thousand people it represented. BC's large Indian population gave it a sizable block of votes and George Manuel began to travel quietly through the province to test support for his presidency.

Clarence Jules, an old friend of George Manuel's and the chief of the Kamloops band, remembers George suddenly showing up at a Union meeting in Prince Rupert. In the hotel room after the meeting, Manuel told them about the suggestion made by Harold Cardinal and the other Western leaders that he run for the NIB presidency and asked them what they thought of it. He let them think it over until they were on the plane back to Vancouver. Then he told them that he had already agreed to stand for the position and that he wanted their support.

As expected, he was promised the backing of virtually every Indian leader in BC. He could also count on the support of the Alberta, Manitoba and Saskatchewan leaders who had convinced him to run. To get the support of Ontario, he and the western leaders got in touch with Omer Peters, a respected leader in the Union of Ontario Indians who had worked with George Manuel on the National Indian Advisory Board, and offered him the job of NIB vice-president on Manuel's ticket, which Peters accepted. To seal this BC-Ontario alliance, Fred Plain, another Ontario leader, was asked to nominate George Manuel for the presidency.

When the delegates arrived in Vancouver on August 19, Walter Dieter knew nothing of the forces aligned against him, so he made no objection when George Manuel was elected to chair the meeting or when the prairie leaders moved a motion declaring the Vancouver meeting as the first annual assembly of the National Indian Brotherhood.

Instead, Dieter went on with his president's report where he outlined what he saw as a limited role for the NIB in the Indian movement. He told the delegates that he would hate to see the NIB overshadow the provincial organizations. "I feel that we should keep the NIB in as small a capacity as we can get it but still be able to call the resources of public opinion of Indians across Canada to put pressure on government for anything that Indian people at the grass-roots level need."[1]

Interestingly, Dieter's approach to the NIB – as a creature of the PTOs – was echoed by Harold Cardinal when he suggested that "first of all in Alberta we are very conscious of our jurisdiction."[2] Cardinal asserted that the NIB had no business in matters related to education or health and he didn't want to have the NIB even studying them in its committees. At the time, Cardinal's restricted definition of the NIB's role passed without comment, but the role of the NIB would soon be a cause of some disagreement between him and George Manuel.

The leadership vote was held the following day, August 21, and three candidates were nominated: Walter Dieter from Saskatchewan, Noel Doucette from Nova Scotia and George Manuel from British Columbia.

To Walter Dieter's surprise, George Manuel was swept into the presidency on the first ballot. The Saskatchewan leader, who had mortgaged his house to give the NIB start-up funds, suddenly found himself out in the cold and he was wounded by the unexpected rejection.

It was an awkward moment for everyone in the room. Sensing this, George Manuel kept his acceptance speech short and low-key. He thanked the delegates for the confidence they had shown in him and promised to "guide the National Indian Brotherhood towards the achievement of its stated objectives." Then he called a meeting of his executive council to plan a new direction for the organization.[3]

The first order of business was a decision to close down the NIB office in Winnipeg, where they were three months behind in the rent and the phones had been cut off. The new NIB headquarters would be in Ottawa where the national Indian leadership would be close to the corridors of power.

To his chagrin, George Manuel also learned that the young organization was already $38,000 in debt and that his only staff would be his vice-president, Omer Peters, and two secretaries who would be transferred from Winnipeg.

The debt problem was further complicated when out of a sense of guilt for dumping Walter Dieter, the executive passed a resolution agreeing to pay his salary for the next year. Financial necessity caused them to rescind the offer a few weeks later and Dieter's salary, which wasn't actually being paid anyway, was officially terminated in September.

At the end of the meeting, Harold Cardinal agreed to pay George Manuel's salary from IAA funds, while George was struggling to put the NIB on an independent financial base.

Along with heading an indebted organization, George Manuel would have to quickly face the challenge of reining in Andrew Delisle's National Committee on Indian Rights and Treaties, which was beginning to swell to unwieldy proportions. In the fiscal year 1970-71, the NCIRT received $550,000 in government funds, $358,000 of which was to be disbursed to provincial research organizations. As George Manuel diplomatically put it, "the NCIRT and the [National Indian] Brotherhood – they were like two organizations. I felt my first responsibility was to bring these two together."[4]

As soon as the executive meeting ended, however, George Manuel found himself making an unscheduled trip to Ontario after Omer Peters and Fred Plain insisted he accompany them on a tour of their province.

George Manuel told them he had no money for travel and said that if they wanted him to make the trip, they would have to pay his way.

The Union of Ontario Indians did pay his way down, but they didn't have any money for his return trip. So George Manuel found himself stranded in Northern Ontario without a dollar in his pocket, and he had to contact Harold Cardinal in Alberta to send him money to get back to Edmonton.

It was an inauspicious beginning to his term in office and a signal of how precarious his financial position was as NIB president. When he contemplated the large debt and his lack of staff he resisted the move to Ottawa that the NIB executive had mandated. At one point he is even reported to have gone to the executive and advised that the NIB be declared bankrupt and closed down.

The executive rejected the proposal and after three months of stalling, George, his wife Marlene and their infant daughter headed east in his Toyota. When they arrived in the capital, they rented a small walk-up apartment in Aylmer, on the Quebec side of the Ottawa River. George and Marlene were happy to find they had a view of the Gatineau hills out of their window – the scene reminded them a bit of the hills behind Neskainlith – but they did not have enough money for furnishings, so for several months they lived in the empty shell of the apartment.

George Manuel's work arrangement wasn't much better. He was operating out of a borrowed corner of Andrew Delisle's NCIRT office at a time when he was supposed to be putting the NCIRT under control. After a short time, however, George Manuel found the fears about the Quebec leader had been exaggerated. While Delisle could be a tough political operator, he was committed to the cause and he and George Manuel got along well. If Andrew Delisle had had dreams of usurping the NIB's authority before George Manuel arrived on the scene, he showed little inclination after the Shuswap boom man showed up at his door.

In the long run, George Manuel would have more difficulty from his own provincial organizations than from Delisle. The first issue of contention was the relationship between the NIB and the government. The idea of the NIB meeting with various ministers, instead of dealing solely with the gatekeeper at Indian Affairs, was one of George Manuel's political priorities. In the wake of the Red Paper presentation, the Trudeau government had agreed to the NIB request for a permanent mechanism to facilitate meetings with various cabinet ministers. For the Indian movement, this was one more important step in their struggle to gain access to the country's centre of power.

News that George Manuel was beginning exploratory sessions of the joint NIB-Cabinet Committee was not universally welcomed, however. In a reflection of the federal-provincial tensions in the larger society, the NIB had a constant pull and push between the national office and the provincial organizations, and many of the provincial leaders feared that the NIB-Cabinet Committee would allow for too much centralization of power within the NIB.

To try to allay the provincial leaders' fears of NIB domination, George Manuel began an exhaustive series of cross-country travels. Including two foreign trips (to be dealt with in a later chapter), he logged more than one hundred thousand miles in his first ten months in office as he met with provincial and local leaders to spread the message that the NIB was their organization and to assure the sceptical that he would make it responsive to their needs.

It was a pattern that he would keep up throughout his six years as the NIB president. He would spend a good third of his time on the road, meeting the people in formal and informal settings, urging them on to greater political action and gauging their reaction to the NIB and its work. As Castilliou had discovered a decade earlier, George Manuel had a knack for walking into a room of ten strangers and leaving with ten friends. This personal touch became a central element in his leadership style at the NIB.

What he found in his initial travels, however, were broad disagreements about the role of the NIB. These problems were complicated by the great disparities, in both numbers and experience, of Indian organizations across the country.

The most powerful block among the PTOs was the prairie block that had put him into power. Ontario and BC had large Indian populations, but in both cases the unity of their organizations was still in a fragile state. Quebec and the Maritimes had relatively small native populations and new and largely inexperienced organizations, while the northern territories had large Indian populations, but weak organizations.

To address both the disparities in the movement and the confusion over the NIB's role, George Manuel called an executive council meeting in Ottawa in late September where he announced that he was going to "test the structure of the NIB" and hoped they would not be tied down by too many restrictions placed on them by the PTOs.

What was bothering him was that the Brotherhood had been "given a mandate but has no machinery to work with." He told his executive that "if you are giving us responsibility we want equipment to go along with that; otherwise, we cannot do the job you want us to."[5]

George Manuel also brought the executive into a discussion over the funding problem. There was a reluctance to go hat in hand to the DIA where, it was feared, every dollar would have a string attached to it. The idea was to get funding from various federal government departments for housing and health services, the same way the provinces did. Doug Sanders, a young lawyer George Manuel had seconded from NCIRT, outlined the strategy:[6]

"If Indian people have access to different departments of government, they can then start playing one branch against another; this really concerns Indian Affairs here as they have been able to go ahead without an effective check . . . What happens when there are four or five departments concerned? The Indians come up better for that."[7]

George Manuel decided to put the case of federal money to the Indian organizations on the same level as transfer payments to the provinces. He looked, for example, at Prince Edward Island, where the entire population was less than half that of the 260,000 status Indians in Canada, and the island's land mass was only a fraction of the size of the total reserve lands. PEI received almost five times as much in federal payments as the Indian people; the comparison was one that he would use again and again in the years ahead. It turned out to be an effective counter to Indian Affairs boasts that they were spending all those millions in programs to help the First Nations.

The initial focus of the NIB's funding drive was the Privy Council office, which was beginning to take on a kind of grab bag funding role in the government for special programs and organizations. The NIB was one of the first to line up at the withdrawal window.

After a great deal of behind-the-scenes negotiation with the Privy Council officials, George Manuel and the executive drew up a $1.7 million budget for the PTOs, with a further $259,000, representing one dollar per status Indian, for the NIB's operation. When the budget was officially submitted to the Privy Council, George Manuel warned that "the urgency of the situation demands that this payment should be made within ten days."[8]

As it turned out, the timing couldn't have been better. At the Red Paper presentation, Trudeau had promised regular consultations with the Indian organizations and George Manuel was able to point out to the government bureaucrats that any discussions with Indian leaders would be as meaningless as Arthur Laing's Advisory Board sittings if the Indian organizations didn't have funding to carry out consultations with their people.

The government reluctantly agreed. Six weeks later, funds were released, although not in the amounts that the NIB had asked them for. Both the PTOs and the NIB budgets had been cut in half and, as the Indian leaders feared, the cheque came with a pointed note that read:

"If after the consultative mechanism becomes operative it develops that you do not have sufficient money available to finance that aspect, we will be prepared to review the situation with you with a view to requesting additional funds."[9]

In other words, those additional funds would be tied to the NIB playing ball with the government. Even though George Manuel still feared that Chrétien was trying to push the policies of the White Paper on them under a new guise, he had no choice but to accept the money. To ensure that the government understood that he was accepting the cash, but not their directives, he set a tough tone in his speeches by attacking the attitude that the First Nations were getting some kind of gift from the government.

"When Arthur Laing was minister of Indian Affairs," George Manuel recalled, "he once said something to the effect that the Canadian taxpayer was spending $127 million dollars on the Indians and the taxpayer deserved a better return on his investment. Well, that statement is only partially true. The Canadian taxpayer did not spend a penny on the Indians of Canada – however the Canadian taxpayer did make available, through parliament, $127 million to the Department of Indian Affairs. The $127 million was then spent by the Department of Indian Affairs, and Mr. Laing was only correct about one thing, you're damn right the Canadian taxpayer deserves a better return on his investment."

The NIB leader then went on to demand that Canadians "stop referring to my people as *our* Indians. We are not your Indians.

"We don't need you identifying with our cause – we need you attacking one of the base roots of our problem – a stifling, condescending, paternalistic attitude.

". . . If you can't attack the root causes of paternalism and racism on your own . . . then get out of our road and don't slow us down by jumping on and off the band wagon."[10]

While George Manuel was serving notice that the First Nations would henceforth look after their own affairs, he was also busy putting the Privy Council money to use in setting up the new NIB office just a few blocks from the Indian Affairs building. As soon as the phones were hooked up, he began putting together his staff.

Before January 1971, his staff in the NCIRT office consisted of Omer Peters and the two secretaries who had been transferred from Winnipeg. His budget only allowed him to hire another secretary, but what he needed was an executive director, someone who could help him put together a solid team and then run things when he was on the road.

Fortunately for George Manuel and the NIB, one of the most capable people for the job happened to be living in Ottawa at the time. Marie Smallface Marule, a Blood Indian from Alberta, had just completed three years working in Zambia as a CUSO volunteer. She had all of the academic qualifications for the job, as well as a strong personality and a quick and incisive intellect. Her years in Africa had also given her a decolonization perspective along with a Marxist strategy on the native struggle that had been rare in the Indian movement in the past.

The two also hit it off on a personal level. When Marie Marule came to his office in October 1970, George Manuel began by admitting that, officially, he only had a job for a secretary. Marie showed she could be as forthright as George when she replied, "Fine, but I don't type and I don't take shorthand." George Manuel smiled and told her she was hired.

Marie Marule began working at the NIB in the first week of January 1971. Over the years, she and George Manuel developed a mutual respect and close political allegiance that would last until the end of his life. Marule recalls that she was taken by him from the start.

"George Manuel had a lot of presence. He had an international awareness and political astuteness. I was also surprised that he wasn't worried about my radicalism at the time. It was easy to talk with him because he was incredibly bright and extremely well read. He was a prolific reader and he had a natural ability to analyze. He was also a great listener and could pump people for what they knew."[11]

By the same token, it would be difficult to exaggerate Marie Marule's importance to George Manuel. In many ways she played the same sort of role in Ottawa – that of trusted confidant, advisor and unquestionably loyal friend and political ally – that Phillip Paul played in British Columbia. Paul remembers that in his frequent visits to Ottawa, the three of them got along "like three peas in a pod in terms of politics. We could sit down and have supper and talk about the whole gamut of national and international questions and how the Indian movement fit into the larger picture."[12]

The second most important person George Manuel hired during this period was Ron Shackleton. A six-foot-five Mohawk, Shackleton was one of the Indian students who was hired by the DIA in 1968 and who gravitated around Walter Dieter.

Shackleton was an intelligent and committed man with a gentle soul that earned him the respect of all who knew him. George Manuel made Shackleton his special assistant, and then had Shackleton's wife, Christine Deom, a Mohawk from Kahnawake, seconded away from her job at Indian Affairs to work with them at the NIB.

George Manuel next brought in Jamie Deacey, who also became involved with the movement from a government hiring program. Deacey wasn't an Indian; he was the son of one of the most influential bureaucrats in Ottawa, a man who had held senior positions with every prime minister since Mackenzie King. Jamie Deacey had been knocking around town, working for the Queen's Printer and trying to decide what to do with his life when he met Marion Young, who was working for the NIB and the NCIRT as a librarian.

Marion Young and Jamie Deacey eventually married, but when they were going together Deacey hung out at the Traviata with her and the other native students. When the NIB hired summer students in 1971 with an Opportunity For Youth grant, Deacey was hired to set up the office equipment.

Jamie Deacey had decided to return to university after the summer, but he got a call from George Manuel in early September asking him to come to work at the NIB as a special assistant for communications. He was surprised by the offer, but didn't hesitate to cancel his university plans and return to the NIB.

The reason George Manuel wanted Deacey was largely for his family connections. Deacey would be useful in guiding him through the complicated tiers of the Ottawa power structure and in introducing him to those in the Ottawa crowd who still thought that the NIB was nothing more than the end of a ballpoint pen.

The office continued to expand throughout 1971 and by the fall it numbered more than a dozen people, as well as the four people working for Delisle in the NCIRT. In April, Manuel had met with Delisle and worked out an agreement where the NCIRT staff would be put under the supervision of Marie Marule and would be expected to report directly to her.

In those early months, the emphasis was on research. In quiet defiance of the provincial leaders who wanted to limit the power of the NIB, George Manuel assigned his staff various portfolios – housing, economic development, social and cultural development and education – to find out what the real requirements of the Indian people were, and then to try to devise strategies for wresting control of each of those dossiers from the DIA bureaucracy.

The workload was considerable and the example George Manuel set with his own work habits demonstrated that the NIB and the Indian movement had to be your whole life. If he was lying awake at night thinking of some problem and he needed information from staff members, he would call them up at four in the morning and ask them. If they couldn't answer right away, they were expected to have the information available when he arrived at the office in the morning.

The actual office, however, was run on democratic lines. Marie Marule remembers that George always showed a friendly concern toward the people he worked with. "He made time to spend with any member of the staff and tried to get to know them, their problems, their strengths and weaknesses. There was a community development style to his approach and he politicized every member in a subtle and casual way."

As another staff member recalled, it didn't matter if you were a secretary, office manager or mail boy, you were expected to take part in the policy discussions and your opinions were weighed alongside everyone else's. In the same way, he gave the staff the broadest possible leeway to carry out their own tasks and continually stressed the fact that they were not working for him, they were working for the people.

George Manuel also took advantage of the ideological differences within his staff to elicit the widest possible views on any subject. One of his favourite ploys was to give the same dossier to a leftist like Marie Marule and to a conservative like Deacey and ask them both for their analysis. Then he would sit in the room and listen to their reports and spark an argument between them so he could get a left-wing and right-wing take on the issue.

There were two areas that George Manuel was firm on, however. One was money. No one, including himself, was paid more than a modest salary, and everyone was expected to account for every penny of NIB funds they spent. The man who went with his wife and kids to gather returnable bottles on the side of the Trans-Canada outside Chase was not going to turn into a profligate spender just because the government was sending him cheques. The money, he deeply believed, did not belong to him or his staff or even to the organization; it belonged to the people and every penny had to be well spent on their behalf.

The second issue was in-fighting in Indian organizations. He tried to ensure that alternative views within the movement were treated with respect and that the NIB staff never publicly criticized other Indian organizations. In this case, however, George Manuel honoured the proscription only on "public" disputes. If he saw individuals trying to undermine the unity of the movement, as Harold Cardinal was soon to find out, he would not hesitate to quietly send his political allies after them.

During this period, the young NIB staff also spent a considerable amount of time socializing together. They went out after work to have a few beers at the Beacon Arms, or if George Manuel wanted to buttonhole some of the guys from DIA or the Privy Council, he'd head down the street to the Berkley Savoy where the bureaucrats hung out.

There were also Saturday night parties at Marie Marule's house in Aylmer. In a sense, these parties were an important part of the work week, because she and her husband, Jacob Marule, a black South African activist, invited CIDA and CUSO types as well as people from the socialist Tanzanian and other African embassies to meet with the Indian activists.

It made for a fascinating and mutually educational mix. George Manuel was always willing to get up to play a little banjo and sing one of the Shuswap songs Dick Andrew had taught him; his sense of fun and jack-o'-lantern smile were particularly popular among the Africans who felt suffocated by the stuffy Ottawa atmosphere. But while he was enjoying himself, George Manuel was also sounding them out on their feelings about Canadian indigenous people and how they related it to their experiences with colonialism in their own countries. As time went on, Manuel began to develop an important circle of contacts among Third World representatives like the First Secretary of the Tanzanian High Commission, Mbuto Milando, which would soon lead to his touring Tanzania at the invitation of Julius Nyerere, and to the development of an international framework around the Indian struggle in Canada.

Another part of the Ottawa job was making contacts with the white power structure in Ottawa. In the past, the First Nations had been completely frozen out, not only by the government but by the press as well. If an Indian Affairs issue arose in the House of Commons, the journalists would run back and forth between the white politicians and bureaucrats in government and the white opposition Indian Affairs critic, and assume that they had found out all there was to find out about the matter. It never occurred to them to ask native leaders what they thought of the issue.

As one NIB advisor put it, "The press was simply not willing to accept Indian competence" and George Manuel had to work to get them "to give him the time of day."[13]

To get more visibility, the NIB leader had Deacey finagle invitations for him on Parliament Hill's social circuit. Deacey recalls that his boss made an immediate impression. When they attended the Ottawa functions, Deacey would find "at the end of the evening that George Manuel had met and talked to everyone. And most of them came to him. He had an ability to attract people without having to – in the white way – be the centre of attention. That quiet wisdom seemed to attract people."

Marlene was usually too shy to accompany George to these social events, but he persisted and she finally relented, agreeing to go to a dinner at the Chateau Laurier where the Prime Minister and the Ottawa socialites would be in attendance. Marlene remembers her nervousness as she sat at a table with men and women she had never met before but had often seen on the national news.

Her nervousness was dispelled somewhat when some of the women got up to go to the washroom and invited her along. Inside, the Ottawa matrons showed how they made it through these events by pulling mickeys of vodka out of their purses and taking a few belts before heading back to the tedium of the official function. That incident helped her dispel any illusions about the high and mighty since she had used the same strategy, a good stiff drink of whisky, before heading off to the Chateau Laurier.

While George Manuel was raising the profile of the NIB in official Ottawa, however, the stresses and strains within the organization were worsening. In early March, he was informed that Harold Cardinal was withdrawing Alberta's delegation from the National Committee on Indian Rights and Treaties and was threatening to withdraw from the NIB, as well.

The problem for Harold Cardinal was, once again, one of jurisdiction. He objected to the fact that the NCIRT seemed to be making policy decisions in its dealing with the claims commissioner and that the NIB was setting up a negotiating committee to deal with the government at a ministerial level. This fear of the national organization undercutting provincial power was not limited to Cardinal. Other members of the Executive shared his fears and his belief that the NIB should act solely as a coordinating body.

Harold Cardinal might have expected that George Manuel, who had been put into power by the western leaders, would immediately address Alberta's concerns. But Manuel was beginning to see a different role for the NIB, and he was able to use Cardinal's threat as an opportunity to exert his authority over his executive.

He invited Andrew Delisle and the executive to a meeting in Calgary, where he announced that he felt strongly that "there is no issue which should ever be allowed to threaten the basis of our political strength and our vitality, which can be assured only through unity. . . . This is not the time for bickering and petty politics."[14]

George Manuel asked Harold Cardinal to reconsider his decision to withdraw from the NCIRT and offered to sit down with him and discuss any problems he had with either the NCIRT or the Brotherhood. Cardinal refused and George Manuel made a brief tactical withdrawal. But at the next executive council meeting, the NIB leader came prepared with a demand for unity that reflected his recent contact with the African diplomats.

"The African subjugated people," George Manuel began, "cry out for UHURU, for freedom. The Indian people should cry out for both

UHURU and UNITY, for it is only through unity that we will achieve real freedom.

"Freedom not as a subjugated race, but freedom formulated by Indian people for Indian people."

According to George Manuel, Indians "had suffered in the past because of lack of unity . . ." and because they didn't have any recourse to an Indian "central government" to bring them together in a unified manner.

"If we had met the white man as Indians of North America rather than as Mohawks, Blackfeet, etc., history and our rightful role in North America would have been quite different. We would have met the white man on his own terms, i.e. 'Might is Right,' and defeated him at his own game."

He concluded with a call for "national unity" among the delegates and urged the delegates to stick together in the battle against the government and in addressing the other critical issues like Indian education, health and economic development. [15]

The speech was a direct challenge to Harold Cardinal, particularly when George Manuel mentioned the need for a kind of Indian "central government." Cardinal had fought that idea from the beginning, so after George Manuel finished speaking, he announced that Alberta would "refrain from active participation in the National Indian Brotherhood." [16]

When a resolution was put forward to give the NIB the right to disperse funds from the Privy Council to the PTOs, Harold Cardinal voted against it, along with Saskatchewan's David Ahenikew. Less than a year after they put him in office, two of the three prairie leaders were in revolt.

As the NIB president, George Manuel was not in a position to declare war on Cardinal or Ahenikew. So, as he often did in these matters, he turned to his friend and ally Phillip Paul. The Union of BC Indian Chiefs issued a scathing attack on the Alberta leader that accused him of using the NIB only when the feeling moved him, and claimed that he "constantly dictated to the executive and the assembly with his amateur theatrics and threats of withdrawal . . . now like a small boy he had stated by his withdrawal that if you won't play my way, then I will take my ball and bat and go home."

The BC statement then addressed the other PTO leaders. "If every time a party is in the disgruntled minority they choose to walk out there is no association . . . If we are not willing to surrender the authority necessary to allow the Brotherhood to be the national bargaining agent for Indian people then we might just as well fall back into the provincial splinter groups we once were, and compete with each other for funds. The Department of Indian Affairs and the government would like nothing better."[17]

Harold Cardinal was too astute a politician not to know that the stinging personal attack out of BC came with at least the approval, if not at the instigation, of George Manuel. If Harold Cardinal considered Manuel "his man in Ottawa" before the summer of 1971, he now knew that George Manuel belonged only to the movement. When push came to shove, no one, not even his family or friends, would deter him from a course of action he believed was necessary for the cause.

At the end of June, George Manuel also put Jean Chrétien on notice that he would not compromise on his principles, even if his funding was at stake. The message was delivered when Chrétien invited Manuel and members of the NIB executive to the Montebello resort on the Ottawa River to "consult" with them on the Department's 1972-73 budget.

When George Manuel and his delegation arrived, they were met with a *fait accompli*. Every detail of the budget had already been determined. Worse still, George Manuel discovered that it contained provisions for yet another major expansion of DIA's administration staff that the NIB had not been informed of.

The NIB leader immediately rounded up his delegation and walked out. Then he went to the press and he denounced the Department in general and Jean Chrétien in particular for wasting money on administration and planning from the top down, when what was important was to give the Indian people the right to govern themselves and the resources to do so.

In reality, the opportunity for a little Chrétien-bashing came as a relief. The NIB was still in a fragile state because of the jurisdictional problem and George Manuel was still not convinced that it would survive. Somehow, he had to turn the attention of the leaders of the PTOs away from their differences and concentrate their energies on their common struggle.

Phillip Paul remembers that during his first year in office, George often spoke about the "discouragements and the fragmentation that was brewing in different parts of the country."

He urged the leaders to put aside their internal bickering and "to keep constantly in mind that we have to develop the peoples' strength. We must not forget that the people make us, the people break us."[18]

In a move suggesting that he expected he might be back in BC earlier than planned, George Manuel went back to Neskainlith to shore up his political base. He took his half-brother, Joe, out for a few beers at the Underwood hotel in Chase and urged him to run for chief in the next band election.

Joe had not been especially interested in politics and he admitted that he was very uncomfortable about taking on the responsibility, but George was persuasive and he agreed. To give Joe a head start in the January 1971 band election, George went to Ben Alexander, Andy Paull's old colleague and one of the most respected figures in the community, and asked him to nominate Joe. Alexander made the nomination and Joe won the election, remaining band chief until 1977 when another Manuel, George's son Bob, took over.

With his political base covered, George Manuel was thus assured that he could go home again. But as he headed into his second year in office in the summer of 1971, his priority remained the unity of Indian nations across the country. He was unexpectedly aided in this task in the fall of 1971, when Harold Cardinal was brought back into the fold. The reason wasn't any change of heart on Cardinal's part, but political necessity, as he found himself under personal and political attack by the wounded grizzly, Jean Chrétien, who in the fall of 1971 had Harold Cardinal treed in his own forest.

## CHAPTER TEN

# The National Indian Philosophy

## 1971-1972

As long as he can continue dividing us, he will continue winning . . .
We, as Indian people, the heart of Canada, must save the white man in
spite of himself.

George Manuel
17 Apr. 1971

During the early 1970s, the White Paper policies remained a kind of
Sword of Damocles hanging over the heads of the Indian organizations.
After the Red Paper presentation, Chrétien said he wouldn't drop the
sword without the Indians' permission, but neither did he remove it and
replace it with a new policy.

So while keeping one eye on Chrétien and the Department, George
Manuel tried to push the NIB into two new policy areas. The first was
Indian control of education and the second was an economic plan for
rebuilding the Indian nations.

As George Manuel put it, "Economics is the key to solving any
human problem. Just as education is absolutely essential to any young
person who is going to take his proper place in society. But there are as
many different kinds of economic development as there are different
kinds of education."[1]

Based on his philosophy of community development, Manuel
believed true economic development could only come from below, by
giving the people the political and financial tools to build their own
future according to their own plan. Similarly, Indian education had to be

controlled by Indian parents and had to include traditional community values as well as academic subjects.

There was a recent model for this type of education in northern Alberta. In the summer of 1970, Indian parents had protested against a Department of Indian Affairs decision to sell off the Blue Quills Indian School by occupying the building and demanding that it be given to the community so they could run it themselves. After negotiations with DIA officials, the school was turned over to the community and Blue Quills became the first Indian-run school in the country.

The education issue came to national prominence in June 1971, when the Standing Committee on Indian Affairs advocated sweeping changes to the Indian education system. The report called for a partnership between Indians and the government to develop and implement curriculum. It also backed the teaching of Indian languages in the early grades and provided for a major role for Indian parents in running the schools.

George Manuel had been following the committee proceedings closely and he described its report as the most important of the decade. "It is the first time an official source has understood what we have been trying to say for the past hundred years or more."

He stressed the importance of the community being involved in all areas of the education process and highlighted the statement that the government should not transfer any of its educational responsibilities to provincial governments "without the express and clear approval of the majority of the parents in each community concerned." The NIB president then called on Jean Chrétien to honour the spirit of the report by putting a moratorium on the transfer of Indian schools to the provincial system.[2]

Chrétien refused. In September, he gave a speech in Thunder Bay where he stated that the transfer of the responsibility for education to the provinces would continue and implied that the Department would not take any responsibility for improving the existing schools while those transfers were taking place.

While Jean Chrétien was disavowing the Committee report and the NIB was working on its own education policy, the issue was again being fought in a much more direct way in Alberta. The result was a major and, as it turned out, premature confrontation with Chrétien over who would control the education of the Cree and Blackfoot children.

On the Saddle Lake Reserve, Indian parents decided to follow the Blue Quills example by keeping their children out of the local DIA school. Originally, they were protesting the poor facilities, but Harold Cardinal and his IAA advisors decided to expand the protest by promoting a province-wide school strike. The immediate demand was to have new schools built on the reserves to replace the run-down facilities, but the ultimate goal was an Indian takeover of the school system.

Harold Cardinal later admitted that the plan was too ambitious and the planners overly confident, but when the school year began in 1971, a significant number of Indian parents kept their children home and numerous schools were shut down. Support for the strike in most communities turned out to be more broad than deep, however, especially in the south where the Blackfoot were reluctant to follow the Cree initiative. When Jean Chrétien dug in his heels and refused to negotiate with the parents until the strike was over, most parents outside of the northeast of the province began to quietly send their kids back to the classroom.

George Manuel had backed the strike from the beginning. As soon as it started, he and Harold Cardinal set aside their differences over the NIB powers and joined forces to fight the government. On September 28, George Manuel travelled to Alberta to attend a number of band meetings in the striking communities and two weeks later he was back at Harold Cardinal's invitation to attend a meeting of the Alberta chiefs at the Blue Quills Indian School, where they discussed the best way to get Chrétien to come and speak to the people directly. In the meantime, George Manuel kept up a steady stream of correspondence with Chrétien, criticizing the deplorable conditions of the Indian schools across the country and urging him to meet with the Alberta protesters.

Jean Chrétien moved a short distance on October 5 when he signed an order for the repair of the dilapidated school buildings in Saddle Lake, but the Indian parents refused to end the boycott until the Minister promised new schools. The following day, Chrétien went on television to accuse the parents and the IAA of trying to blackmail him and the Canadian government.

During October, the poor organization of the strike began to show as school after school quietly returned to operation. By the end of the month only five schools were still out. Sensing that the strike would soon collapse on its own, Chrétien returned to his hard line. He declared that he would not negotiate with the Alberta parents or with the IAA leadership until every last child was back at the DIA schools.

In desperation, the IAA organized a sit-in by fifty young activists at the Edmonton office of the Indian Affairs Department. The sit-in had little effect, however, because by this time Chrétien was holding secret talks with individual band chiefs and, as Harold Cardinal put it, "Unfortunately, Indian Affairs found allies within our ranks."[3]

Chrétien's breakthrough came in the second week of November when Chief Gordon Youngchief from the Kehewin reserve met the minister in Winnipeg and agreed to end the strike in his community in exchange for the promise of a new school. The following day, the students from two of the last five reserves went back to school and the strike was essentially over.

It had been a test of strength between Jean Chrétien and the Indian organizations, and Chrétien had won. After the humiliation of the Red Paper presentation, he had proved that with DIA funds and a divide-and-conquer strategy, he could still split off bands from the provincial and national organizations and shape events in Indian country.

For two weeks after the strike, Cardinal lashed out in anger at Chrétien's double-dealing and the two men quickly found themselves engaged in a bitter verbal battle in the press with both accusing the other of bad faith and attempted blackmail.

Jean Chrétien then proved his ability to go for the jugular when he turned up at an Indian Affairs meeting waving documents that he said showed that Harold Cardinal's IAA had not accounted for $125,000 of its $330,000 community development fund for 1970.

Cardinal hotly denied the suggestion that there had been any wrongdoing, but he had been seriously wounded by the charge. George Manuel appeared before the Indian Affairs Committee to offer Cardinal moral support, but the NIB leader already knew that his backing couldn't save the young Cree. Cardinal's outspoken style had put off many people in his own province and there was a growing sense among the Alberta chiefs that the Cardinal–Chrétien dispute had become too personal and was costing their people in government services.

Harold Cardinal acknowledged this fact himself in December 1971, when he resigned from the IAA leadership. That resignation lasted only a few months; in June 1972 he ran and was re-elected to the post, but he never regained his former prestige in the national movement.

Harold Cardinal was not the only casualty of the school strike, however. Before the strike, George Manuel had been working with various government ministries on setting up the Joint NIB–Cabinet Committee that would give the Indian organization regular access to key cabinet ministers. When Chrétien was under fire, the cabinet members drew their wagons around him and cut off all negotiations with the NIB.

All George Manuel could do about the failed strike was to use it as an example of Indian frustration over the DIA educational system.

In early November, he gave a barn burner of a speech at the Eighth Annual School Committee Conference of Indian Teachers in Sydney, Nova Scotia. The trip started badly when he and Ron Shackleton went to check into the CN Hotel Nova Scotia and were told that no rooms were available. Remembering his experience at the Plaza Hotel in Kamloops a dozen years earlier, George Manuel phoned back and tried to make a reservation. The desk clerk told him, yes, the hotel had available rooms, so George contacted the Nova Scotia Human Rights Commission and filed a discrimination charge.

The confrontation at the CN Hotel and the crushing of the school strike put George Manuel in an aggressive mood. When he addressed the teachers the next day, he began by stating that "speeches aren't worth a damn unless they are backed by action."

He criticized the fact that the 150 delegates had been selected by the DIA, rather than by Indian organizations. "I'm surprised that you came under the system," George Manuel said, "because you are indirectly saying that the government system is right.

"We have abandoned our principles, and become slaves of a system completely alien to our way of life, our beliefs and our background."

Then he added to the room packed full of Indian teachers and white bureaucrats: "The people of British Columbia say I'm so successful because I dropped out at grade two."

George Manuel urged the Indian delegates to "make their school committees more than puppets of the government," because the government officials who make the decisions "don't know hunger, or know lack of water, or had to go through a snow drift to get to a school that condemns your culture, your values, your dignity."[4]

While he was lashing out at the status quo in education, George Manuel and his team at the NIB were also working on their own solution in their *Indian Control of Indian Education* brief, which called for a

National Indian Educational Authority that would be made up by band educational authorities funded from existing DIA spending on education. The bands would then be given leeway to start their own schools or to negotiate the conditions for their participation in the provincial schools. Whatever means of delivery they decided on, Indian parents were to be put in control over the education of their children, and all of the old 1950s- and 1960s-style integration programs would be abandoned.

"Integration viewed as a one-way process is not integration, and will fail," the NIB brief stated, because "In the past, it has been the Indian student who was asked to integrate: to give up his identity, to adopt new values and a new way of life. This restricted interpretation of integration must be radically altered if future education programs are to benefit Indian children."[5]

All Indian children would be given an opportunity to study in their own language and to learn about their own peoples' history and culture. George Manuel knew from his own experience that it was vitally important for Indian children to have access to the wisdom of their peoples' traditional beliefs if they were to make sense of the world around them.

As he saw it: "Indian culture and values have a unique place in the history of mankind. The Indian child who learns about his heritage will be proud of it. The lessons he learns in school, his whole school experience, should reinforce and contribute to the image he has of himself as an Indian."[6]

When the NIB's education brief was handed to Jean Chrétien in November 1972, the Minister accepted it in principle, but refused to discuss the mechanics of its implementation.

It was a tactic that Chrétien would use again and again over the next three years. In many ways, it was more frustrating than a blanket rejection, because it allowed him to stall on the issue until another arose and pushed it off the agenda.

This DIA ploy was repeated with the NIB's study of economic development, which was presented to the Department in October 1972. The study had begun in February at a conference in Halifax where a team of outside experts was brought in to examine various government departments and their funding of development projects. Other experts discussed the mechanics of setting up Indian corporations and finding sources of start-up capital.

At a second economic development conference a month later, George Manuel stressed the importance of Indian control of economic development and heaped scorn on the department's past record in the area.

"Ever since the White Paper of 1969 declared the old Indian policy the New Indian Policy," he told the DIA representative, "a new formula for solving all our problems has swept across the land. ECONOMIC DEVELOPMENT!" But what kind of economic development was the department interested in? "Is this economic development to solve our problems as Indian people? Or is it economic development to solve Ottawa's Indian problem? Is it medicine or is it witchcraft?"

He then went on to trace the destruction of the Indian economy with the usurpation of the basis of that economy: the Indian land. Putting things in the BC perspective, he remarked:

"It is no coincidence that it was the continued presence of the Land Question, the heart of any economic development program, that led first to religious persecution, potlatch prohibition, and later to political persecution, when we were forbidden to raise funds for organizing, travel restrictions were imposed, and children were carted off to distant schools."

Real economic development, then, was intrinsically linked to political power. Without political power there could not be the type of development that would help the people at the grass-roots level, and without an independent economic base controlled by the people, political power was "an empty farce, a paper tiger."

To back this up, George Manuel pointed to the "nations of Africa, colonized at the same time by the same European powers that came to our shores, who call themselves independent Republics today.

"So many of them are still producing raw materials for the industries of the Imperial Powers' home territory. Those countries with honest leadership know that they do not have real independence . . . They, like us, are having to recover their land base, and work with the people to discover how it can be used to lift up the common standard of the community."[7]

The NIB economic development brief was presented to John Ciaccia, Chrétien's new assistant deputy minister. Ciaccia was at the time considered a very sympathetic figure by many in the Indian movement, but in this case his response to the NIB brief was the same as Chrétien's. He offered a blanket endorsement of the theory behind the proposals, but refused to make any concrete commitments.

Aware that he was facing a departmental stonewall, Manuel went on the attack. In a letter to Jean Chrétien he outlined the various dossiers on his desk and concluded that "we as Indian people are not going in the direction we committed ourselves to – the advancement of our people in the social, educational and political future of our country.

"Mr. Minister," he added, "if you saw such a bleak future for your own people, would you not have broken negotiations or discussions and tried to find another way?"[8]

George Manuel's frustration at the lack of movement toward eliminating the day-to-day pain of his people came out in his speeches to all-Indian audiences. In a springtime speech to the Iroquois and Allied Tribes on the St. Regis Reserve, he spoke about the old and new battles against the white man "who has no heart and abuses all that is placed before him – even his own kind.

"What kind of a man is this White Man?" he asked. "He has divided some of us and has made some of our brothers feel culturally ashamed that they are Indian . . . [they] even try to imitate the white man so that they can feel important again. We must, I say, not look down on these people but hope that one day they will become Indian again. . . ."

The only solution, George Manuel would repeat time and time again, was to build a unified activist movement.

"Some of us are still fighting, every day, the white man who is trying to make us as he is: a cold, heartless animal that only cares for himself and no one else.

"As long as he can continue dividing us, he will continue winning. . . . We, as Indian people, the heart of Canada, must save the White Man in spite of himself. We must teach him of the Great Spirit, the Mother Earth and how to be human beings again. Let us not die, as the White Man has, by only caring for ourselves."

What Indians needed to develop, George Manuel argued, was a "national Indian philosophy" that they could use to offset the white man's philosophy. This philosophy would cover the whole spectrum of self-government issues and set priorities on radicalizing the people at the community level and on setting long-term as well as short-term strategies of struggle.[9]

But George Manuel would have little time in the immediate future to pursue that avenue. The NIB, as would so often happen, was caught up in events beyond its control when a Federal Court of Appeal made a decision that had the potential of seriously dividing Indian communities.

In October 1972, the Court unanimously reversed an Ontario court decision on the issue of Indian women losing their status upon marriage to a non-Indian. The woman contesting the case was Jeannette Corbière Lavell from the Wikwemikong Band. Her lawyers argued that the provisions under the Indian Act that took away a woman's status when she married a white man, and gave a white woman status when she married an Indian, contravened the Canadian Bill of Rights.

For George Manuel the ruling required a painful decision. Personally, he supported Lavell's case; during the consultation hearing in Nanaimo in 1969, he had argued that all Indian women should be allowed to retain their status on marriage. But when he asked Doug Sanders to spell out the legal ramifications of the case, he discovered there could be harmful consequences for Indian people as a whole.

From a legal point of view, the problem was the grounds, rather than the content, of the Lavell case. Her lawyers had based their case on the fact that the Bill of Rights took precedence over the Indian Act, and in agreeing with their arguments, the Court brought into question the validity of the whole Act. If the Indian Act was overturned before aboriginal rights were entrenched in the constitution, it was feared that white hunters could use the anti-discriminatory provisions in the Bill of Rights to challenge Indian hunting rights, or real estate developers could challenge the provisions in the Act protecting Indian lands against sale to outsiders.

Along with these major legal considerations, there were also fears at the band level that the thousands of Indian women who had lost their status would return to their communities with their children and greatly increase the strain on the already scarce housing and community resources.

The women who had unjustly lost their status, however, insisted that the Federal Court decision be respected. In December, they met in Ottawa with white feminists to demand that the government change the restrictive laws. The genuine emotion at the gathering was reflected by the leader of the Equal Rights for Indian Woman organization, Cecilia Dore.

She waved a picture from *The Montreal Star* at the delegates, show-ing an animal cemetery at her home reserve and explained:

"It is a picture of some stones, a dog and a tree. Why am I showing it to you? It carries a message. You realize that dead pets are treated with more respect than the Indian woman who has married a non-Indian! Even when I am dead I cannot go home."[10]

Despite his sympathy for the woman's cause, George Manuel was forced to quietly ask Prime Minister Trudeau to have the Attorney Gen-eral appeal the decision to the Supreme Court and argue against it to protect the aboriginal rights clauses in the Indian Act. If the Supreme Court upheld the Federal Court's finding, he asked that the government take the further step of inserting a "notwithstanding clause" into the Indian Act that stated that the Act would operate in its "present form notwithstanding the Canadian Bill of Rights."[11]

Chrétien later publicly endorsed George Manuel's position; interest-ingly, he and Trudeau used the same sort of "notwithstanding clause" to get their Charter of Rights accepted by the reluctant premiers during the patriation of the constitution a decade later.

When the Lavell case went to the Supreme Court all ten Indian pro-vincial organizations as well as the NIB and the Department of Indian Affairs argued against Lavell and her feminist allies. On 27 August 1973, the Supreme Court overturned the Federal Court and declared the Indian Act supreme over the Bill of Rights because "it is not the right of every Canadian to be or to become a 'registered Indian'."

A dozen years later, another Indian woman took a similar case to the UN Human Rights Commission, which censured the Canadian govern-ment for discrimination against Indian women. The government then moved on its own to restore status to those women who had lost it by marriage to a non-Indian.

Typically, though, the government did not supply adequate funds to the bands to cope with the influx of women and children to the reserves. This victory of justice for women was accompanied, as a result, by increased economic hardship for the men, women and children already living in the poorest bands.

Although his lawyers had argued on the winning side in the Jean-nette Lavell case, the outcome was not a particularly happy one for George Manuel and many other native leaders. It preserved the legal protection of Indian status in the Indian Act, but it also served as a reminder that the legal decision of who was and who wasn't a citizen of an Indian Nation resided in an Act over which they had no control.

In the wake of the decision, George Manuel argued that indigenous people should be able to decide on their own Indianness outside of the Act. In a speech to the BC Association of Non-Status Indians, he reminded them that "the Indian Act was made by a white government and the Indian people had no say in it. It did not take into consideration the Indian people, only white society.

"All boundaries dividing the native people of this country were made by the white man . . . reservations, U.S. border, and legalities which divide Indian people were made by white people."

He went on to stress the common struggle of all native people, no matter what the Indian Act said, by referring to the great Métis leader, Louis Riel, who "was hanged in Regina for the very thing I'm talking about . . . independence."[12]

For George Manuel the fight for independence still involved as many internal battles as external ones, and he was forever walking the tightrope between the competing interests of the member organizations. At one point, the leaders of the PTOs even began to grumble about Marie Marule because they feared that she was wielding too much power within the organization.

In fact, Marie was in charge of running the day-to-day NIB operations when George was on the road, which was a great deal of the time. During these long absences, provincial leaders contacting the NIB office were told to deal with her, and some of them suspected that Marie Marule was shielding the boss from them.

In her day-to-day work, Marie Marule did, in fact, come to know George Manuel so well that she could anticipate his reactions and George encouraged her, along with everyone else, to take initiative and solve problems on their own, without having to constantly check back to him for approval.

More serious than whispers that Marie was "smothering George" was the fact that he was losing his executive assistant. Ron Shackleton had decided to leave the NIB to go to law school. Shackleton's wife Christine remembers that they were both surprised by George Manuel's reaction. Despite his long advocacy of further education, Manuel opposed Shackleton's return to school. He told the young Mohawk that it was a critical time in the development of the movement and he needed him at the NIB.

Shackleton had been a tireless worker at the NIB in both arranging Manuel's extensive travels and taking care of all of the details along the way, but he also had a deeply humanist spirit and was a valued counsel in political matters. Christine Deom remembers that George and Ron not only had a kind of father and son bond, they also had similar backgrounds.

Shackleton had been taken away from his natural mother when he was very young and had been adopted by a white Ottawa couple. He had only managed to locate his birth mother a year before her death, but by then she was in an advanced stage of alcoholism and wanted nothing to do with him.

When she died, George and Marlene attended the funeral and, in the name of the National Indian Brotherhood, sent an enormous wreath of flowers with a card that read "From the Indians of Canada."

The gesture moved Shackleton to tears. He was sorry to be disappointing George with his decision to go to law school. But he believed that it was the best way he could contribute to the struggle, so he refused to back down.

With Ron Shackleton leaving for university, the only person trained to replace him was Jamie Deacey, so George Manuel gave him the job. By all accounts, Deacey performed the executive assistant job well, and his connections continued to be valuable to George Manuel and the NIB. But soon after Deacey was promoted, George Manuel began to think he had made a mistake. Deacey recalled: "I tried strenuously and strictly during my time at native organizations to be a servant" and "I always tried to bear in mind – I don't know how successfully – that it wasn't my culture."[13] Others in the NIB thought Deacey was not all that successful in recognizing his place and described him as "a hotshot character" who sometimes seemed to think that he alone knew what was best for the organization.

George Manuel was concerned about the rumbles of discontent Deacey was creating and he decided to get rid of him. He realized, though, that Deacey would need a cooling-off period because he knew too much about the NIB workings and its short-term strategies. He feared that if he just fired him, Deacey would go over to the other side and get a job with Indian Affairs where he would spill the NIB beans. So he had to come up with a way to put the young white man on the shelf for a while.

What George Manuel and Phillip Paul decided on was a Machiavellian plot to send Deacey to work for the Union in British Columbia for a stint as the executive director. In return, Paul would send someone the Union was having problems with to Ottawa to work on a special project for the NIB. To make sure that Deacey wasn't aware of the deal, the Union held secret meetings with him and pretended to lure him away from the NIB.

The plan worked. After a bit of courting from the Union, Deacey walked into George Manuel's office and told him that the Union had made him an offer and he had decided to take it. Although Manuel went through the act of feigning surprise and injury at losing his special assistant to his BC buddies, Deacey was soon dispatched to the west coast where he replaced Bill Mussell as the executive director of the Union. (Ironically, after Deacey and his wife Marion Young divorced, Bill Mussell replaced him as her second husband.)

Eventually, Deacey figured out that he had been "traded for future draft considerations" to the Union and although he began with a two-year contract, he worked barely a year in BC before he was quietly told it was time to leave. As George Manuel had feared, Deacey's first job after he left the Indian movement was as a communication advisor to the minister of Indian Affairs.

Even though some time had elapsed since he was at the centre of things, Phillip Paul believed Deacey still posed a threat. Shortly after Deacey arrived at Indian Affairs, a brown envelope was slipped under someone's door, suggesting that he was leaking information to the Union of BC Indians. Deacey knew it was a plant by the Union to burn him at Indian Affairs, but he was able to keep his job when he convinced his superiors of this.

Deacey went on to work as a Liberal Party operative in Ottawa but looking back, he has few hard feelings about his time in Indian politics. He understood that the basic issues were the survival and the welfare of dozens of small besieged nations and this often left no room for compromise or other niceties. Today, Deacey's attitude is that: ". . . if I could survive four years of Indian politics, white politics is a walk in the park."[14]

In his first two years at the NIB, George Manuel had done more than survive. During his term of office, he had led the NIB from an indebted paper organization to a significant presence in Ottawa. For the first time in Canadian history, the First Nations and the Indian question were not abstract legal issues to be dealt with somewhere out in the great beyond: they were camped out at the door of Parliament demanding redress to age-old grievances. By 1972, George Manuel had become a familiar figure on the Ottawa scene and his straightforward and uncompromising manner had won a grudging respect for both himself and the Indian cause.

During his first term, he had also managed to keep the twelve very disparate provincial and territorial organizations, representing dozens of First Nations and six hundred Indian bands, inside the Brotherhood. That in itself was a considerable accomplishment. Through initiatives like the education and economic development briefs, the NIB under Manuel had also begun to take the first steps in defining Indian government.

It wasn't surprising, then, that when George Manuel ran for a second term at the General Assembly in Winnipeg in July 1972, he was unopposed and had the active backing of every provincial and territorial leader in the country.

On a personal level, though, the job was a gruelling one; his life was dominated by work. Marlene remembers that he was on the road almost half the year and when he was home he would have to spend long hours in his room with a bulging briefcase of reports, strategy papers and government documents. On an intellectual level, he was also deepening his knowledge of the historic place of the First Nations in Canada and trying to apply that knowledge to their place in a rapidly changing country and world.

This left him with little time to spend with Marlene and their child. To escape the loneliness of Ottawa, Marlene made an extended visit back to Neskainlith to visit her family and friends.

George found a refuge of his own. During Marlene's visit back home, he slipped away for a weekend of camping in a park in the Gatineaus. While he was there, he met a couple of men from the adjacent Maniwaki reserve who invited him to camp on reserve land. During the rest of his time in Ottawa, George Manuel would occasionally disappear to the Maniwaki Reserve for a few days to fish, sit by a campfire and forget the responsibilities of leading the First Nations movement.

A less traditional escape was the occasional drinking sprees with his friends and, just as in his work, his stamina was considerable; at times, however, these blowouts got him into trouble. Once at a reception in a Victoria Hotel with a group from the Union, someone mentioned the Slavic custom of breaking the glasses after a toast. George was feeling pretty good by this time and decided to follow the ritual by breaking his glass against the mantle. Everyone joined in with a rain of crystal and the police were called. George took the rap for the mess and was led out of the hotel while his supporters hurled insults at the police.

The NIB president tried to calm everyone down by telling them, "Let them arrest me," but when they had him out of the hotel the police let Manuel go and the matter was dropped.

George Manuel was always careful, however, to make sure that these occasional binges did not interfere with his work. Some of his fellow leaders, who went on to confront serious battles of their own with the bottle, remember that no matter how much partying he did, he was always back in shape in time to take on his responsibilities.

As it turned out, he would need all his wits about him in the ensuing years. In his second term of office he continued to push the education and economic development dossiers, but he also turned his attention to the one issue that had always dominated his political life: the land issue.

By this time, George Manuel had reached the conclusion that it had been a mistake to accept the idea of researching Indian land claims because they were already owners of the country. Henceforth, he would insist that the onus was on the white pretenders to prove their right to the lands they claimed.

When George Manuel discussed the new approach at a Union of BC Indian Chiefs meeting, Don Moses asked him how they could force the land issue to the top of the agenda. George Manuel replied that they might have to march on Ottawa to demand their aboriginal and land rights. When asked how many people the Union should send, George Manuel smiled and suggested that the answer was the same as to the question of "how many Indians are in British Columbia? Every Indian should go! I put it to you as leader of the National Indian Brotherhood, if it's necessary to walk to Ottawa to gain some recognition, then we should do it and I will be right there with you."[15]

# PART THREE

# Indian Shogun

We began to call him *Shogun* because he was way ahead of the Canadian political leadership . . . a generation ahead.

Dave Monture

## CHAPTER ELEVEN

# International Travels

## 1971–1972

If the motivation of the CIDA people is to remain high it would be of some help . . . to arrange some tangible indication in the press that the Canadian halo has not slipped too far.

Telex from Dar es Salaam to External Affairs, following George
Manuel's 1971 visit to Tanzania

While George Manuel was working out the details of his national Indian philosophy, he was also beginning to shape an international one.

Manuel was aware of the importance of seeking international recognition of the Canadian Indian struggle as early as 1960, when he and Henry Castilliou worked on a brief for the United Nations on the BC land question. By the time it was submitted to the UN, he had left the NAIB, but the idea of internationalizing the struggle was a tactic he always favoured.

In the spring of 1971, the NIB president began a series of travels that would culminate in the founding of a new indigenous organization under the aegis of the National Indian Brotherhood. The first trip was to New Zealand and Australia as part of a Department of Indian Affairs delegation. Planning for it had begun after the Red Paper presentation. At the time, Prime Minister Trudeau had referred to New Zealand as a model for Canada's relationship with its indigenous people. After the meeting, Trudeau called Len Marchand into his office and asked him if he would lead a group of MPs to take a closer look at the Maori's place in New Zealand society.

When Chrétien heard about Marchand's project, he wanted in and he eventually took over the leadership of the delegation with Marchand's role reduced to that of an advisor. One piece of Marchand's advice that Chrétien took, however, was to invite George Manuel to accompany them on the tour.

When the invitation arrived at the NIB office, there was a great deal of discussion about whether it would be appropriate for the NIB president to travel with the minister but it was decided that the opportunity for George to meet with Maori and Aborigine representatives would outweigh any problems caused by his appearing in a few photographs with Jean Chrétien.

When the delegation, which also included Bill Mussell, Len Marchand and three other MPs, left for the South Pacific on 26 March 1971, George Manuel was concerned that he "might be compelled to spend a lot of time listening to government officials from one country telling officials from another country about their Native people." He also worried that the only Maoris he would be allowed to meet would be those "who share the same sentiments on integration" as the white politicians in Canada and the host countries.[1]

To counter this, he was determined to do what he could to break away from the official tour and to try to use his first trip outside of North America to meet with indigenous people who had faced the same wave of European expansion and settlement as the North American Indians.

The historic link between the BC Indians and the indigenous peoples of Eurasia was, in fact, particularly strong. The first European to make contact in both regions was Captain James Cook. Both areas had then been subject to British settlement and developed under the British imperial system.

As George Manuel had feared, however, holding discussions with the Maoris and Aborigines in an informal setting would not be easy. As soon as the plane touched down at the Ohakea Air Base, a New Zealand air force jet whisked them off to the capital for a series of official meetings. The first was with Chrétien's counterpart, the minister of Maori and Island Affairs, who "described with great enthusiasm his government's policy for the Maori people."

"We were told by the minister," George Manuel reported, "that the Maoris are integrating quite rapidly; more Maoris are moving into the city than ever . . ."

As the New Zealander went on to list his department's achievements in education, George Manuel observed that the country's approach "seems to be complete assimilation and the dissolution of all special rights and status of the Maori people.

"In fact, the longer I listened to the learned gentleman, the more I thought I was listening to Mr. Chrétien describing the White Paper to a visiting Maori anthropologist."[2]

This sense was reinforced when George Manuel was leaving the minister's office and met three Maori men outside. He was surprised to discover that they held three of the four seats set aside for the Maori people in parliament, and yet they had not been invited to the minister's briefing.

From the three Maori MPs, George Manuel also learned that Dr. Pat Hohepa of the Maori Council, the New Zealand equivalent of the NIB, had asked to be included in the meeting, but the government had not issued him an invitation. Before the attending Canadian diplomats could drag him off to the Canadian High Commission to be entertained by Maori dancers, Manuel invited the three MPs to his hotel room that night so they could hold their own discussions away from the prying ears of government officials.

At the High Commission, Maori dancers were delighted to discover the North American Indians among the Canadian delegation and during the ceremony they invited George Manuel to join with them and demonstrate one of his peoples' traditional dances. George accepted the invitation and performed a traditional Shuswap dance and sang one of his grandfather's songs. Later, however, when he read the High Commissioner's report to Ottawa on the incident, he felt he had made a mistake. The High Commissioner had written that "the President of the National Indian Brotherhood donned his buckskin robes and feathered headdress and to everyone's delight performed several Indian dances and chants and gave gifts to many of the locals . . ."[3]

When George Manuel saw the patronizing words, he regretted having put on a show for the white officials. "They are still trying to keep us in our place," he told a friend, "dancing and singing. It was the type of report I would be ashamed to show anybody."[4]

After the ceremony, however, George Manuel got down to his specialty: politics. He invited the Maori entertainers to his hotel for the evening meeting with the Maori MPs and as it turned out, he found himself hosting an impromptu Maori convention in his room. Along with the Maori politicians and the entertainers, Dr. Pat Hohepa and members of the Maori Council showed up to meet the North American Indian leader. The discussions were wide-ranging and both George Manuel and his guests discovered they shared a common point of view on the land and aboriginal rights questions, as well as the related issues of education and the preservation of their ancient cultures.

George Manuel was especially interested in finding out more about the New Zealand electoral system, which set aside four seats for the Maori MPs, a model that he had mentioned in his 1960 Parliamentary brief. The Maoris told him they were generally pleased with the system, but admitted it was only part of the solution. It gave them a voice in parliament, but more often than not, their voice was drowned out by that of the dominant society.

At the end of the evening, Dr. Hohepa agreed to take George Manuel around to Maori villages when the official tour was over and the Canadian delegation flew off to Australia to meet the government officials in Sydney. But first, Manuel had a meeting with Prime Minister Holyoake, where he planned to underscore the fact that he was representing the First Nations of Canada and not the government. Jean Chrétien was already in Holyoake's office when George Manuel limped in wearing his chief's headdress and carrying a painting he was offering as a gift. The Prime Minister took one look at him, turned to Chrétien and asked, "Is he tame?"

It was an awkward moment, but Manuel put the prime minister at ease by explaining that he had brought a painting as "a gift given to him by the Indian people of Canada in a spirit of good will which in their tradition meant freedom, justice and the brotherhood of mankind."

The New Zealand prime minister recovered sufficiently to accept the gift, but his remark had stung George Manuel, who later told Marie Marule how insulted he'd felt for himself and his people. Holyoake tried to make up for his gaffe a few days later when he sent George Manuel a carved Maori totem, but the slight was not forgotten.[5]

The trip greatly improved for George Manuel when he was able to visit the Maori villages with Dr. Hohepa. During the visits he often donned his ceremonial headdress and at every stop on this informal tour he was warmly met. Children crowded around him; the sight of a North

American Indian in buckskins and headdress reminded them of American movies and, to George's great amusement, they shouted "Cowboy! Cowboy!"[6]

Manuel's tour of New Zealand ended with a Maori-organized ethnic bash that included Polynesian peoples such as Samoans, Tahitians and Fijians, who had moved to New Zealand and who shared a common culture with the Maoris, as well as a Yugoslavian dance troupe that had somehow wandered into the party.

He found this encounter with the peoples of the South Pacific invigorating, and was interested to learn that they, too, shared a love of the land and a fierce pride in their traditional cultures. By the time George Manuel left the island to meet with the rest of the delegation in Northern Australia, he was leaving friends.

George Manuel caught up with the rest of the Canadians in Gove, Australia. As was the case in the first days of the New Zealand visit, he was given little time away from government officials.

When he had the opportunity to speak with two white teachers in an Aborigine village about the problems in education, he was "left with the impression that on an individual basis there is some sentiment for helping the Aborigines but overall there is not much indication that they are receiving the kind of assistance that springs from real sympathy."

To an even greater extent than the New Zealanders, the Australians were pursuing an assimilation program. One official told George Manuel that the whole education system, from pre-school to adult courses, was aimed in that direction, and "he explained that they regard integration as giving too much recognition to the collective Aborigine community.

"Assimilation," he told us, "concentrates on the individual personal adjustment to the Australian community as a whole. He may retain much of the elements of his own culture but he [wants] to be able to move in Australian society much the same as a Turkish migrant."[7]

When it came time for George Manuel to address an Aborigine student assembly, he showed his disapproval of the paternalistic Australian attitude by telling the kids to "be proud that you are dark. We have every reason to be as proud as the white man. And maybe more . . .

"Just as much as the Maoris and the Aborigines, the Indian people in Canada are dark people in a White Commonwealth."[8]

The NIB leader elaborated on that theme in his report back to his executive. "We share with the Maori and Aborigine, and I suspect also with the many different African peoples," he wrote, "not only this common struggle but also the very real progress that we have made in the past decade. Progress measured . . . by the success of our struggle for survival."[9]

By the time George Manuel left Australia, he was thinking not about the fight for survival but about the battle to regain the political and literal ground that had been lost over the past centuries. And he began to see that struggle more and more with an international perspective. On the long plane ride back, he counted up the people in the indigenous world. With the Indians of Canada, the United States, Central and South America and the indigenous peoples of Eurasia, the movement would represent not hundreds of thousands of people but tens of millions and could force the issue of indigenous rights onto the world stage in a way never dreamed of before.

On his arrival back in Ottawa, Manuel began to plan an international conference that would lay the groundwork for "some more lasting institution. One that, by making us look outward to our dark brothers across the seas, will also help us to see inward to the course of progress within our own communities."[10]

A few months later, he was describing his vision of an international organization of indigenous peoples to the First Secretary of the Tanzanian High Commission, Mbuto Milando. He told Mbuto that if they could somehow stand together, the voices of the millions of indigenous peoples could reach beyond their national borders and be heard by the world.

Mbuto thought for a moment, and then suggested that what George Manuel seemed to be talking about was the emergence of a "Fourth World." George Manuel seized on the phrase and over the years popularized it to describe all of the indigenous peoples trapped within settler societies in conditions that were close to those of the peoples of the Third World.

In an interview a couple of months later, George Manuel outlined the direction of the new movement.

"Aboriginal people of the world must unite to prevent the white race from destroying mankind. White people have a need to destroy, conquer, to suppress, this is not found in the aboriginal value system.

"There is an urgent need for aboriginal peoples all around the world to unite to give direction to the white race before it destroys itself and all mankind."[11]

The New Zealand trip also demonstrated the potential of the NIB for winning international respect for the native cause. As the representative of virtually all of the Indians of Canada, even the Prime Minister of New Zealand's door had been opened to George Manuel, and he was in a small way able to demonstrate that "Indians still exist as a people and that we are still fighting for our rights and that we will not be white-washed or silenced by the government that so willingly stole our land."[12]

The photo of George Manuel presenting the Indian painting to the foreign prime minister and the account of the trip to New Zealand and Australia was heavily publicized in NIB publications (although Holyoake's slight was edited out of the official version). To bring the importance of the meeting between North American and Eurasian indigenous people to the reserve level, George Manuel enlisted a CUSO friend of Marie Marule, Michael Posluns, to put together a slide show with a voice-over script.

When Michael Posluns finished that task, he also began working with George Manuel on a book, *The Fourth World*, which combined autobiographical sketches and a political analysis of the forces of assimilation that Manuel's people had faced in the past.

Like a good politician, George Manuel was able to use the Michael Posluns book (Posluns interviewed George Manuel for forty hours on tape, and then wrote the manuscript), the slide show of his New Zealand/Australia trip and the subsequent foreign trips to win prestige points back home. As he expanded the role of the NIB onto the international stage, he was able to expand his influence in Canada far beyond that of the provincial leaders who had put him in power.

At the end of 1971, just after the collapse of the Alberta school strike, George Manuel was given another opportunity to mount the international stage when he received an invitation from the Tanzanian embassy to attend its tenth anniversary of independence in December 1971.

As Marie Marule recalled, it had been a last-minute invitation. Originally, only Jean Chrétien had been invited. When she heard about this, she suggested to a friend at the Tanzanian embassy that they invite George Manuel as well. The Tanzanians agreed. But just before Manuel and Chrétien were to depart, Chrétien had to back out because of pressing parliamentary business. So George Manuel and his executive assistant, Ron Shackleton, left for Tanzania as the only Canadian guests at the independence celebration.

The two-man NIB delegation attracted a great deal of attention in an African country where most people had assumed that the North American Indians had long ago been wiped out by the US cavalry, as they had seen so often in Hollywood movies. "George Manuel was," as an NIB press release put it, "happy to dispel that impression."[13]

Manuel and Shackleton arrived in Tanzania just as the independence celebrations were getting under way and were invited as official guests to the military parade and various parliamentary ceremonies. Through the NIB's contacts with the Tanzanian diplomatic community in Ottawa, a private meeting was arranged with Julius Nyerere for later on in the trip.

Before that meeting took place, however, the NIB president found himself in a scrap with the Canadian High Commission. Canadian diplomats had only found out about his presence in Tanzania when they read an article entitled "Canadian Indians Seek Ties With Us" in Dar es Salaam's daily paper. George Manuel was pictured on the front page in ceremonial dress and quoted as having come "to seek solidarity with other members of the Third Humanity."

In the article he was quoted as describing the Europeans in North America as colonialists and said that the objectives of the Indian movement were akin to those of socialist Tanzania. He told the reporter that he was impressed to see that Tanzanians were able to run their own affairs and that he "almost shed tears" when he saw Africans at the head of every activity in the country.

In an offhand remark that caused a great deal of concern for the listeners at the Canadian High Commission, George Manuel responded to the question about whether North American Indians would resort to arms in their struggle by stating that he was "extremely impressed by your military parades."[14]

To find out if Manuel was hinting that the Canadian Indian movement was considering engaging in an armed struggle, a representative of the High Commission was sent to a meeting George Manuel had arranged with a group of CIDA workers in Tanzania. Despite the many attempts, the High Commission operative was unable to pin George

Manuel down on the armed struggle issue and in a report sent back to Ottawa, he accused George Manuel of taking "the Delphic approach to the question as to whether the Indians are prepared to resort to arms in the fight for their rights; he does not answer it but like the lady in the poem he doesn't say yes and he doesn't say no."[15]

The discussion with the CIDA people that evening grew heated when some of the CIDA workers took offense at George Manuel's description of white Canadians as "colonizers" and accused him of idealizing Tanzania and its socialist policies. The aid workers also criticized him for hinting that Canadian Indians might take up arms and for damaging his country's reputation in Tanzania. The discussion ended with George Manuel and Ron Shackleton shouting that Canada belonged to the Indians and the whites had no business to it anyway. As the High Commission operative saw it, "Chief Manuel appears to have adopted many tactics of Black Power which until now has been an alien technique in the relations between the Indians and the authorities of the Canadian government."[16]

The scrap between George Manuel and the CIDA workers was picked up in the Tanzanian press, which began to publish articles critical of Canada's treatment of Indians. For the High Commission, the most damaging was one condemning CIDA programs as imperialist and urging the Tanzanian leadership to drop Western aid altogether, following Cuba's example of turning to the Soviet bloc for support.

When that article was published, a CIDA official wrote to the High Commission, demanding that it take action to refute George Manuel's statements. As the CIDA official put it:

"As a Canadian citizen I would like to express hope that the Canadian High Commissioner will do something to correct the false and immensely harmful impression caused here by Chief Manuel of the so-called CIB [sic]. . . . In my own case, I have time and again been called upon to assure my working partners that Canada has no colonialist attitudes. . . . Today my words appear farcical."[17]

The High Commission telexed back to Ottawa for background information on George Manuel, the NIB and the situation of Canadian Indians and asked that someone "outside official channels" write an "impartial factual" response to Manuel that could be planted in the local newspapers. To be effective, the government telex explained, the person selected to author the piece would have to be someone who was known for his or her "sympathetic approach to Nyerere" and yet would be willing to portray Canada's Indian policies in a favourable light.[18]

The damage control had come a little late. The High Commission was already receiving detailed questions from the Tanzanian press about the difference in the mortality rate of white Canadians and the Indians of Canada, and the relative education, income and employment levels of the two groups. When the NIB leader left the country, diplomats at the High Commission were left muttering that they could only hope that Canada's "halo" had not slipped too far as a result of George Manuel's visit.[19]

For George Manuel, the battles with the CIDA workers and the High Commission had been marginal. The highlight of his visit was his meeting with Julius Nyerere. As he saw it, Nyerere's philosophy of self-reliance, frugality and leadership-by-example closely paralleled what he was trying to accomplish with his own "national Indian philosophy," and he was struck by the Tanzanian leader's sincerity and dignity.

As part of his leadership-by-example method, Nyerere often went out into the villages to work with the people. It was in one of these villages that George Manuel was introduced to him and for George Manuel, the man Nyerere most resembled was his grandfather, Dick Andrew.

"We only have to watch Julius Nyerere," he wrote, "the president of Tanzania, taking time from his executive duties to work alongside the day labourers in a small village to know that the traditions of our grandfathers have a place in the modern, technological world."[20]

In the same vein, George Manuel was also impressed by Tanzania's bottom-up philosophy of rural development, in which he saw parallels for the development of the reserve lands in Canada. As he put it, "the background of Indian life was socialism. How they lived, how they shared with one another,"[21] and he thought that it was important that they retain some of those values in the modern world.

One area of discussion with Nyerere that would have long-range consequences for George Manuel concerned the role of tribalism. In Africa, the re-emergence of tribal blocks after independence had at times led to civil strife and political paralysis; Nyerere warned Manuel about the effects of tribalism in the Fourth World movement. George

Manuel took the warning seriously and he later stood in opposition to a tribal movements in BC, even though Nyerere's advice was in some ways a poor fit for the Canadian movement.

George Manuel continued his African education with a side trip to Kenya. He had read about the heroism of Jomo Kenyata as a man who had taken up arms and suffered imprisonment to free his people during the independence struggle.

When George Manuel looked at the results of the struggle, however, he found Jomo Kenyata using "the same bureaucratic system against his own people as the very white race. . . . that he accused of exploiting them. . . . He just took over the system and placed black-skinned people there."

Kenyata, he observed, was being wheeled around in a white Cadillac with a showy police escort and living with "all the trimmings of a very wealthy European. But when you go into the country, you see how poor his people are. Just as poor as they were when the English controlled that country. So there hasn't been any change."[22]

Over all, the African trip also gave George Manuel the opportunity to consider the complexity of the struggle of the Canadian Indians for self-government. In Africa, he witnessed first hand how even a minority of whites had managed to dominate the overwhelming majority of blacks through economic control. How much more difficult it would be to win justice in Canada, where the whites had the weight of numbers as well as economic might, to frustrate the numerically small First Nations.

While acknowledging the difficulties, George Manuel was determined to carry on building the Fourth World movement, and on his return to Ottawa he and Marie Marule held a brainstorming session in which they addressed the enormous logistical problems involved in arranging the international indigenous conference.

While the planning was still in its formative stage, the NIB leader made a third international trip that only added to the complexity of the Fourth World. In 1972, he visited the Sami reindeer herders in the northern reaches of Scandinavia, and he discovered a Fourth World people whose skin was white.

The occasion of that trip was the UN Conference on the Human Environment in Stockholm. The NIB hadn't been on the original invitation list when Canada's National Preparatory Committee met in

November 1971, but once again Marie Marule was able to use her NGO contacts, in this case with the head of the Canadian Labour Congress, James MacDonald, to get an invitation for the National Indian Brotherhood president.

When the invitation arrived in February 1972, George Manuel accepted it "enthusiastically" because the growing environmental crisis represents "a threat to the very existence of the culture and way of life of thousands of native Canadians."[23] But he also saw in the invitation an opportunity to put forward the Canadian Indian cause among the Europeans and the larger UN community that would be attending the conference.

In the lead up to the Stockholm trip, Marie Marule worked to get George Manuel meetings with groups like the Copenhagen-based International Working Group for Indigenous Affairs (IWGIA) and Survival International, which largely comprised white anthropologists, but which had good records in promoting indigenous rights.

Through IWGIA, the NIB was also able to locate a lawyer who had contacts with the Sami, and Jamie Deacey, who was still working as George Manuel's executive assistant, was sent off to finalize the details of Manuel's meetings with IWGIA and to try to get him an invitation to visit some Sami communities in the north.

In his travels, Deacey ran into Gun Leander, a reporter from *Dagens Nhyeter*, Sweden's largest newspaper. She was intrigued by the idea of the Canadian Indian leader visiting the Sami, and offered to fly George Manuel up to meet with them at the paper's expense while she produced a photoessay on the historic meeting of indigenous peoples from two continents.

George Manuel arrived in Stockholm on June 3, with a hastily assembled NIB position paper on the environment that was highly critical of the Canadian government's record. Perhaps because of this, he found himself "excluded from the mainstream of the Canadian delegation." So he went off on his own to cultivate contacts with the Chinese, Brazilian, German, Australian and East African delegations.

From his own soundings, he discovered that most of the delegates placed Canada at "a half-way point between the developed and undeveloped countries." It was a role that the Canadian delegation – a self-described "honest broker" in world affairs – also seemed to welcome.[24]

George Manuel took the time to visit some of the leftist "alternative conferences" that had been organized to coincide with the UN conference. He wanted to see if they were ideologically in line with the NIB but found them "to be lacking in basic organization and shaky in their presentations."[25]

As in the South Pacific, George Manuel's real priority was meeting with indigenous people, and when he left for the north with the Swedish reporter on June 8, he was full of anticipation. He found the 1,200 kilometre flight fascinating and described the terrain as "similar to the Northwest Territories. It [was] barren but beautiful country."[26]

The delegation stayed in Kiruna overnight and in the morning they flew by helicopter to the village of Rensjon where he was welcomed by the chief who was wearing his ceremonial costume. The Swedish photographer snapped pictures of the historic meeting of George Manuel shaking hands with the Sami chief on the heli-pad.

George Manuel was also impressed by his first look at the chief's house, which even in that remote area had electricity and was, by Canadian Indian standards, quite comfortable. But when he began to discuss problems with the chief and other Sami representatives, he discovered that the issues the two peoples were fighting were, as in the case of the Maori and Aborigines, remarkably similar: "Their major problem – as is ours – is the question of land rights and who actually owns and has the right of usage of the land."

The chief explained to George Manuel that the Sami "had herded their reindeer through the area that is now the town of Kiruna during the change from summer to winter pastures and vice-versa." When the town was built, the Sami were forced to take one of two alternative routes. But then a mine development blocked one of those routes and the mining company and the government proposed building a road that would effectively shut off the last route to their traditional winter pasturing land.[27]

This threat of loss of their livelihood was made even more serious by the Swedish practice of recognizing people as bona fide Samis only as long as they were reindeer herders. If the people could no longer herd reindeer, they would cease to exist as a distinct people in the eyes of the Swedish government.

For George Manuel, this bureaucratic threat sounded painfully familiar. He told the chief "that we have undergone quite a bit of the same type of government exploitation and deliberate attempts at eroding and destroying both our land and treaty rights."

One similarity between the Sami and the Canadian Indians that was not at all painful to discover was the feast the local people put on after all the "heavy political talk."

The meal, which "consisted of smoked reindeer, bread very much like bannock, and wild berries," was, George Manuel said, the best he had had in Europe. He was struck by the fact that he had been served almost the identical meal in Indian homes in the Northwest Territories and the Yukon. His vision of the Fourth World of indigenous peoples that had grown during his trip to the South Pacific, became even more concrete as he ate the country food of the Sami people ten thousand miles away in northern Sweden.

During the feast, he tried out his idea of an international indigenous peoples' conference on the chief. In George Manuel's words, the chief "did not disappoint me and told me that the idea had long been a concern of his as well, and that he would be very pleased to participate in such a conference."[28]

In itself, the agreement of the Sami chief to attend a conference of the world's indigenous peoples would have made the northern trip a success, but there was another benefit. Manuel and the delegation returned to Stockholm on Saturday night and woke up Sunday morning to see on the front page of the paper a photo of George Manuel meeting the Sami chief. There was a half-page story about how the great chief of the Canadian Indians had explained that his people had similar problems as the Sami and, in many instances, were even more badly treated by the Canadian government. When you flipped to page six, there were related stories based on interviews with George Manuel that had as their theme, as Deacey remembered it, that Canadian Indians "were treated like shit" by the federal government.[29]

George Manuel was staggered by the amount of coverage his visit had received and the Canadian NGO delegations shared in his delight. The head of the official delegation, Maurice Strong, however, was not at all happy by the beating Canada took in the Sunday paper. Part of his job had been to promote Canada in Europe and the front-page treatment of the Indian issue cast a cloud over Canada's image.

The atmosphere was tense when the Canadian delegation met on

Monday morning for what was supposed to be a routine get-together. To break the ice, James MacDonald stood up and said that he "thought it was marvellous that some member of the Canadian delegation was receiving some publicity."[30] The government representatives didn't laugh at the joke and George Manuel never heard anything in the way of an official reaction, but he noticed that afterward, the officials and the ministers were much more concerned about him and went out of their way to include him in all the activities of the delegation.

The last week in Sweden also gave George Manuel an opportunity to examine some of the byzantine workings of the international community. He came to understand that North American Indians "are in direct competition with the developing countries for funds and other resources that our Indian organizations have been demanding from the Federal Government."

As he put it, "There is only so much water in the well. In terms of prestige, the developed countries would much sooner help out a country 2,000 miles away than a disadvantaged minority in their own country."

That realization was a bit disheartening. George Manuel concluded "that if the National Indian Brotherhood and Indians in Canada are to accomplish their goals they must achieve international recognition and aid. But we should not suffer under any illusions, instead, we should look at our position with reality and make the necessary moves to assure our international participation."[31]

The conference wrapped up on June 15, but George Manuel's journey was far from over. Although tired from his two-week sojourn, and filled with new concerns about the course of the international struggle, he headed off to other European capitals to try to gather the recognition he felt the movement needed.

His first stop was Copenhagen, where he met with representatives of the International Working Group on Indigenous Affairs and held a press conference with the Danish press. In his private discussions with IWGIA, George Manuel discovered that they were planning a forum in Chicago to discuss how their progressive anthropology differed from the paternalistic approach of the classic anthropologists.

George Manuel told them point blank that what he wanted was "an International Indigenous Peoples' Conference with indigenous people being the participants as opposed to being studied." He was pleased to find that the European anthropologists didn't argue against the idea, but instead reacted with enthusiasm. They spent the next two days discussing the conference, with IWGIA agreeing to cancel their forum and use the money to help fund George Manuel's project.[32]

From Copenhagen, George Manuel flew to London to meet with the Society of Friends, the Anti-Slavery Society and finally Survival International, which was made up of a group of wealthy Englishmen who were involved in supporting the Indians of Brazil. He was trying to enlist all of the British groups into supporting the conference and he was rewarded with polite encouragement.

Deacey recalls, however, that some of the people they met in Britain tended to be "a bit eccentric. If you didn't collect odd butterflies from the Amazon, you could have a Canadian Indian" or some other native representative around." This was particularly true of the Anti-Slavery Society, which was headed by a relative of Aldous Huxley, who thought the indigenous peoples' conference was a grand idea, but felt he would be more competent in organizing it than the indigenous peoples would.

Before leaving London, George Manuel had an opportunity to meet a number of British MPs and ex-cabinet ministers and discuss the conference; he was surprised to find they supported the idea and offered to try to get British government financial backing for it.

A British Lord, Sir Geoffrey de Freitas, then led George Manuel on a tour of Westminster. As they passed through Westminster Hall, Manuel "thought of all the decisions that had been made here so carelessly for centuries that had affected our people. It was not a sense of nostalgia which overcame me, but one of weariness in that we have not really progressed but merely traded one white government in London for another in Ottawa."[33]

His spirits were lifted that afternoon when he was honoured at a luncheon by the Society of Friends and he discovered that the last person to be so honoured was the American civil rights leader, Martin Luther King, Jr.

The final stage in George Manuel's journey was Geneva, where he met with representatives of the International Labour Organization who told him quite clearly that they "were not interested in embarrassing the Canadian government." George Manuel was surprised at the cool response and made a mental note that in the future he would try to get

James MacDonald and the CLC to meet with the ILO leadership and explain the situation to them.

His final meeting in Geneva was with Newaz Dawood of the World Council of Churches, who greeted him warmly and pledged full support for the idea of the indigenous peoples' conference. Dawood went further, discussing with George Manuel the methods that an indigenous peoples' organization could use to get non-governmental observer status at the UN. In fact, the WCC sent a representative for a follow-up meeting with George Manuel soon after he arrived back in Ottawa.

The end of his European tour marked George Manuel's second anniversary as NIB president. While he was entering his third term of office, however, his attention once again swung back to the domestic scene where a landmark court case put the land claims and aboriginal rights issues centre stage in Canada as they had never been before.

## CHAPTER TWELVE

# Land Title and the James Bay Battle
## 1972-1973

There is no Trail of Tears that can be drawn on Canadian maps as it
must be drawn for the Cherokee Nation. We were not banished from
our land. It is as though the land was moved from under us.

George Manuel
*The Fourth World,* p.32

In the fall of 1972, the NIB was still far from achieving the "national
philosophy" that George Manuel had spoken of at the annual assembly.
But the organization had achieved enough internal cohesion to begin to
focus its efforts on what would always be one of the fundamental issues:
the rights of the First Nations to their traditional lands.

In a November speech to the Union of BC Indian Chiefs, George
Manuel signalled that he was not only ready to move on the question of
aboriginal land rights, but also to try to reopen the whole treaty question.
He began by speaking of the great Plains Cree chief Big Bear.

"A hundred years ago Big Bear was resisting the signing of the
treaties. He continuously cautioned his colleagues against consenting to
the conditions of the treaties by the commissioners. He, like Pound-
maker, believed that this is Indian land, it isn't a piece of pemmican to be
cut off and given in little pieces back to us. He was totally opposed to the
entire spirit of the Canadian treaty terms."

As George Manuel saw it, "The frustrations, humiliations and anger
of that time are also present today. Attempts to subjugate our people
continue in spite of centuries of our resistance. Some of our people are
tired of passive resistance. All we want is justice and freedom from

tyranny and subjugation. Big Bear wanted the same things for his people a hundred years ago as we want for our people today – Justice, Freedom, Social, Cultural and Economic Independence."[1]

Harold Cardinal had come to the same conclusion after speaking with the elders in Alberta. The elders, he discovered, never viewed the treaties as a surrender of land or sovereignty. Instead, they considered them as peace treaties between nations.

According to Cardinal, "we did not, by treaty, surrender our water, our timber, our mineral resources; we did not surrender our way of life. The only thing that we agreed to do was to live in peace with the white man, and to share with him the available land so that he could come into this country, and bring his livestock, and support his families."

Cardinal went on to argue that if "our elders understood the treaties to be peace treaties rather than bills of sale for land and resources, how legitimate is the government's claim to ownership of those resources . . ."[2]

The government's claim to legitimacy over the unceded lands in British Columbia was put before the Supreme Court in the fall of 1972 and the answer, which was given in January 1973, caught both the government and the native organizations by surprise.

The case was the Nishga land claim, which was filed under Frank Calder's name with Tom Berger serving as the Nishga lawyer. Berger based the claim on unextinguished aboriginal title, a concept that had been rejected by Trudeau and all preceding Canadian governments. In the past, the Canadian courts had also always agreed with the government and there had been fears among Indian leaders that the Nishga case would be just another legal door slammed in their faces.

But that didn't happen. The seven-member court ruled three for recognizing the Nishga's aboriginal right to the Nass Valley, and three against. The seventh judge did not rule on the contents of the case, but only on procedural grounds. That meant that the Supreme Court had split on the idea that the non-treaty parts of Canada, which included Labrador, the Northwest Territories, the Yukon and almost all of Quebec and British Columbia, were still under the legal title of the First Nations who resided there.

The ruling had the greatest implications for the BC and northern lands because the court rejected one of the key arguments the federal and BC governments had used to deny the existence of aboriginal title in these areas. Successive governments had argued that the BC and northern Indians were not covered by the Royal Proclamation of 1763, which explicitly recognized the existence of Indian "nations," because no British subject had reached that far when the Proclamation was issued.

In his review of the case for the NIB, Doug Sanders pointed to Justice Emmett Hall's decision that the Proclamation was "confirmatory and declaratory of the common-law position on Indian title."

According to Hall, the "Proclamation was like the Magna Carta in being a fundamental document of English law. It followed the flag and came to apply in British Columbia by virtue of the Colonial Validity Act."[3]

Before the decision was handed down, Frank Calder, James Gosnel and a group of Nishga leaders had gathered in Len Marchand's office on Parliament Hill. When the outcome was announced, Marchand called George Manuel at the NIB headquarters on Albert Street and invited him to come over. Then he arranged for the whole group to meet with Trudeau in the prime minister's office.

For George Manuel and the others it was a precious moment. The NIB had presented its position paper on aboriginal rights to a commons committee in 1971. They had asked the government to recognize that prior to the colonial settlement of North America, the Indian people "had uncontested dominion over their tribal territories and all the people therein." As the brief put it, the First Nations "could govern, make laws, wage war, and had their own political, social, educational, economic and property systems. Each tribe had absolute control over the resources and products of its lands."[4]

George Manuel had followed up with a lengthy personal letter to the prime minister in June 1972, asking Trudeau to expand the terms of reference of the land claims commission to include aboriginal rights. The prime minister didn't bother to answer. Now he found himself confronted in his office by George Manuel, Len Marchand and the Nishga leaders clutching a court decision that gave strong legal backing to their claim of aboriginal title over vast areas of the country.

Trudeau's response was a smile and the enigmatic statement that, "Perhaps you have more rights than I thought."[5] After a polite discussion, the group left the meeting without a clear commitment, but they were encouraged by the fact that the prime minister seemed to be taking the aboriginal rights question seriously.

To keep the pressure on Trudeau, George Manuel immediately issued a press release that stated that he wanted "the prime minister to resolve this question without further delay" and asked him to keep in mind "that Canada is supposed to be a Just Society."[6]

The Calder judgement and the pressure from Indian organizations seemed to have some effect on Ottawa. When the Yukon Indian Brotherhood presented its land claims brief to the government in February 1973, Jean Chrétien announced that the government was, for the first time, prepared to enter into discussion "with a group that has never signed treaties."

Marchand remembers that he and the others kept up the pressure throughout the summer of 1973 for a more explicit recognition of aboriginal rights. He was told during a July lunch with Trudeau and Chrétien that the government was prepared to recognize the concept of aboriginal rights, but it would only negotiate the exact content of these rights with the different Indian groups involved.

When the new position was announced, there was a sense of elation in Indian country. It was felt that a major breakthrough had been made and that the Indian nations in the non-treaty areas were only years away from just and comprehensive land settlements. It was in this spirit of optimism that Phillip Paul called up Doug Sanders and asked him to move back to Vancouver Island to help set up a land claims research centre and put together a claim that would encompass virtually all of mainland British Columbia.

George Manuel expressed regret that Doug Sanders was leaving for Victoria, because in their years together at the NIB the two men had developed a close working relationship. But Sanders also had the impression that George Manuel thought that he, too, would soon be heading back to help negotiate the British Columbia land claim and the subsequent self-government protocols.

That sense of optimism was slowly eroded, however, as it became clear that what Trudeau and Chrétien considered aboriginal rights were a far cry from what the First Nations were dedicated to recuperating. For George Manuel, the goal was recognition of the Indian Nations as equal partners in the country with the French and English nations, and that the Indian people should have at least the same powers over their land, resources, health systems and education as the non-Indian people of Ontario or Prince Edward Island, or as the French majority in Quebec.

But in the federal government's view, aboriginal rights were considered as something that had to be "extinguished" during land claim negotiations, and the DIA strategists began to develop plans for modern-day versions of the nineteenth century treaties, with the government of Canada offering cash settlements and reserve lands in exchange for agreements from the Indian nations that they had no further claim on their traditional homelands.

This narrow, and from George Manuel's point of view, genocidal approach to aboriginal rights was first pursued in Quebec, where the Cree and Inuit were facing a determined push from the provincial government that wanted to expropriate their lands for the James Bay hydroelectric project.

The government of Quebec had quietly begun studies for the project in 1965 on lands the federal government turned over to the province in 1912 under the condition that the aboriginal claims be settled. Quebec had never fulfilled its obligations and after details of the James Bay project leaked out in 1969, leaders from the Indians of Quebec Association (IQA) began to protest the province's failure to address the land claim. As a result, a committee of the federal and provincial governments and the IQA was set up in to look at the question of aboriginal land, hunting and fishing rights in the region.

Before any progress had been made, Premier Bourassa announced the "world would begin tomorrow" with his "Project of the Century," the $6 billion James Bay Hydroelectric Project that would instantly create 125,000 jobs and eventually serve as "the key to the economic and social progress of Quebec."[7]

The northern Cree leaders reacted with shock to the announcement of the massive development of their lands by outside forces. After a meeting of the local Cree leadership in Mistassini, they drafted a resolution for the minister of Indian Affairs stating that the Cree opposed the project "because we believe that only the beavers had the right to build dams in our territory" and requested that Chrétien "use his legal jurisdiction to stop any attempt of intrusion of our rightful owned territory by the government of the province of Quebec, or any other authority."[8]

In Quebec City, Bourassa ignored the Cree concerns and passed the James Bay Development Corporation Act that put a large portion of Cree and Inuit lands under the board of a five-man government.

George Manuel was shocked by the speed and the callousness with which the government of Quebec was moving against the Cree and Inuit. In the past, he had always been sympathetic toward the demands of Quebec *vis-à-vis* English Canada and he expected that the Québecois would be sympathetic to the demands of the native people for formal recognition of their nationhood, since they were asking for essentially the same thing from English Canada. The events surrounding the James Bay Project, however, suggested otherwise.

"The experience of living in a land of minorities," he told a Montreal audience, "has taught the people of Quebec to find their own greatest strength and to expect the same from others. But recently I have had to wonder whether this experience has developed a capacity to consider the needs of others.

"The decision of the Government of Quebec to proceed with the James Bay Hydro Development Project is a decision to displace or take away the livelihood of seven thousand Indian people. Without even the kind of consultation exercise with which the federal government indulges us."

George Manuel went on to warn that if Quebec persisted with the project, the result would be "conflict and disharmony between north and south inside Quebec."[9]

As the debate over James Bay heated up, George Manuel's tone became harsher. He accused Quebec of having tried to starve native people into submission in the 1930s and suggested that little had changed since then.

The James Bay battle was to be a seminal one for the Indian movement. It would show the strengths and weaknesses of the movement and it would set the ideological tenor of the land battles in the future. It would also lead George Manuel to draw a line in the sand over the issue of the extinguishment of aboriginal rights.

In his fight against the James Bay project, the only real ally George Manuel had inside the government was Len Marchand, who announced in the House of Commons that he was tempted to "take out his tomahawk" on the James Bay issue, and claimed that if his Indian ancestors had had a different immigration policy there would be no question about human and environmental disasters like the James Bay project.

Marchand then produced the preliminary environmental study which broadly indicted the effects of the project on the rivers and wildlife of northern Quebec, but which stressed that the most devastating effect would be on the native people in the region. The development, he claimed, would not only disrupt traditional Cree hunting areas and pollute Cree waterways, it would cut roads and airfields into the region that would bring the isolated Cree communities all of the pressures of modern life without giving them time to prepare for them. Indian leaders and anthropologists feared that the result would be the social disintegration of what was one of the last few traditional hunting societies in North America.

It was around this time that Billy Diamond, the young Cree leader, and Charlie Watt, the equally young Inuit leader, showed up in Ottawa looking for support from the NIB. George Manuel arranged a meeting for them with Chrétien, himself and the IQA lawyer, James O'Reilly. When Diamond and Watt asked Chrétien for funds to help them launch a legal challenge to Quebec's assault on Cree and Inuit lands, Chrétien is reported to have stated flatly that "There is no way the government of Canada is going to support you in a law case against the government of Quebec. James Bay is a reality . . ."[10]

But three months later, Chrétien bowed to pressure from Indian leaders, and from advice in his own department suggesting that the federal government had a trustee role toward the Quebec Cree. He agreed to give the IQA funds to take the James Bay Corporation to court.

In the spring of 1973, Quebec Justice Albert Malouf agreed to hear the case for an injunction against the project and announced he would take the testimony of the hunters and trappers of the region before making a decision.

When Malouf wrapped up the public testimony in late June, there was some hope that the native cause would be supported by the courts. But that sense of optimism was offset by a sudden rift in the Quebec–Indian coalition when the twenty-four-year-old Billy Diamond informed Andrew Delisle, the head of the IQA, that he would handle the land negotiations on his own. Diamond eventually brought in James O'Reilly to work on the Cree claim and then he withdrew his people from the IQA entirely.

George Manuel was concerned about Diamond's sudden withdrawal from the Quebec wing of the NIB, but he and others had known that trouble was brewing between the Crees and the Indians in the southern part of the province. For Delisle, a Kahnawake Mohawk, the James Bay battle was a means not only of solving the Cree claims, but also of forcing Quebec to address Indian land claims across the province.

As Dave Monture, who was then working for the IQA in Quebec City, remembered it: "Andrew [Delisle] wanted George's support for a larger land claim in Quebec and the Crees wanted to draw a line and negotiate on their own behalf. They didn't want southern, and in their view, more assimilated Indians, who didn't even know how to trap any more, messing around in their claims."

The young Crees had also scorned the southern Indians for their three-piece suits and for always being surrounded by white lawyers, but as Monture recalled, "it wasn't eighteen months later that Billy Diamond was well-dressed and surrounded by lawyers."

During the Malouf hearings, Diamond, Watt and O'Reilly met several times with the provincial government to try to put together a deal, but according to Diamond's biographer, Roy MacGregor, the two sides were "light years apart."

"The bureaucrats were talking about a cash sweetener and the setting up of reserves just like the ones where the poverty-stricken Crees on the Ontario side of the bay had lived since 1905."[11]

What the government did succeed in doing, however, was to get Diamond and O'Reilly focusing on a cash offer in leading them toward extinguishing Cree title. In a private meeting in May with John Ciaccia, who had moved from Chrétien's office to the provincial Liberal Party, Diamond and O'Reilly offered Ciaccia a wish list of changes to the project that included greatly expanded land and fishing rights and a billion-dollar cash settlement.[12]

This behind-the-scenes offer was a clear departure from the position Billy Diamond had taken in public. In his speeches Diamond insisted, and continued to insist for some months, that Cree land was not for sale and only beavers had the right to build dams in their territory.

After his secret billion-dollar offer to Ciaccia, however, he had put a price on his people's land and all that was left from the government point of view was the haggling.

On the surface, the Cree and Inuit cause appeared to be strengthened on 15 November 1973, when Justice Malouf presented his 170-page decision that granted the Cree and Inuit an injunction against the construction of the James Bay Hydro-electric Project and recognized that "the rights of the Cree Indian and Inuit populations have never been extinguished."[13]

The head of the James Bay Corporation treated the whole matter with contempt and announced that "The injunction will not slow the rate at which our work is progressing. . . . There are five thousand of them and five million of us. They can't keep it all for themselves . . ."[14]

The Corporation then went to the Quebec Court of Appeals and had the injunction suspended. The bulldozers were once again sent rolling across the Cree and Inuit lands as the five million *of us* began to push the five thousand *of them* from their lands.

With the project moving ahead and Billy Diamond's secret billion-dollar price tag on the table, the government of Quebec went to the Cree and Inuit with a counter-offer. Ciaccia's opening figure was $100 million in cash and two thousand square miles of land.

The indigenous leaders refused the deal and Bourassa waited two months, until January 1974, before going public with the $100 million offer. Quebec government and Hydro Quebec officials then began to portray the northern Indians and Inuit as extortionists trying to squeeze more millions out of the government.

When George Manuel heard of the $100 million offer for extinguishment and saw how Bourassa presented it, he knew the Crees and Inuit were in trouble. His suspicions were heightened when Jean Chrétien came out and publicly supported the Quebec offer.

In a January 1974 statement, George Manuel launched a vigorous attack on what he saw as Chrétien's sudden acquiescence to Quebec.

He accused the DIA minister of "grossly misleading the general public, deceiving the federal Parliament and attempting to manipulate the Indian people by his recent statement in support of the Quebec Government's termination policy for the Indians and Inuit people of the James Bay area."

The NIB leader then attacked the ambiguity of the offer in the area of government jurisdiction over the Indian lands. "The social and economic development services to be provided by the Government as stated is extremely ambiguous. If 'the Government' referred to in this proposal is the Provincial Government of Quebec then this is an enormous transfer of federal responsibility to provincial authority, a complete implementation of the 1969 federal Liberal government White Paper proposal which has been vigorously opposed by all Canadian Indian groups."

George Manuel then took aim at Chrétien's duplicity.

For Chrétien "to repeatedly inform the House of Commons that he is upholding his responsibility to the Indian and Inuit people of James Bay area by partially financing the James Bay Court battle," and then turn around and pressure "the Indian and Inuit people to accept an unrealistic termination proposal illustrates a complete inconsistency and an apparent dangerous deception."[15]

By the spring of 1974, however, George Manuel and everyone else knew that the Crees were cornered. Quebec would not back down on any of the essentials of their James Bay development plans and the federal government would no longer help the Cree pursue the matter in the courts. All Diamond and Watt could do was to stall and try to get Quebec to sweeten its offer. But even here, they could not hold out forever. Public opinion in Quebec had been whipped up against the multi-million dollar demands of the Cree and Inuit and it was becoming politically easier every day for the provincial government to withdraw its offer and simply shrug off the whole issue of the Indians and Inuit in the north.

In November 1974, when Quebec came with what it said was its final offer, the Cree and Inuit and their lawyers decided that they had the best deal possible under the circumstances and signed an agreement in principle to extinguish their aboriginal title to much of their homeland.

In return, Billy Diamond and Charlie Watt won for their people a cash settlement of $150 million, a small land base, a larger area of land use, and a role in regional government. In exchange they renounced "all claims to collective title" to their traditional lands in Northern Quebec.[16] Hydro Quebec would join the beavers in having carte blanche in damming what had been, since time immemorial, the homeland of the Cree and Inuit people. Indian land which, as late as February 1974, Billy Diamond had described as "not for sale, not even for millions and millions of dollars," had been sold.[17]

George Manuel reacted to the news of the final settlement more in sadness than in anger.

"Extinguishment of aboriginal rights means to me the extinguishing of Indian identity, totally and completely," he told an *Indian News* reporter, "and that is why I am against it and that is why the people I represent are against it."

When he analyzed, what, exactly, the Cree had received for giving up their heritage, he was even more disturbed. The $150 million turned out to be "the equivalent of a payment of $805 per year per native person for the first ten years of the agreement.

"And half of the $150 million mess of potage is dependent on the generating capacity of the James Bay power plant – the plant responsible for stealing our birthright."

Still, George Manuel refused to attack Billy Diamond or any of the other Cree leaders personally. Instead he took a parting shot at Diamond's legal advisor when he concluded that "The only person to benefit from the James Bay settlement is the lawyer for the Crees."[18]

As it turned out, George Manuel was right. Sixteen years after the deal was signed, even a Hydro Quebec-sponsored study indicated that the Cree in Northern Quebec were just as poor as they had been before the agreement became Canadian and Quebec law in 1975. The costs of social and environmental destruction caused by imposition of the "The Project of the Century" on the Cree land remain incalculable and the agreement has opened the way for Hydro Quebec to pursue countless other projects, large and small, on the lands the Cree and Inuit leaders signed away.

For George Manuel, the success of the federal and provincial governments in pushing forward with the James Bay project was a bitter blow, especially when it had come after the apparent victory in having aboriginal title recognized in principle by the federal government. After all, what did aboriginal title mean if a provincial government could move onto Indian lands and develop them as they saw fit? Of what significance were negotiations when one side could unilaterally determine the outcome?

Looking ahead, George Manuel was also concerned that the Quebec settlement would be used by the federal government as a precedent for the negotiations it was carrying out with the Yukon Indians, and in future negotiations with the Indians of the Northwest Territories and British Columbia.

Those negotiations, he feared, would also be geared toward the extinguishment of aboriginal title and he told his friends that he would rather die without an agreement with the government and pass on to his children "the legitimacy of the struggle" than sign a deal like James Bay "that they could not live with."[19]

As he saw it, the failure to stop the James Bay development pointed out the continued weakness of the movement. To try to re-invigorate it, Manuel organized a retreat for himself and the provincial and territorial leaders.

The meeting was designed to provide an opportunity for the Indian leaders to build a common front against any deal with the government that involved the extinguishment of Indians' aboriginal title to their traditional lands.

As George Manuel saw it, "the co-operation to reach this goal could only become a reality if every provincial and territorial leader co-operated with each other in complete honesty, in opening their minds, hearts and feeling in respect to a national strategy for the goals and objectives of economic independence for our people."[20]

During his closed-door meetings with his fellow leaders, however, George Manuel was disturbed to find that many of them were wavering on the issue. He believed that they had a very narrow political perspective, so he launched an information campaign that saw NIB staffers and his Third World friends travelling across the country to speak of the anti-colonialist struggle and the philosophy of liberation behind it.

While he was working at politicizing the grass roots in Canada, George Manuel was also continuing to build the international indigenous movement. He began by bringing in two new figures to help prepare for an international conference.

The first was Guy Lavallee, a Métis priest from St. Laurent, Manitoba, whose enlistment to the cause occurred in what had become a typical George Manuel recruitment technique. Lavallee had been appointed to head the permanent Indian Pavilion after Expo '67 and he invited George Manuel to speak at the "Indians of Canada Day" he organized in 1971.

He had just arrived back in Montreal from a stay in Manitoba in January 1973, when his phone rang at 2 p.m. on a Friday afternoon. It was George Manuel calling from Ottawa and he said, "Guy, I want to see you."

Lavallee said fine, he'd head up to Ottawa on Monday or Tuesday to meet with him. George Manuel said, "No, I want to see you this afternoon."

Lavallee was a bit taken aback by what amounted to a summons to the NIB office, but thought "what the hell" and jumped in his car for the two-hour drive to the capital. When he entered George Manuel's office, George shoved a bulging file across the desk and asked Lavallee if he would read it on the spot and tell him what he thought of it.

The dossier contained all of the planning work that had gone into the international aboriginal peoples' conference. When he finished going through it a couple of hours later, Lavallee told George Manuel he agreed with both the contents and the objectives of such an organization and George said, "Good, you're hired."

Lavallee asked, "What for?"

George Manuel smiled. "Hired to raise money for this project. We need hundreds of thousands of dollars in six weeks and we want you to raise the money . . . The only problem is that we don't have any money to pay you. So you have to raise your own salary."

Lavallee remembers standing there "listening to this man, sitting behind this huge desk with the conviction of a Jean Drapeau in front of a thousand people. But at the same time, he's gentle and firm. It was at that very moment that I came to know George Manuel as a person. As a man of conviction, as a man of vision. Not just George Manuel the politician or the tough negotiator around a table with politicians. But really a man of deep conviction, a man who was very sensitive to humanity and who had a vision for indigenous people.

"And I got on the bandwagon because I agreed with his objectives, but I also felt that he could lead us onto greater heights . . . Which he did afterwards. History proves that."[21]

Lavallee soon found himself dispatched to Europe where he began to tap the contacts George Manuel had made in 1972, to get the funding for the indigenous conference.

At the same time, George Manuel was busy recruiting another international operative through one of Marie's contacts. His name was Rodrigo Contreras, a young Ecuadorian who had landed in Canada in 1969 and began working with the NGOs in Ottawa. He had seen George Manuel for the first time at the consultation meeting in Ottawa in May 1969, and he remembers that two things struck him about George Manuel: the fact that in the late 1960s he had a very short brush cut and that he came across as "a very lucid alternative kind of leader."

Over the years, that latter impression was confirmed when Rodrigo met George informally at Marie's parties in Aylmer, where Rodrigo also lived. He first heard of the plans for the indigenous peoples' conference from Marie in 1973, and he was immediately taken by the idea. When Marie told him they were looking for someone to help organize the Latin American side of things, he expressed an interest, so she arranged for a meeting between the two men.

Contreras claims the meeting changed his life. Like Lavallee, he was struck by the depth of George Manuel's conviction and the breadth of his vision. Rodrigo also observed that "it was a turning point in my life that I met a man of such stature and nature that made me feel equal, almost for the first time in my life."

"I think [George Manuel] felt equal and unequal many times in his life, but I think he tasted equality and he fought for it until he died . . . And now I strive and I struggle and I fight for equality because I know what it feels like to have a feeling of complete equality."[22]

Finally, George Manuel hired a new special assistant, Clive Linklater, a young Saultaux from Ontario whom he had trained as a community development officer in Edmonton. George Manuel had first used Clive Linklater as a liaison worker with the James Bay Cree, but he soon also put him to work as an organizer of the aboriginal peoples' conference with Marie Marule, Guy Lavallee and Rodrigo Contreras.

By October, enough contacts had been made internationally for Marie Marule to make the first trip south to Georgetown, Guyana, where they hoped to hold the first preparatory meeting. Marie met with high officials in the Forbes Burnham government and they agreed to host the meeting in the following April. When she left Georgetown, she made stops in Colombia and Ecuador to meet with the local indigenous leadership and issue invitations to the April conference. Back in Ottawa, she drew up the final invitation list and sent it out to indigenous representatives from four continents.

George Manuel's dream of an international organization of indigenous people was one step closer to becoming a reality. But at the same time, the battle on the home front was heating up, as young militants began to push the issue of native rights in Canada onto the streets.

## CHAPTER THIRTEEN

# Red Power

## 1973-1975

The younger generation of our people are organizing silently, and things will be different when they take over. It is unfortunate that Indians may have to use militant action to achieve their rights. Even now the mood of Indians is explosive.

George Manuel
Apr. 1971

In May 1973, Marlene and George had a second child, a son named George, Jr. Like George Manuel's other children, George, Jr. would barely see his father during his childhood. But by 1974, George Manuel's work was bringing him into close contact with two of his grown sons, Bob and Arthur, who were both drawn into the increasingly radical youth wing of the Indian movement.

Arthur Manuel had been elected president of the Native Youth Association in 1971 and he preached the unity of all the indigenous people of North, South and Central America so they could "form a majority over whites in the Western Hemisphere." He also called on the Indians of Canada to have as many children as possible so that in a generation or two, the armed struggle would become a viable option. A fiery speaker, the young Manuel ended his speeches with a Black Panther style clenched fist and a shout of "Power to the People!"[1]

In the past, George Manuel had often used the radicalism of the younger generation to urge the government to negotiate. He once told a *Calgary Herald* reporter that his son said he was "too mellow, that I don't know what politics are all about, and that I will never win anything this way."

He then pointed out that the situation among the young was reaching the "explosive" stage and that if the government didn't act, violence was a real possibility. [2]

The youthful explosion that came in 1973 turned out to be a controlled blast, however, with the NYA organizing a twenty-four-hour takeover of the Indian Affairs building in Ottawa to demand that the federal government stop the James Bay project and begin serious negotiations on the BC land question.

George Manuel got wind of the plan and asked his half-brother Joe, who was still the Neskainlith band chief, to come east to keep an eye on the young people in the NYA.

Arthur Manuel had arranged for 150 members of the Native Youth Association to meet at the Akwesasne Reserve on Cornwall Island on the afternoon of August 29. As a courtesy, he called his father at three in the morning to let him know about their plans. George Manuel only asked his son, "Do you know what you are doing?"

Arthur said, "I think so."

The elder Manuel replied, "Fine," and then quietly arranged to have the NIB lawyers outside the Indian Affairs building in the morning in case trouble broke out.

The group arrived at the building at 8:30 a.m. and the takeover went off without a hitch. The young militants marched into the building with blankets and sleeping bags while they chanted and drummed. The few employees who were already at their desks were ushered out while the RCMP and the Ottawa City Police surrounded the building.

After Arthur Manuel assured the police that they were carrying out a peaceful sit-in that would end in twenty-four hours, the tension was relieved and the police sat back to wait it out.

During the morning, the police even allowed George Manuel to pass through their lines to the door of the building and he spoke briefly with Arthur, asking him if they needed anything. Arthur said everything was fine and went back upstairs where filing cabinets were being emptied and the photocopy machines were kept busy. The young activists were especially interested in documents concerning James Bay, and along with the photocopies, they stuffed a number of sensitive original documents into their bags and blankets.

Shortly after the incident, packages of photocopied and original government documents began appearing in the mailboxes of Indian chiefs across the country. Some of the more wary chiefs, seeing the government seals and the "secret" and "confidential" designations, were reported to have quietly taken them out and buried them in the bush. For the NIB and its affiliate organizations, however, the documents supplied a wealth of information on government strategies, in particular those dealing with Indian opposition to the James Bay project.

The government didn't find out about the missing documents until much later, when the RCMP began an investigation. So when Arthur Manuel and the NYC members walked out of the Indian Affairs building the next morning, they were surrounded not by police but by reporters and television cameras and they stopped to make statements before walking away with the government documents hidden inside their sleeping bags and blankets.

With their mission accomplished, Arthur Manuel led his NYA contingent across the river to Quebec where they stopped at a *depanneur* to buy a few cases of beer before heading to his father's house to celebrate the takeover and the document haul.

Arthur still considered his father something of an establishment figure, so he wasn't sure of the reception he would get when they arrived. But his father welcomed them into his house and sat with them as they celebrated their act of defiance.

It was typical of George Manuel that he never hesitated to back any form of Indian resistance. As the Canadian diplomats in Tanzania had discovered, he would not even renounce the right of Indians to engage in armed struggle in their fight for justice. Many times he would say he was "not suggesting physical violence" but add parenthetically that in the fight for Indian sovereignty, violence "can never be discounted. . . ."

While George was quietly backing Arthur's radical approach, he was also working with his oldest son, Bob, within official circles in BC and then in Ottawa. During 1971 and 1972, Bob Manuel was working as a self-described "foot soldier" for the Union of British Columbia Indian Chiefs. He was married by this time and as had been the case with his father, his travels in the movement were taking a toll on his marriage. When George Manuel met him in Saskatoon in 1972, he was attending a course to prepare him to teach at Camosun College.

George knew Bob was having problems at home and he told him about the difficulties of his own separation from Marceline. "It was a very tough thing," he said. "You start to get back together with your wife, you separate and get back together, you know it just causes a lot of misery for everybody." He advised Bob not to go back to BC and suggested he come to Ottawa to work with him. Bob Manuel was at first reluctant; he explained that Phillip had already offered him the teaching job, but George offered to pay his way, or at least the balance of his ticket, and his son agreed.

When Bob Manuel arrived at his father's house a few weeks later, though, he discovered that his father had had second thoughts. George Manuel realized that hiring his son to work for him at the NIB would leave him open to charges of nepotism, so instead, he arranged for Bob to get a job with the DIA, similar to the community development job he had had with the Department of Indian Affairs in the mid-1960s.

Bob Manuel recalled that his father had used more than a little pull to arrange it. George came home from the office one day and told him that John Ciaccia had a meeting with Marie Marule the next day and that Bob should meet him there. The next morning, he waited outside Marie's door until she made an excuse to leave the office and indicated that Bob should slip in and talk to Ciaccia.

Ciaccia was apparently expecting him, because he had just one question: "Are you ready to travel?"

Bob Manuel said he was and Ciaccia replied, "I'm not sure, but if we can get all the paper work done this afternoon, you'll be on a plane to Alberta tomorrow."

As it turned out, Bob Manuel flew to northern Alberta the following day, where he coordinated funds for a number of small economic development projects. It was while he was in Alberta working for the DIA that he was tipped off about Arthur's plan to take over the department's headquarters in Ottawa. He caught a discreet bout of diplomatic 'flu and went home for a few days until the furor died down.

During his trips back to Ottawa, Bob Manuel also had the opportunity for serious political discussions with his father, and he discovered that despite his father's apparent political and organizational success in building the NIB, he was greatly frustrated by the organization's inability to push forward on the self-government front.

From his experience watching how Quebec and the James Bay Development Corporation were moving against the James Bay Cree,

George Manuel shifted his thinking away from the "national philosophy" and toward the idea of building a "peoples' movement." He was beginning to believe that only if the mass of people were politicized and energized and put in the forefront of the movement could they take on the powerful government and private-sector interests that were blocking the political, social and cultural rebirth of Canada's First Nations. Like Arthur, Bob Manuel saw the change in his father's approach to Indian politics and gained a new respect for his willingness to lay his own position on the line to further the cause.

He recalled that what his father "really wanted to see was the emergence of the people. He never fought against the AIM movement or anybody. He always welcomed them. He had a kind of philosophy that the Red Power movements are the ones that make change, that make uprisings."

It was the radicals at the base, George Manuel knew, that allowed him to go to the politicians and tell them, "you're not listening to us, to the policies that we are trying to put forward . . . That's why these things occur." Marches, demonstrations, civil disobedience and even the threat of violence, George Manuel came to believe, were essential in getting the government's attention.[3]

He believed the movement would not be built only by Indian lawyers and university graduates, but by school dropouts and even by those who had spent time in jail. To bring them into the struggle, he proposed setting up a Cultural Education Training Centre that would politicize school dropouts and former Indian inmates. He wanted fighters as well as intellectuals.

During the summer of 1974, those fighters were coming into evidence. Indian road blockades began to appear across British Columbia to protest the lack of movement on the land issue. More serious was the occupation of the Anicinabe park near Kenora in Northern Ontario.

The park was taken over by a group of a hundred young armed Indians who called themselves the Ojibway Warrior Society and modelled themselves on the American Indian Movement activists who had been involved in a ten-week stand-off and a bloody gun battle with the FBI at Wounded Knee in 1973.

The Ojibway Warriors claimed that the park land had been illegally expropriated by the federal government from Indian lands, and then sold to the city without the Indians' consent. The Warriors were besieged by a contingent of the RCMP for more than two months before they finally surrendered to the authorities.

A few weeks later one of the leaders of the Warriors Society, Louis Cameron, turned up in Montreal where he met a group of radical urban Indians, both status and non-status, and hatched a plan to storm the Parliament buildings in Ottawa during the opening of the new session on September 30. To gain native support and national publicity, they organized a cross-country Caravan that left Vancouver in rented buses on September 14.

While attracting a certain amount of press attention, the Caravan found little support from the Indian communities or Indian leadership. One problem was that their demands were unfocused and in some cases were considered to border on the silly. They asked that Indians receive "payments in perpetuity from all levels of government" and for $500 million to be made available "for legal defence." The oddest demand, however, was that the NIB leader, Chief George Manuel, be made minister of Indian Affairs.[4]

The group was being funded in part by the pariah of the Canadian left, the pro-Albanian Communist Party (Marxist-Leninist). Because of what were seen as unsavoury elements in the Caravan, and the naivete of its leadership, most Indian leaders avoided contact with the group.

The aloofness of the mainstream Indian organizations changed after September 30 when two hundred Caravanners assembled on Parliament Hill and were badly beaten by the police. George Manuel was one of the first to step in and condemn the police action. He then met with the group's "Central Committee," but it was not a particularly fruitful meeting, with some of the young activists leaving his office and muttering about Manuel's paternalistic attitude toward them.[5]

It was a surprising remark, since George Manuel had always shown a great talent for communicating with the young and inspiring them to the cause. But then again, with the Caravan he was dealing with people who were demanding, in all seriousness, that he become the minister of the Department he had dedicated his life to dismantling.

George Manuel was probably even less enamoured with the group when they took over the building on an island in the Ottawa river that he had selected for the Indian Cultural Centre and set up their own "Indian Embassy." The building was burned down a few months later under suspicious circumstances – the Caravanners blamed the Mounties, the

Mounties blamed the Caravanners – and George Manuel's dream of a Cultural Centre died in the ash heap.

Still, the NIB leader was able to use the park occupation, the Caravan and the fistfights on Parliament Hill to a political advantage. With the spectre of Indian political violence hanging over their heads, government ministers were suddenly receptive to George Manuel when he walked into their offices and told them it was time to deal with him or face the *deluge* of the young radicals on the streets.

The result was a relaunch of the Joint NIB – Cabinet Committee where he could once again escape the suffocating bureaucracy of the Indian Affairs Department and face the various government ministers on a more equal basis. At the first meeting on 9 October 1974, he reminded the Cabinet that the First Nations were in a very critical time in their history. "We are surrounded by immigrants from other lands. Our lands are no longer ours in some places. Despite this, we are determined to maintain our special place, our special rights and our special status as Indian people."

George Manuel went on to list the statistics on the debilitating poverty that was still a fact of life for the overwhelming number of the First Nations people. He called on the government to attack the problems at source: the lack of funds and the lack of local control over those funds. He pointed out the waste of the DIA money on a new $43-million office tower in Ottawa and the $80 million that was spent on "special services" that had nothing to do with helping the development of the Indian people.[6]

In a sense, George Manuel was going back to the beginning to instruct the Cabinet on the simple facts of life for his people. The reason was not only the long hiatus between meetings, but because he was now, for the first time as the NIB president, facing a new minister of Indian Affairs.

In the fall of 1974, Judd Buchanan, a former Alberta insurance man, took over from Jean Chrétien, who went to the Treasury Board. There was a great deal of apprehension in Indian country about facing the devil they didn't know, because Buchanan's only contact with native people had been a brief stint as Chrétien's parliamentary secretary in 1970.

As it turned out, the Indians' fears about Buchanan would be justified in the long term. In 1974, however, the minister was still getting his bearings and his Department was following the Chrétien strategy of fencing with the NIB over each issue as it arose, but not initiating any new policies.

The main battles during this period were over economic development and housing, two issues that George Manuel saw as intimately related.

The NIB's economic development position was set out in a report that was published in *Indian News* in the fall of 1973; the report was heavily influenced by George Manuel's exposure to African socialism and by his international perspective.

It began: "In economic terms the present situation of the Canadian Indian Reserve communities is comparable to that of underdeveloped countries. If the Indian community of Canada was placed on UNESCO graphs it would compare, in respect to several economic indicators, to Botswana . . ."

George Manuel's strategy for relaunching the native economy began with a proposal for a massive housing blitz on reserves across the country.

"House building," he believed, was "the one industry capable of providing employment at all levels of skill development. It lays the foundation through training for skills which can be carried over into the widest variety of economic endeavors."[7]

For George Manuel, house construction on the reserves was not only a means of improving shelter, but of driving the local economy and providing jobs and marketable skills to the people. In this way, the housing program was part of his stated philosophy that "both political and economic independence must progress simultaneously." To achieve this, he advocated the community development approach of using "the end as a means of achieving the end." That is, when developing a program or a plan of action for cultural, political, social or economic advancement, you always tried to maximize the advantages in all of the other areas as well.

As soon as the Department of Indian Affairs discovered that the NIB was working on a housing plan, the bureaucrats went to work trying to set up their own Housing Task Force. But when the Department's Task Force coordinator turned up at the Brotherhood's housing symposium in March 1973 in Winnipeg, he was immediately challenged by the delegates and ejected from the hall.

George Manuel wrote to the Minister asking that he dissolve the

DIA's Task Force, "transfer the budget of the Task Force to the National Indian Brotherhood Working Committee on Housing" and restrict DIA's role to that of an advisor only.

The Minister said he would work closely with the Indian organizations on the housing issue "whenever possible," but insisted that the Department had to take a leading role in developing the housing policy; he suggested the DIA and the NIB set up a coordinating body.

George Manuel rejected the offer. Before the NIB became mixed up with the government, he insisted, it must have its own study complete so they could bring the Indian view to the table. He wrote back to the Minister that "Indian people have repeatedly been asked to endorse other people's assessments of our needs, with little time allowed for us to reflect upon our own needs, determine our priorities and put forward proposals for change. I feel sure that you would agree that a return to such token consultation is neither desirable nor tenable."

By the time the DIA came up with their housing proposals in the fall of 1974, Judd Buchanan was at the helm and, as expected, there were substantial differences between the NIB and the DIA plans.

The DIA's goal in the housing drive was merely "to achieve expansion and improvement through the construction of new housing and the rehabilitation of existing houses." In effect, the Department of Indian Affairs philosophy hadn't really changed since the 1930s, when the housing crisis was addressed by giving each family a small lumber allotment.

For George Manuel and the NIB, housing construction and improvement was part of a much broader drive toward economic development and political independence. To realize any important gains, the Indian people had to be in control of the entire housing project, from financing to design to construction.

The conflict over the housing issue was the first serious skirmish between Judd Buchanan and George Manuel, but that battle would soon escalate into a sort of guerrilla war between the National Indian Brotherhood and the Department of Indian Affairs.

» «

While that battle was still brewing, George Manuel was also pursuing his international agenda. In organizing the international conference, the greatest obstacle he faced was locating and identifying legitimate indigenous organizations that could represent their people at the conference.

Those initial contacts were difficult to make, since most of the Indian organizations in places like Central and South America were weak and local in nature. Many of their leaders were also suspicious of the NIB because they feared it might be another organization of anthropologists who were trying to co-opt their organizations rather than join with them in the struggle. For their part, the NIB organizers also had to be very careful that they weren't dealing with government-controlled organizations.

These issues were of particular concern to George Manuel. Rodrigo Contreras recalled that he would get calls in the middle of the night to check on the government links of some group in Guatemala or to present a complete breakdown of the political situation in Paraguay by morning. As with everyone else, he was expected to get the information, even if he had to stay up all night to do it.

One important task that George Manuel took on personally was getting Non-Governmental Organization status at the United Nations for the NIB. He flew to New York to present the NIB's NGO case and when the UN agreed to accept the NIB's membership on 6 February 1974, he described the day as "the most historic event" in his life. Representation at the UN, he hoped, would "lead the Indian Canadians and the indigenous minorities of the world into the arena of world politics by having their problems heard in an international forum."[8]

George Manuel was not planning to use the UN status solely for the NIB. From the beginning he intended to transfer it to the international indigenous body when it was set up, and he took a major step in that direction in early April when he left for the preparatory meeting in Guyana with representatives from the Maoris, the Australian Aborigines, the Sami, the National Congress of American Indians and several Latin American indigenous groups. The Guyanese government hosted the meeting and the prime minister of Guyana, Forbes Burnham, showed up at the opening social.

Along with George Manuel, the NIB delegation included Marie Marule, Doug Sanders and Guy Lavallee; the Canadian delegates had only one question to ask the other representatives: was the idea of an indigenous peoples' organization feasible? The answer was unanimous: not only was it feasible, it was a necessary and long overdue step in the battle to regain their national sovereignty.

As Doug Sanders recalled, the meeting "faced the problem of virtual instant agreement by the delegates to proceed with the proposal of the National Indian Brotherhood to hold the international conference."[9]

The rest of the four-day conference gave the delegates a chance to hammer out a more precise definition of "indigenous people." According to the delegates: "The term indigenous people refers to people living in countries which have a population composed of differing ethnic or racial groups, who are descendants of the earliest populations living in the area and who do not as a group control the national government of the countries which they live."[10]

The group then made arrangements for a follow-up meeting in Copenhagen early in 1975, and for a founding assembly of a new organization that would be held in Canada later that year.

When the meeting broke up, George Manuel was invited on a junket to eastern Brazil by the Guyanese interior minister, where they were able to meet with a small group of Brazilian Indians. Lavallee recalls that George Manuel's first reaction when he got off the plane was to stroll into the village to meet not only the leaders, but also the ordinary people who were as drawn to the limping round-faced Canadian Indian leader as he was to them.

When George Manuel returned to Ottawa, he was optimistic about the progress on the international front, but he soon found himself mired in housekeeping work. He was approaching the end of his second mandate and it was time to make some staff changes. With his increasing workload in setting up the international organization, he decided that he would need a vice-president who could take charge of things when he was away. Omer Peters was still respected in the Indian world but he was getting on in years and was finding the amount of travel required difficult. Peters had mentioned this a few times and said he was thinking of retiring before the August general meeting of the NIB in Vancouver. But by the spring, he still hadn't made any definite moves so George Manuel decided to give him a nudge.

In April, he sent Peters to represent him at the UBCIC's general assembly in Williams Lake. The DIA minister was also attending the meeting and George Manuel arranged for Peters to travel in style with the minister on the Department of Transport Jet Star.

When Peters arrived in Williams Lake, he was surprised to find that the Union had organized a retirement party for him and he was feted with warm speeches about his four-year tenure as the vice-president. News of Peters impending retirement spread across the country, and if Peters hadn't totally made up his mind about retiring before the trip, there was no question that he was on his way out afterward.

George Manuel had Peters' replacement, Clive Linklater, lined up, and when the Vancouver assembly was held that August, George Manuel was once again unopposed for his third two-year term as the national chief of Canada's First Nations.

Linklater's arrival on the scene was part of a general infusion of younger blood in the leadership positions of the NIB. The organization began to profit from a wave of young Indian lawyers and other professionals who were coming out of graduate schools in the mid-1970s.

Ron Shackleton graduated from law school and returned to work full-time with the NIB in 1974. While in school, Shackleton had continued to do contract work for the NIB, and he and Roberta Jamieson, a Mohawk law student who later went on to become Ontario's Ombudsman, founded the Native Indian Law Students' Association, an organization that acted as a talent scout for the NIB.

George Manuel had been the featured speaker when the Association was launched. Once again, though, he cautioned the Indian students about the "European educational system that teaches and encourages individualism, a school system that has driven our people and communities apart and is destroying our cultural powers, identity and independence of Indian peoples in Canada."

When speaking about education, George Manuel began to put the emphasis on the traditional Indian values that had to be reinforced by Indian education as much as on the issue of Indian control.

"We want our children to learn Canadian history which gives honour to the customs, values, accomplishments and contributions of this country's original inhabitants and First Citizens.

"We want our children to learn how to add, subtract, multiply and divide, but we don't want them to become greedy and grasping in the process. We want our children to learn science and technology so that they can promote the harmony of man with nature – not destroy it. We want our children to learn about their fellow men in literature and social studies, and in the process to learn to respect the values and culture of others."

But he was afraid that along the way they might lose the Indian wisdom his grandparents had learned from their grandparents and had passed on to him along with the language and the culture of the Shuswap nation.[11]

Shackleton and Jamieson were among those who managed to combine academic achievement with the traditional values George Manuel had spoken of. They were both valuable sources of expertise for the NIB and engaged in research, prepared submissions to government departments and represented the NIB at various meetings. Jamieson was sent to trade-union and related conferences to give workshops on Canadian Indians and their struggle for sovereignty, and Shackleton represented the NIB at a national conference of the Canadian Law Teachers Association. Both of them also sat on a committee on natives and the law headed by Warren Allmand.

Along with the two Indian lawyers, a young Mohawk law student at Queen's University, Bill Badcock, was employed to work with native inmates in Kingston and became a good friend of George Manuel's and eventually an NIB staffer. Badcock and others remember some mighty all-night parties that were somehow fitted around their hectic work schedules and George was generally in the thick of it.

His stamina seemed, at times, almost superhuman. As the movement advanced, more NIB staffers were hired until he was heading a team of almost fifty people. At the same time, there were always more meetings with ministers, more briefs to be drawn up, more strategy sessions to be conducted and endless travels to consult with the provincial and local leaders.

There were few opportunities for him to go out to dinner with Marlene or to enjoy his favourite form of relaxation: sitting at home with the phone unplugged and watching a western on television. It was inevitable that the twenty years of struggle, relentless travel and sleepless nights would take a toll. Early in 1975, a medical check-up revealed irregularities in his heart. George Manuel's doctor told him that he was headed for trouble and told him to take a prolonged rest or he would find himself with serious health problems.

George Manuel had, in fact, been feeling the strain after four years in the Ottawa pressure-cooker. He knew he could use a couple of months back in Neskainlith to recharge his spiritual as well as physical batteries, but this was impossible. He was still pressing the DIA to implement the NIB's Indian Control of Education brief and their economic development and housing proposals, but under Judd Buchanan the Department was offering even more resistance than it had under Jean Chrétien. On the international scene, he was trying to finalize the arrangements for the indigenous peoples' conference. But one of George Manuel's biggest challenges in 1975 was one that even he could not have foreseen: the sudden and uproarious self-destruction of the Union of British Columbia Indian Chiefs.

## CHAPTER FOURTEEN

# Political Eruptions in BC
# 1975

The 1975 Union assembly assumed a life of its own. It became a political
and cultural revival meeting . . .

Paul Tennant
*Aboriginal Peoples and Politics*, p.178

After the Guyana meeting in April 1974, the National Indian Brotherhood set up a Secretariat, headed by Marie Marule, with a mandate to
organize the international peoples' conference and outline the structure
of a permanent organization. George Manuel's enthusiasm for the idea
continued to grow throughout 1974 and by the spring of 1975, the organizers were ready for a second preparatory meeting where the final details
of the conference and the shape of the new organization would be ironed
out.

That meeting was held in Copenhagen in May 1975; George
Manuel, Marie Marule and Rodrigo Contreras represented the NIB.
The first item on the agenda was to decide on the date and the location
of the founding meeting. The delegates chose Canada in the fall of 1975,
but in reality they were only confirming a decision George Manuel had
already made. With the sponsorship of the UBCIC, he had arranged to
hold the conference in October on a Nootka Reserve near Port Alberni
on Vancouver Island.

During the Copenhagen meeting, a six-member provisional policy
board was also set up with George Manuel at the head and with board

members from New Zealand, the US, Norway, Sweden and Greenland. The board finalized a list of organizations from twenty countries that would be invited to the founding meeting and reviewed the organization's financing, which had reached a modest total of $87,000 in two years.

The last item on the agenda was to choose a name for the organization. Marie Marule suggested they take a leaf from the World Council of Churches book and call it the World Council of Indigenous Peoples (WCIP). The name was accepted and after four years of planning, the international indigenous organization was about to become a reality.

The NIB delegation headed home with a sense of elation. But their high spirits were dashed when they arrived in Ottawa and heard that one of their closest friends and comrades, Ron Shackleton, was dead.

Shackleton's death had come without warning after a typically busy week and weekend devoted to the cause. On Friday, June 20, he had been in Toronto to attend the annual conference of the Association of Friendship Centres. On Saturday, he had driven to La Macaza, Quebec, to attend a Métis and Non-Status Indians Conference and on Sunday he was back in Ottawa to attend a meeting of the Native Law Students' Association.

On Monday he was supposed to attend a seminar on Natives and Criminal Justice, but the twenty-six year-old Mohawk lawyer had a heart attack early Monday morning and he was dead within hours.

George Manuel was devastated by the news. At the funeral he said that Shackleton had represented the best of the new generation of Indian activists because he was someone who truly understood the people. Manuel suggested that he had seen in Ron Shackleton a future leader of the NIB.

"Ron and I came from the same background," he added. "A very poor background. He understood my commitment to the Indian people because his commitment was just as strong . . . I can only say, that when I heard of his sudden death, I thought, why him? Why not me? He had his whole life in front of him and I have my life behind me."[1]

Shackleton's death was a great personal as well as political loss for George but he would have little time to mourn his fallen comrade as he found himself locked in an escalating series of disputes with the new minister of Indian Affairs. The problems began in the spring of 1975, when Judd Buchanan issued a wide range of new guidelines on DIA funding without consulting the Indian organizations. When Manuel heard about the changes, he felt that he was back in 1969 when Chrétien had done precisely the same thing. He protested Buchanan's unilateral guidelines and the response was the same as it had been from Chrétien six years earlier: a bureaucratic stonewall.

While Manuel and Buchanan were exchanging angry letters over the issue, the Department announced it was backing out of the previous NIB–DIA agreements on education. Despite DIA foot-dragging under Chrétien, a number of important steps had been taken to implement the NIB education policy, and by early 1975, sixty bands, representing roughly twenty per cent of the Indian population in the country, had total or partial control of their schools.

The DIA decided to shelve the policy in March 1975, after Buchanan stated that there would be "no more transfers of Indian children from provincial schools to reserve schools under Indian control" because the program was too expensive and was "a set-back to integration."[2]

George Manuel then began quietly working on a counter-strategy that focused on the areas where the DIA had already dismantled its infrastructure for delivering education and other social services. If negotiations between the NIB and the DIA became deadlocked, he would threaten to walk away from all cooperation with the government and drop everything back into its lap. For the DIA, this would create a bureaucratic nightmare and he was counting on that threat to win negotiating points.

Even more troubling for George Manuel than the moratorium on education reform was Buchanan's land claims policy. From the start, the Minister made it clear that he would try to make the same sort of cash-for-land deal in the Yukon as the Quebec Cree had been forced to sign. In the spring of 1975, Buchanan announced that he had reached an agreement in principle with the Yukon Indians for the extinguishment of their land claim in exchange for $50 million and a parcel of land.

This time George Manuel did not stay in the background as he had when Billy Diamond was signing away the Crees' aboriginal title to Northern Quebec. A Yukon deal that extinguished aboriginal titles, coming so close after the Quebec deal, would set an almost ironclad precedent that would make the recognition of aboriginal title in BC and the NWT impossible.

For the first time in his tenure at the NIB, George Manuel went public and denounced not only the federal government for its extinguishment policy, but also the Yukon Brotherhood for agreeing in principle to the government's offer. He then used every ounce of behind-the-scenes influence he had to force the Yukon Brotherhood to withdraw from the agreement.

With his public denunciation and back room politicking, George Manuel succeeded in blocking the deal. As a Canadian Press report put it, "After Manuel's intervention, a 'no aboriginal rights extinguishment policy' was adopted by the Yukon Brotherhood as a condition for signing the final deal with the government."[3] The government, however, held fast to its extinguishment demand and the whole package was sent back to the negotiators.

It was in this charged atmosphere that another cabinet minister, the multi-millionaire defense minister James Richardson, made his contribution to native and non-native understanding by telling *Maclean's* magazine that he couldn't understand why the Indians were kicking up such a fuss.

"I mean, what did they ever do for Canada? Did they discover gas? Did they discover oil? They didn't even invent the wheel. Why, when we came here, they were still dragging things around on two sticks."[4]

George Manuel responded to the Richardson statement with an open letter expressing frustration and outrage:

"When your people came we helped you because you were men, like us, and there was so much you did not know. We taught your people how to hunt, how to eat, how to travel. But your people learned only how to survive, you would not learn how to live.

"Many of us died from your weapons and diseases. Many of us have died inside because you have taken away the surroundings on which our inner lives were built. This land was our soul. And it is upon the souls of thousands of our people that this country has been formed."

He concluded by stating that in "the quality of living based on relationships with the world around you, your people have contributed little to this country. With all the material comforts of your outside lives, you have not yet learned how to live. We feel sorry for you."[5]

The fact that the same kind of ugly prejudice toward Indian people that was common in the 1930s was still flourishing at the highest levels was disheartening for George Manuel, who saw the education of the non-native majority as a crucial part of the Indian movement. How much education remained to be done was confirmed a couple of months later, when a Conservative Ontario MPP for the Timiskaming riding, Edward Havrot, dismissed the whole idea of settling land claims with the Indians because they were "just a damn nuisance.

"I could buy the Indian chiefs off with a case of goof . . . These damned Indians have gone absolutely wild. We should have given them a bunch of tepees and some cord wood and that's all."[6]

In the furor that followed, Premier Davis asked for and received Havrot's resignation, but Havrot's resultant "apology" was even more insulting to the Indian people. He said his "life-long and best friend is Jewish, another is Estonian and married to a squaw."[7] Havrot then defied his own government and ran for the Conservative nomination in his riding. He won the nomination.

The battles with the Department of Indian Affairs, and the racist interventions by Richardson and Havrot, put George Manuel in a fighting mood for the Joint Cabinet-NIB meeting in April.

Pierre Trudeau had appointed his right-hand man, Marc Lalonde, to head the government side of the committee, which met in both the spring and the fall of 1975. George Manuel opened the April meeting by telling the ministers that Indian Nations would no longer settle for cash in land deals like the James Bay agreement or in the offer made to the Yukon Indian Brotherhood.

"We cannot consider nor accept any proposal or agreement which undermines or extinguishes our interests in Canada based upon our aboriginal and treaty rights."

He kept the same tone when he moved on to his report on economic development, where he criticized the government's record and warned that the situation of "despair is creating a growing atmosphere of unrest, especially among the Indian youth, under the age of twenty-five, which comprises more than fifty per cent of the total Indian population. The high Indian crime rate and the establishment of militant Indian Red Power in Canada is a reflection of mounting frustrations . . ."[8]

The guarded threat of Indian violence seemed to have some impact on the Cabinet because by the end of the meeting, George Manuel had won a number of important concessions. In a joint press release, he and Marc Lalonde announced the creation of a new protocol for relations between Indians and the government. At the heart of it would be an expanded joint NIB–Cabinet Committee which would preside over a host of sub-committees addressing everything from Indian health and education to the reform of the Indian Act and the Indian land question. Both sides would have equal representation and the NIB influence was ensured when George Manuel arranged to have Marie Marule elected as the first chair of the joint committee.

It was a significant breakthrough in securing the First Nations access to the government; it is also interesting to note that the structure of the new committee was almost identical to the one George Manuel had drawn up after his discussions with the Cabinet in 1971. Above the accompanying chart, he wrote INDIAN PEOPLE, and he warned his colleagues in the NIB that they would always have to keep their constituency in mind if they were to avoid being co-opted by the powerful political figures they would be dealing with.

George Manuel's success with the Cabinet Committee only seemed to intensify his battle with the Department of Indian Affairs. In the fall of 1975, he and the Department were locked in a war of words over Buchanan's unilaterally imposed DIA guidelines. Buchanan had infuriated George Manuel when he tried to pull an end-run on the NIB by claiming that twenty-two Saskatchewan bands supported his reorganization guidelines. Manuel quickly pointed out to the minister that a Saskatchewan all-chiefs conference had already unanimously condemned the guidelines and he challenged the minister to produce the names of the twenty-two bands Buchanan claimed were in his corner.

Buchanan refused. In late September the dispute came to a head when George Manuel received word that the regional directors of the DIA were holding a private meeting in Winnipeg to discuss how the Department should deal with Indian organizations. He dispatched his vice-president, Clive Linklater, to the meeting with a formal request that Linklater be accredited as an observer, in the same way that DIA representatives were invited to NIB meetings, and with a scathing statement to read to the DIA officials.

When Linklater arrived during the morning coffee break, he received a cool reception. When he asked the deputy minister, Arthur Kroeger, for observer status, Kroeger responded with the incomprehensible comment, "It's a nice day out, Clive."

Linklater then requested that he be allowed to make a statement to the DIA staffers, but Kroeger repeated more forcefully, "It's a nice day out, Clive!" Linklater then asked the assistant deputy minister, Peter Lesaux, for a copy of the meeting's agenda and he received the same childish response: "It's a nice day out, Clive!"

A reporter who had heard the exchange asked Lesaux why he refused to listen to Linklater's statement; Lesaux brushed him off by stating that "It's just the same thing we have heard before."[9]

In the end, Clive Linklater was forced to read the NIB message to the directors' empty chairs, as all but three DIA officials left the room when he began to speak. As it turned out, it *wasn't* a message the Department had heard before.

Linklater told the near-empty room that the NIB and its member organizations "do not consider that Indian people are responsible to the Department of Indian Affairs; rather that the Indian Affairs officials should be responsible to the Indian people."

The statement accused the bureaucrats of treating the NIB and its member organizations "as a 'third force' – maybe even as an enemy force.

"If you consider the Indian organizations to be your 'enemies', then by the very nature of our organizations, the Indian people at the Band level are also your enemies.

"Maybe you should simply declare open war on the Indian people. That way, you could accomplish your cherished goal of TERMINATION of the special federal responsibility and relationship to the Indian people by the simple expedient of the actual physical EXTERMINATION of the Indian people."[10]

The statement ended with a warning that "If you persist to view us as the enemy, we will be forced to act as the enemy."

When George Manuel later recounted the snub of Linklater to the prime minister, he warned that his organization's relations with Judd Buchanan were steadily deteriorating and charged that Buchanan was "setting back Federal Government–Indian relations by at least ten years."[11]

Trudeau apparently agreed, because in less than a year, Buchanan was out and a new minister, Warren Allmand, was in. From the Indians' point of view it was a welcome change. Allmand had begun to take an interest in Indian Affairs a couple of years earlier when he was the solicitor general. On a tour of some northern reserves, he had discovered conditions that were not much different from the crushing poverty he had seen in India.

Allmand also had a first-hand experience of problems between the Indians and the justice system when he was driving at night through Prince Albert, Saskatchewan, with a couple of local Indian leaders. An RCMP car began following them and the Mounties pulled the Indians over on a pretext. They began to harass the Indians until they realized that their boss, the solicitor general, was sitting in the back seat.[12]

This incident led to Allmand working with the NIB to set up a National Conference on Native Peoples and the Criminal Justice System in February 1975. The conference explored a wide range of injustices toward Canada's native people by the courts and the police, and Allmand emerged as a noted backer of the Indian cause.

When he became the Indian Affairs minister in September 1976, however, his good intentions quickly fell victim to the bureaucracy. His open policy toward Indians led to a mini-revolt in his own department, led by his deputy minister, Arthur Kroeger. The row with Kroeger and the rest of the hard-line DIA bureaucrats resulted in Allmand being shifted out of the portfolio barely a year after his appointment.[13]

For George Manuel, though, the battle with the DIA in the summer of 1975 reflected his growing impatience with progress he was making in Ottawa. When he attended an April 2 Land Claims Conference sponsored by the UBCIC in Terrace, BC, he showed just how far his frustration was when he told his BC friends that he felt he was wasting his time in Ottawa.[14]

To illustrate the point, he told them about a recent visit to the DIA office in Ottawa with the NWT Brotherhood leader, James Wah-Shee. The federal court had recently awarded the Indians of the Northwest Territories a caveat on the lands north of sixty and James Wah-Shee had come to Ottawa to demand that the government begin land claim negotiations. The DIA official shrugged off the court order. He told Wah-Shee that all it did was force the Department to bargain with Indians. "If you push too hard, that means if you demand too much, then we are not going to settle with you and our negotiations will break down, then we will have to go to Parliament and they will have to hand down a decision settling the claims with or without your participation."

In other words, the NIB leader explained, "there is no way the Federal Government is prepared to settle the land claims within your terms. They are saying . . . we recognize Aboriginal Rights, Land Claims, only if you accept the terms under which we recognize it . . . Only if you accept the settlement we are prepared to give you. That is what they told the Indians of James Bay and they accepted it."

As George Manuel saw it, that "is not justice, that is white supremacy, that is racism."[15]

In a statement that revealed something of Manuel's future strategy, he spoke about the government only responding to political power and pointed out that since the native people didn't have the votes to pressure the government, they would have to find other means. Once again, he wouldn't rule out violence. In fact, it might even be inevitable.

"Younger people," he said, "are going to be forced to resort to the politics of violence. I think it is going to come even if we don't want it."[16]

George Manuel's musings in Terrace were not entirely in the abstract. Radicalism was growing in BC with young Indian activists threatening road and rail blockades and other acts of civil disobedience to get government action.

The youth wing of the BC movement was also adopting an increasingly leftist analysis of the Indian struggle, which identified with the anti-capitalist and anti-colonialist movements in Canada and abroad. Young activists like Bob Manuel began holding workshops around the province detailing the corporate role in usurping Indian lands and in blocking the modern-day movement to recuperate them.

Within the Union, that point of view was being pushed hardest by a number of non-native consultants who were also working the back rooms to urge the young activists into more and more radical actions – including breaking off all relations with the government and refusing government funding so they couldn't be 'co-opted' by the system. This outside pressure, combined with an internal challenge to the Union's leadership, resulted in a political eruption in BC that would lead to the near destruction of the UBCIC.

The internal opposition was led by Bill Wilson, who had begun working for the Union in 1970 when he was a law student and had been given the job of assisting Davie Fulton in putting together the Union's constitution and position paper on aboriginal title and land claims. Wilson had come from a wealthy coastal family and he had no real experience with the Indian movement at the band level. But he was convinced that it was time for a new generation of leaders, those with university educations, to take control of the movement.

As early as 1971, the twenty-eight-year-old Wilson explained that he thought "the reality of the situation is that people with a grade-eight education can't confront people with law degrees."[17] It was around this time that George Manuel, the national leader with a grade-two education, went out to dinner with Wilson in Vancouver. As Bill Wilson tells it, George Manuel didn't know how to eat *escargot*, nor did he know that he was suppose to taste the wine Wilson ordered to accompany the meal and give his approval to the waiting wine steward. When he finally got that straight, George Manuel reportedly turned to the waiter and said, "That's good, bring us a galloon!"[18] For Bill Wilson, it was an indication of George Manuel's lack of sophistication. Others who have heard Bill Wilson tell the story suspect that George Manuel was putting the young "sophisticated" law student on.

Despite Wilson's elitist sensibility, he made himself a spokesman for the grass roots in both the Union and the British Columbia Association of Non-Status Indians (BCANSI), with whom he worked for a time. As Paul Tennant observed, the fact that "Wilson should emerge as the leading advocate of grass-roots politics was a paradox, for among all the young Indians playing leading roles in BCANSI or the Union, he had the least grass-roots experience. He had had no local political or administrative experience in either an Indian band or a BCANSI local. His reputation rested on the prominence of his own family among the Kwagiulth."[19]

In both organizations, Bill Wilson's specialty was assailing the "brown bureaucracy." His prominence grew after 1974 when the Union set up its own programs for social services, housing, education and cultural matters with the aim of replacing the DIA in the province with an Indian-controlled administration.

Bill Wilson attacked not only the expansion of the Union, but the whole philosophy behind accepting core funding from the government. As he put it: "Core funding robbed us of the kind of leaders we once had. It's robbed us of the Andy Paulls . . . We now have these welfare recipients who exist on core funding and who would not be in the movement if there were no financial gain."[20]

Bill Wilson's calls for a return to the romantic past of Andy Paull dovetailed neatly with the agenda of the radical activists, and his sniping at the Union leadership as "brown bureaucrats" and the Council of Elders as opportunistic boozers fostered suspicions between the local and provincial leaders.

But Wilson had another important issue to pursue. He was fighting for the removal of the distinction between status and non-status Indians. He had a personal stake in this, in that his own mother had lost her status when she remarried a white man, but instead of addressing that obvious injustice directly, he appealed for one big organization of status and non-status Indians, which he defined as people with at least one-quarter Indian ancestry. Not surprisingly, he found little support among the status Indians, who understood that while their battles were often complementary to those of the non-status Indians, they were not identical.

As Phillip Paul explained, "politically, it's a good idea to have status and non-status together, but there are different objectives. When it comes to negotiating the land issue you have to have something to give from both sides. The government has to want something and you obviously want something from them."[21]

The status Indians had a bargaining position because they had their reserve lands and a recognition under the Indian Act of a kind of special status. The non-status and Métis people were not included in the Act and were, in fact, under provincial jurisdiction. Status Indians feared that by including the non-status and Métis people in the movement they would be weakening their case in any negotiations with the federal government.

The issue remained a touchy one, however. Non-status and Métis people often felt hurt by the rebuff they received from the status Indians, and the status Indians were often uncomfortable with the fact that by holding onto the status/non-status distinction they were perpetuating divisions in their ranks that had been made by an Indian Act they had no control over.

All of these currents – leftist radicalism, internal criticism and status/non-status tensions – came together in an electrical explosion on the floor of the Union's annual assembly in Chilliwack in April 1975.

As Paul Tennant saw it, the Chilliwack meeting "assumed a life of its own. It became a political and cultural revival meeting that had a profound emotional significance for many of those taking part." The speeches became increasingly radical as the meeting wore on and this radicalism was fired still further by the traditional drumming, dancing and singing. Bill Wilson then stepped into this euphoric combination of cultural pride and political defiance to present a resolution that the Union reject core funding from the government.

Just as the delegates were about to vote on the matter, a telegram arrived from George Manuel, who was back in Ottawa and unaware of what was transpiring at the assembly. The telegram spoke of the strategy he and the NIB were developing to fight Buchanan's cutbacks in education and other social services by threatening to turn the programs back to the government. George Manuel asked for the Union's support for his tactical manoeuvre.

When the telegram was read on the floor, however, it was misinterpreted to mean that the NIB leader had joined the radicals in backing the rejection of all government funding. If there was any chance of defeating the motion before Manuel's words were read to the assembly, it disappeared afterward. The resolution that BC Indian organizations and Indian bands immediately reject all government funds passed by a massive majority and the young activists believed they were starting a national snowball that would roll across the country, liberating all native people from the government's shackles.

As Tennant pointed out, "Without having consulted the grass roots, the advocates of grass-roots control were now demanding that Indian communities and individuals give up all government financial support, including local administration grants, educational financing and welfare payments."[22]

When it came time to elect the new three-person executive, Bill Wilson and George Watts, who had backed the funding refusal, were elected along with Phillip Paul. Paul and Watts eventually found it impossible to work with Wilson and resigned. The Union was in tatters. It had no funds, no central machinery and worse, no plans to back up the dramatic gesture made in Chilliwack.

Paul and the original Union leadership met in Victoria to try to analyze what had happened. They watched videotapes of the meeting to try to see who the hell had organized the disorder. Bob Manuel was present at this meeting. Unknown to the rest, he had been one of the radicals who helped whip up the assembly and he found himself watching the video and hoping that Paul and the others didn't see his role; his nervousness increased when Doug Sanders pointed at the screen and exclaimed, "Can't you see, the staff did it!" Bob Manuel sunk down in his chair. He was relieved when Sander's comment went unanswered and the final conclusion was that what had happened was a spontaneous "peoples' movement."

After the Victoria meeting, Bob Manuel and the other young activists drifted home to wait for further orders from their leaders. As Bob Manuel put it, after the euphoria of Chilliwack "everybody was waiting for our political masters to call us together and say, here, let's plan out the next phase, let's move on. They didn't do that . . . Among the workers, we thought that somebody else was working on the Second Phase, the Master Plan. And finally, when we gradually got together . . . we discovered that there was no Master Plan."[23]

In fact, the only one with any plan at all was Bill Wilson, who tried to take advantage of the confusion to transform the Union into a status and non-status organization. To accomplish this, he began to push for a formal merger of the Union with the British Columbia Association of Non-status Indians, which was reportedly giving him funds to help with his living expenses after the Union payroll was cut off.[24]

By this time, however, George Manuel was quietly moving back into the picture. He began a tour of British Columbia at the end of May with stops in Kamloops, Lillooet, Vancouver, Mount Currie and back to Vancouver to try to assess the situation. Before heading east, he stopped in Kamloops again where Bob Manuel and some of the younger workers had called a thinly attended meeting that turned into more of a powwow than a political event. After it was over, George and Bob headed to Neskainlith and took a drive up to Neskainlith Lake in the hills behind the reserve to have a little chat.

George and his son, who had had a rather turbulent relationship in the past, were about to become close political allies in a bid to salvage what they could of the wreckage of the Union.

Through his contacts inside the DIA and elsewhere, George had learned that the Native Brotherhood was making a move to get the Union's core funding, and he told his son that they had to get the money back "or the Union's dead. The fact of life is you've got to have money. I've worked without money and I know what it's like. Without money, you've got no base to organize."

George suggested his son push for an all-chiefs meeting and "run for the executive. You've got to get elected."[25]

The opening for the all-chiefs conference came after Phillip Paul and George Watts had resigned. Bob Manuel and others immediately began to call for a new election at a special all-chiefs conference. When the conference was called, Don Moses was given the job of coordinator and Bob "pulled in behind him and said, okay, I'll work with Don as an assistant coordinator for the logistics."

Bob Manuel explained that "Don's job was to go around and promote the conference and my job was to get the facility, get the tables and chairs and all that kind of stuff." But Bob unilaterally expanded his job description. Without telling anyone he intended to run for a place on the executive, he travelled around the province meeting with chiefs and sounding them out on their feeling about the Union and the issues of the day.

The fact that everyone still considered him as just a worker allowed him to get information that would have been denied an official candidate. On the eve of the conference, he found himself sitting in a Kamloops bar with Bill Wilson and a few others while Wilson explained his strategy. When the elections took place, Wilson said, he would have Bill Lightbown, the head of BCANSI, run with him for one of the three executive positions. With he and Lightbown controlling the Union executive, the merger between the Union and BCANSI would be a *fait accompli*.

Up to that point, it looked like Don Moses was the only one who could stand up to Wilson, but during the conference Moses took such a verbal beating from Wilson that his star was fading and Bill Wilson and Bill Lightbown appeared assured of victory.

But when the nominations were called for, the Manuel camp began to move. Word of Bob Manuel's candidacy spread through the hall and the young radicals who had worked with him and the older leaders who had worked with his father, began to line up behind him.

As promised, Wilson had Lightbown nominated along with a few others who were considered long shots. When the votes were tallied, Bill Wilson had retained his place on the executive and Bob Manuel had been elected to his first leadership position with the same number of votes as Bill Wilson. The third member, however, was not Lightbown, but Steve Point, an artist who had been urged to run by his Sto:lo people.

Bill Wilson was disappointed that his strategy hadn't worked, but he was apparently comforted by the fact that his co-executive members were young and inexperienced. Immediately after the vote, he called an emergency meeting of the executive and tried to have himself installed as the head of the Union executive. As Bob Manuel remembered it, Wilson said something to the effect, "Well, fellows, I've got the most seniority here. So I guess you guys should concede that I'm the chairman."[26]

Bob Manuel's reaction to Wilson's move was not so much political as personal. He knew there would be hell to pay from his father if he let Wilson walk all over him, so he told Wilson that "I didn't run to give everything over to you. I got a lot of people who are supporting me out there."

Steve Point echoed Bob's protest and suggested that they forget the whole idea of a chairman for the moment and just try to work together.

When Bob Manuel came out of his first meeting with Wilson, he found his father waiting for him. George Manuel had slipped into town on his way to an NWT Indian Brotherhood assembly where the Dene people were about to release their historic declaration of nationhood.

He wanted to talk to his son about what he felt needed to be done to protect the Union so he told him that he was "seconding" him to Yellow-knife.[27]

On the plane, Bob Manuel was still pleased by his victory, but he remembers telling his father that he didn't feel any different now that he was a leader. George Manuel nodded. When they arrived in Yellow-knife, Bob called Steve Point and Steve had some interesting news. Bill Wilson had offered the use of his downtown Vancouver apartment, his telephone, everything, for the Union's head office.

At first glance, Bob Manuel considered it a generous offer. After all, the Union had no funding and nowhere else to go. When he told his father about it, George Manuel was silent for a moment. Then he said, "You know, Bobby, you said you didn't feel any different. Well, I'm going to tell you, you better start feeling different right now. That guy is taking over on you guys. With your consent, he's going to control the Union. You're going to get squeezed right out. You better get back on the phone to Steve and call an executive meeting and you better meet with Steve privately."

George Manuel went to bed early that night. The international conference was only a few months away, he had declared war against Buchanan and the DIA bureaucracy in Ottawa, and now he also had to figure out how to untangle the political mess in British Columbia. It was the kind of moment when even the most politically committed would wonder if it was all worth it. But George Manuel had an uncanny ability to look at the positive side of things, no matter how hard he had to squint to see it. He had learned from Chilliwack that there was a grass-roots protest movement developing in BC that could be harnessed in future battles. The rejection of funding had been a serious tactical error because it was premature. But the motivation behind it, to get the Department of Indian Affairs off the backs of the First Nations, was one of the goals he had been striving for since he had confronted the Indian Agent at the Adams Lake meeting twenty years earlier.

The next day would also bring a positive development. His reason for being in the north was to attend the Fort Simpson Assembly where the Dene Declaration of nationhood would be unveiled. While it was specifically a Dene document, the principles it expounded fit closely with George Manuel's political goals for the movement in Canada and throughout the Fourth World, and it remains one of the most important statements on Indian nationhood ever written in Canada. It began with the simple, direct statement:

"We the Dene of the N.W.T. insist on the right to be regarded by ourselves and the world as a nation.

"As once Europe was the exclusive homeland of the European peoples, Africa the exclusive homeland of the African peoples, the New World, North and South America, was the exclusive homeland of Aboriginal peoples of the New World, the Amerindian and the Inuit.

"The New World like other parts of the world has suffered the experience of colonialism and imperialism. Other peoples have occupied the land – often with force – and foreign governments have imposed themselves on our people. Ancient civilizations and ways of life have been destroyed.

"We the Dene are part of the Fourth World. And as the peoples and Nations of the world have come to recognize the existence and rights of those peoples who make up the Third World the day must come and will come when the nations of the Fourth World will come to be recognized and respected . . .[28]

The Declaration, with its brief historical analysis, its reference to the Fourth World and to independence and self-government for the Dene Nation within Canada, reflected the main currents of George Manuel's thought. As it turned out, though, he would not be present when the Declaration was formally made.

The next day, George and Bob Manuel met with James Wah-Shee in their hotel lobby in Yellowknife for the drive over to Fort Simpson in a rental car. But before they got under way, George said he wasn't feeling well and asked Bob to drive while he lay down in the back seat. Bob had assumed that his father was just tired, but when they were a short way out of town George said, "Take me back to the hospital. I can't go on."[29]

Bob Manuel dropped his father off at the emergency room and found out that George had just had a heart attack. The doctor's warning that George Manuel had to curtail his activities or face a serious health crisis had come to pass.

The NIB president remained only a few days in the Yellowknife hospital before he was flown to a hospital in Ottawa. His doctor told him that the damage had been minimal, but reiterated his warning about slowing down. At the age of fifty-four, however, George Manuel would not, or could not, get off the buckin' horse. The founding WCIP meeting was just months away, the Union was still teetering on the brink and Judd Buchanan seemed bent on rolling back the gains the NIB had made over the previous five years. So he would deal with his heart problem the way he had dealt with his twisted hip: by ignoring it.

By mid summer, he was back on his feet and ready to take on Judd Buchanan, who in the final weeks of his tenure as minister of Indian Affairs compared the Dene to Quebec-style separatists.

The NIB leader pointed out that the Dene Declaration had stated clearly that what they sought was "independence and self-determination *within the country of Canada.*[30]

"When Mr. Wah-Shee speaks," George Manuel added, "he speaks for an underdeveloped colony (you may say territory if you wish). Yet no less a person than the minister, the highest official responsible as a trustee for Mr. Wah-Shee and his people, deliberately chooses to misinterpret the intent of the Dene Declaration, and drag these lofty principles down to the level of a separatist movement."[31]

George kept up his denunciations of Buchanan during a cross-country tour that fall that took him as far east as Labrador and then back across to BC to meet with the interior chiefs to try to restore their lost faith in the Union.

Then, on October 25, he headed still farther west, to Port Alberni on Vancouver Island, to meet with the indigenous leaders from all over the world who were assembling for the founding convention of the World Council of Indigenous Peoples.

The Fourth World, an idea that George Manuel had formed four years earlier, was about to get a body and a voice of its own.

## CHAPTER FIFTEEN

# A Voice for the Fourth World
## 1975-1976

And rising up after centuries of oppression
evoking the greatness of our ancestors
in the memory of our Indigenous martyrs:

We vow to control again our own destiny and
recover our complete humanity and
pride in being Indigenous People.

wcip Declaration.
October 1975

Rodrigo Contreras was given the job of meeting the international indigenous leaders as they arrived at Vancouver Airport on 24-25 October 1975, and he remembers it as one of the most emotional moments of his life.

One by one they came, Maoris from New Zealand, Aborigines from Australia, Maya from Guatemala, Guaymis from Panama, Miskitos from Nicaragua, Inca from Bolivia, Sami from Scandinavia, Inuit from Greenland and representatives of a dozen First Nations from Canada and the United States.

In all, fifty-two delegates and more than two hundred official observers from nineteen countries were ferried across the Georgia Strait to Nanaimo and the Nootka community on Vancouver Island. As they arrived, a feeling of history-in-the-making began to spread among the participants as they met and spoke with one another for the first time. Together they represented millions of people who had been fighting for five hundred years against the European invasion, which brought deadly diseases, a tidal wave of settlement and political domination under regimes that pursued policies ranging from assimilation to the outright extermination of indigenous societies. Against all odds, the Fourth World had survived and was now prepared to take a step together toward regaining lost lands and liberty.

The first item on the agenda was a celebration of their mutual survival at a welcoming feast. Most of the delegates were dressed in their national costumes and the Nootka produced a lavish seafood banquet of their traditional foods, followed by a cultural celebration of indigenous dancers, drummers and singers from around the world.

The meetings began the next day with George Clutesi, a Sechelt artist and elder, chanting an opening prayer.[1] George Manuel and other members of the Canadian delegation then gave brief welcoming speeches and the delegates settled down to work. The first item of discussion was affiliation of the international indigenous organization with the United Nations. The idea won overwhelming support, and the assembly broke into workshops to discuss the struggle for social and political justice, cultural identity and indigenous lands and resources. The only problem the delegates faced in the workshops was the one they had discovered in the first preparatory meeting in Guyana: they were in agreement on virtually every item on the agenda. They decided, therefore, to drop the remaining workshops and go directly into a full conference assembly to debate, and where necessary amend, the draft charter of the organization.

George Manuel was careful not to impose his own views on the delegates. The draft charter, after all, had been largely drawn up in his office and he wanted everyone to have chance to study it and to make whatever additions or deletions they thought necessary. When it came time to elect the first president of the World Council of Indigenous Peoples, however, there was no question of who the leader of the international movement was. George Manuel was unopposed for the presidency and won unanimous support from the delegates.

Sam Deloria, from the U.S., was elected as George's vice-president, and Julio Dixon from Panama, Clemente Alcon from Bolivia, Nils Sara from Norway and Neil Watene from New Zealand made up the founding executive.[2]

After the election, the delegates passed what they called a Solemn Declaration that addressed the spiritual as well as political unity of the indigenous nations. It began and ended with an expression of historic pride and served as a manifesto for the struggle of regaining sovereignty. It read in part:

> We glory in our proud past:
> > when the earth was our nurturing mother,
> > when the night sky formed our common root,
> > when Sun and Moon were our parents,
> > when all were brothers and sisters,
> > when our great civilizations grew under the sun.

> Then other peoples arrived:
> > thirsting for blood, for gold, for land and all its wealth,
> > carrying the cross and the sword, one in each hand,
> > without knowing or waiting to learn the ways of our worlds,
> > they considered us to be lower than the animals,
> > they stole our lands from us and took us from our lands,
> > they made slaves of the Sons of the sun.

> And rising up after centuries of oppression
> > evoking the greatness of our ancestors
> > in the memory of our Indigenous martyrs:

> We vow to control again our own destiny and
> > recover our complete humanity and
> > pride in being Indigenous People. [3]

Before the assembly was brought to a close, the delegates agreed that one of the first tasks of the World Council of Indigenous Peoples would be to set up an international solidarity network to alert the member organizations and the world to any threat to the land, livelihood or culture of the indigenous nations. As the delegates left Vancouver for the far corners of the world, they left with a sense of hope. They would no longer face oppression in isolation. The World Council would allow them to work together toward their common goals and give them a collective voice in the world through the United Nations.

During the fall of 1975 and the spring of 1976, George Manuel devoted much of his time and energy to the WCIP cause. Once again, though, the main problem was one of financing the new organization. The NIB had covered most of the expenses of the WCIP Secretariat and all of George Manuel's travel expenses, but to become a viable organization the WCIP needed to arrange its own funding sources.

The member organizations could offer little in the way of financial contributions since the WCIP was, to an even greater extent than Canadian Indian organizations, a poor peoples' organization. Just holding the conference had drained its coffers, and when it was over there was a need for a major fund-raising drive. So in March 1976, George Manuel travelled to Geneva with his executive to attend an international conference of the United Nations NGOs where he was both promoting WCIP United Nations membership and trying to get financial support from wealthier organizations like the World Council of Churches. The Secretariat had also targeted the Canadian and Scandinavian governments as possible funding sources and began to lobby for funds from their foreign aid budgets.

During this period, George Manuel found another valuable ally in his World Council work when he bumped into Dave Monture at the Saskatoon airport during one of his cross-country trips. They had known each other since 1970, when Monture reported on the NIB's Winnipeg conference for *Indian News,* and they met often in Ottawa through mutual friends. George Manuel had asked Dave Monture to come to work with him a couple of times before, but Monture had always turned him down with the excuse that he didn't think he had much to offer.

This time, George Manuel had him cornered on the plane, and by the time they reached Ottawa, Monture had agreed to work with the WCIP. The catch, though, was the same one that had confronted Guy Lavallee a couple of years earlier: Monture would have to find a way to pay his own salary. He accomplished this by arranging his own seconding from his job with the Public Service Commission to work for the WCIP.

In June, George Manuel and Dave Monture left for Inari, a small resort town in northern Finland, to attend the Ninth Nordic Sami Council conference. Here, George Manuel quickly signalled that his leadership of the WCIP would be a hands-on affair.

The two men had been billeted in one of the resort cabins on the lakeshore, while most of the Sami were camped in tents, eating out of doors and drinking a fair bit of vodka in the Sami tradition of blowing off steam in the summertime.

George Manuel and Dave Monture ate most of their meals in the restaurant at the lodge and were surprised to find that reservations were required for every meal. They didn't understand the meaning of this until they came in for lunch with a couple of Sami friends and were told that the restaurant was prepared to serve the Canadians, but not the Sami, because they didn't have reservations.

George Manuel suspected the Sami were facing the same type of discrimination that native people faced in Canada, so he started to raise hell. His English was so colourful that the manager had to get a translator and George Manuel explained that he would go on Finnish television to say that he "had come all the way to Scandinavia only to witness blatant discrimination against the Sami people."

As the manager listened, he became more and more fidgety and when George Manuel finally finished, the manager mumbled something about a mistake and promised to take care of it. And he did. Not only were George Manuel's Sami friends served their lunch, the embarrassed manager opened up the restaurant that evening to the Sami staying in tents and paid for a couple of rounds of drinks. [4]

Needless to say, George Manuel's intervention was popular among the rank and file, but it was not that welcome with the more conservative Sami leadership, who were concerned that the Canadian Indian was trying to undercut their leadership.

That concern increased as George Manuel spent most of his time with the ordinary people on the lakeshore. After the conference, when he took a tour of Sami reindeer-herding villages and studied their handicraft programs in Finland and Norway, he also made a point of meeting with and listening to the local people and the local leadership.

Dave Monture recalled that while the national Sami leadership looked nervously on, many Sami began to see George Manuel not as a Canadian Indian who headed the WCIP, but as their own leader on the international front. [5] This sense increased in later years as George Manuel often proved to be more successful at tapping the Scandinavian governments for funds than their own leadership. In the future, the identification of the Sami grass roots with the Canadian Indian leader would be repeated with other indigenous groups and, as in Finland, it would often create resentment among the national leadership.

Over all, though, the Scandinavian trip served as a valuable tool in raising the profile of the WCIP in northern Europe, and after he returned, Manuel decided to make the same sort of tour through Central America.

The Central American trip was one that he had wanted to take since he began planning the international organization four years earlier. The region had a large Indian population, and in countries like Guatemala the Indians were in a clear majority. George Manuel believed Central America was "essential to the search for common solutions for the most oppressed peoples of the world."[6]

It turned out to be a major, and in many ways, historic undertaking. He and Rodrigo Contreras flew off to Mexico City on July 26. They stayed with Luis Lopez Hierra of the Centre for Popular Organization and went to visit the Toltec ruins in the outskirts of the capital. George Manuel, with his bad leg and damaged heart, insisted on struggling to the top of the pyramids to gaze at the remains of the spectacular city that his southern cousins had created. It was a bittersweet moment. His first reaction was one of pride at the beauty his fellow American Indians had built. But Rodrigo Contreras remembers George Manuel wondering out loud how such a tremendous civilization could have been crushed. What it meant for the indigenous people of today, he decided, was that the road back would be a long one. It wasn't enough to merely start an organization, publish a newsletter and travel around; it was going to take "blood, money and sweat" for the indigenous peoples to win back their birthright.[7]

While in Mexico, George Manuel visited a number of indigenous organizations as well as government officials. During the meetings, he was struck by "the paradox of a society attempting to free itself from imperialism and underdevelopment – economic and political oppression – yet through its policies and programs repressing indigenous communities and exploiting their economics without any realization of the consequences of such policies and programs."[8]

After leaving Mexico, they travelled to Guatemala where George Manuel gained some insights into the workings of the Western Hemisphere's most notorious apartheid regime. In Guatemala, almost two-thirds of the people are Mayan Indians but they have been stripped of all economic and political power in their own land and have been subjected to centuries of brutal repression.

During George Manuel's visit, the Highland Indians were also recovering from one of the most devastating earthquakes to hit Central America in this century and most of the Indian organizations were involved in trying to feed and house the survivors. George Manuel had heard about the earthquake just before he left and he had set up a relief fund through the NIB and WCIP. He was able to bring a modest $8,257 contribution to the relief effort.

In Guatemala, Manuel contacted the local delegates from the Port Alberni conference and they took him and Rodrigo Contreras on a tour of the Highlands to meet with local Indian leadership. It was an exhausting ordeal for George Manuel, who was asked to give three or four speeches a day and then go to public meetings in the evening.

They couldn't afford to rent a car so they travelled on the crowded mountain buses that were frequently stopped by the army for ID and weapons checks, which led to long sessions standing on the dusty roadsides with their hands on their heads while they were frisked and questioned about their activities in Guatemala.

For George Manuel the ordeal was complicated by a nasty bout of dysentery, and he often found himself having to plead with Rodrigo Contreras to "get the bus to stop" so he could find a bathroom. Rodrigo Contreras would then ask the driver in Spanish to stop but, as he put it, there were "a lot of close calls."[9]

One close call turned into one of the George Manuel stories that still circulates in Indian country. Rodrigo Contreras had asked the driver to pull over and George Manuel dashed into one of those none-too-clean but, in his case, very welcome Central American public toilets. All the stalls were occupied but George could not wait. So he flung open the door of one of the stalls and when he saw a man sitting there, he literally picked him up by his lapels, set him down outside the door and took his seat. While he was freeing up the stall, George Manuel apologized profusely in English, but once he was inside he realized the man couldn't understand a word, so he yelled for Rodrigo Contreras to translate.

When Rodrigo arrived, he began to convey George Manuel's apologies and he explained that George was very ill. When George was finished, he offered the Guatemalan another round of what were for him incomprehensible apologies and George headed, sheepishly, back to the bus.

In the Manuel lore, the incident is usually used to illustrate George's aggressive strength, with the emphasis on his picking up the surprised Guatemalan and setting him down outside the stall. But what Rodrigo Contreras remembers most is how badly George Manuel felt about unceremoniously unseating the small Guatemalan and how concerned he was that Rodrigo explain the situation and apologize for having caused the man such an indignity.

Yet despite his uncertain health and loose intestines, George Manuel was able to make some very interesting observations about what he saw in Guatemala and to tie them in with his Canadian experience. In the zones he visited, the earthquake reconstruction programs were well under way, but he observed serious flaws in the international aid effort.

"People from many Western European cultures, applying their knowledge and methods with good intentions," he reported, "were failing to appreciate the detrimental impact of their ideas, methods, mechanisms, etc. on the totally different lifestyles and experiences of the indigenous peoples of Guatemala."[10] There had been no consultation with respect to the goals, objectives, processes, systems for restoration or reconstruction, or development programs for the communities.

This point was probably best illustrated by Canada's aid to Guatemala, which consisted of a gift of large quantities of powdered milk. The Canadian aid givers didn't bother to find out that few of the Guatemalan Maya could digest the product and it was therefore useless to those it was intended to help.

Another effect of the ignorance of this invading force of well-intentioned foreigners was that their money and materials often found their way into the pockets of wealthy Ladinos or onto the thriving Guatemalan black market. By not insisting on delivering their aid directly to the Highland Indians, much of it was siphoned off long before it reached the people in need.

The fact that the foreign aid was being lost did not diminish the Maya's own reconstruction efforts. Instead, the people drew on their tradition of mutual aid and used the reconstruction campaign to revitalize their indigenous organizations. After seeing how the people were able to quickly erect a leadership and an organization to deal with the crisis, George Manuel suggested that as tragic as the situation was, the earthquake could lead to a strengthened Indian movement in the future.

As it turned out, he was proved correct. In the aftermath of the earthquake, political and cultural organizational activity increased dramatically in Guatemala and within a few years, the Guatemalan Maya would organize the nation-wide Campesinos Unity Committee (CUC) that would push for basic economic and social justice for the Mayan people. The CUC became a major force in the countryside's political life until a hurricane of government-backed terror swept through Guatemala at the end of the decade.

When their Guatemalan tour was over, Manuel and Contreras moved on to Nicaragua where they were met at the airport by a couple of their Port Alberni contacts, along with the deputy member of Parliament representing the Miskito people and a group of Miskito university students.

The visitors were first taken to the home of one of the members of the reception committee where George briefed them about the goals of the WCIP and held informal discussions which, in Rodrigo Contreras's words, turned into "a marathon session." In the politically charged atmosphere of Nicaragua in the mid-1970s, the students wanted to know if George Manuel was advocating independence for Miskitia and whether that meant they should engage in revolutionary violence. George Manuel simply told them, "If you have to, you have to. But nobody can tell you how to carry out your struggle," but by whatever means they chose, they should fight relentlessly for their liberation.[11]

George took the same message to the Miskito Coast, where he met with the local Miskito leadership and with the Miskito people. Their reception was, Rodrigo Contreras recalled, astounding. Word had passed through the towns and villages that George Manuel, the leader of the Indians of the world, was passing through, and people began to line the roads to catch a glimpse of him and wave. When Rodrigo Contreras realized that the fanfare was in their honour, he asked why they were coming out to see George Manuel. The answer was simple. "When Somoza comes, he comes to visit Nicaraguans. But George Manuel is our President. We are Indigenous."[12]

Manuel and Contreras weren't the only ones to be impressed by the sudden and unexpected outpouring of affection from the people. As the tour through the jungle villages began to draw crowds of up to eight hundred people, they suddenly found themselves escorted by the local army officers, who attended every one of George Manuel's planned and impromptu speeches.

Rodrigo Contreras remembered being surprised that George

Manuel was so friendly with the military men, and particularly amazed when he would give Somoza's guardsmen his address and suggest that they come up to visit him in Canada. When Rodrigo asked why George was doing this, the WCIP leader explained that if he invited them, they would believe he was not a threat. And anyway, they would never get to Canada. The strategy seemed to work, because the army officers were suddenly eager to please their future host in Canada by giving him a little space for private discussions.

His message to the people was the same one he had been giving in Canada for so many years: *Organize and unify around a clear set of objectives. Battle against all the forces of assimilation and try to build your nations economically, culturally and politically. Consult the people, politicize the people and never get too far ahead of them, because when all is said and done, they are your masters.*

During these meetings, one expectation he frequently had to dash was that George Manuel, from a rich country like Canada, was about to shower them with development wealth. He had to explain time and again that the Indians of Canada were not rich and that the people would have to rely on their own means. He could offer them leadership and international solidarity, but he could not solve their need for a new well or new housing. That was part of their own struggle for political, social and economic independence.

The informal discussions and formal meetings were beginning to take a toll on George Manuel's health and his exhaustion was worsened by the stifling Nicaraguan heat. In Mexico and Guatemala, they had been in the mountains, but in Nicaragua they were in the middle of the steamy jungle and George was finding the heat almost unbearable.

Rodrigo Contreras remembers that George Manuel began to wish the people would let him rest, but they wouldn't. They would come to the room or trailer where he was staying at eight in the morning and drag him off to a meeting where he would encourage them to keep up the fight for their rights. Then they would take him off to another village, and another, all day long until ten, eleven or even twelve o'clock at night. The next morning, they would be back for another round of meetings and assemblies with their president.

When George and Rodrigo finally left Nicaragua, they were exhausted, but both had been inspired by the solidarity they had witnessed and the vitality of the people. For George Manuel it reinforced his hope for a viable World Council that could link the struggle of the Shuswap Indian in the interior Rockies, to the Miskito Indian along the Caribbean coast of Nicaragua, to the indigenous peoples of Eurasia and northern Europe.

The final working stop on the tour was Panama, where they met with Julio Dixon, the twenty-seven-year-old secretary general of the National Association of Indigenous Peoples of Panama. Dixon had also been a WCIP delegate for his Guaymi people at Port Alberni and had been elected as the Central American representative. George Manuel had been so impressed with his leadership potential that he had invited him back to Canada after the Port Alberni meeting to discuss the problem of government infiltration of indigenous organizations. From his experience in Latin America, Dixon had told Manuel this was an unavoidable evil, and he suggested that he wouldn't be surprised if among the delegates at the Port Alberni conference there were people reporting back to their governments.

During George Manuel's visit to Panama, the main item on the agenda was the regional WCIP conference that was to be held in Panama the following year. George Manuel had been promoting the conference during his travels through Mexico and Central America. He saw it as almost equal in importance to the Port Alberni meeting because the region, with its large indigenous population, would eventually form the heart of the WCIP.

Along with his meetings with Dixon, George Manuel managed a few forays into the countryside to the Guaymi communities. But Rodrigo Contreras remembers he was near the end of his rope. The heat in Panama was just as oppressive as it had been in Nicaragua, and he often found George in his hotel room with his face close to the air conditioner "like he was listening to a radio."

At the end of the long sojourn, they took a quick trip to Ecuador, Rodrigo Contreras's home country. George stayed in a hotel in Quito while Rodrigo visited his family and he used the time to take a look at Indian life in the capital. He was appalled when he saw Indians being used as pack animals to carry huge piles of merchandise on their backs. "That, for him, is something that could be denounced," Rodrigo Contreras remembered, "and he certainly did."

On the plane back to Canada, though, George Manuel was in an upbeat mood. He had met dozens of local and national leaders and spoke to literally thousands of Central American Indians about their common struggle. Along the way, he had gained valuable insights about the native cultures to the south and about the machinery of repression that was used against them. He also discovered that the people at the village level were ready to assume the burdens of fighting back. All they needed was leadership.

For the past several years, he had been trying to provide that leadership at the international level, while at the same time leading the national movement in Canada and trying to keep the shaky coalition together in BC. Even before his trip south, he knew he was spreading himself too thin and he had decided that something had to give.

No one knows exactly when George Manuel decided not to run for a fourth term as the NIB president. But by the summer of 1976, he was already deeply committed to both the international struggle and to rebuilding the movement in British Columbia.

Around this time, George Manuel received some help in his decision to return to BC from Phillip Paul. Paul was worried about the future of the Union and he had decided that the only person who could pull things together was George Manuel. To lure him back, he drew up plans for a commission that would travel through the province discussing aboriginal rights and the BC land question. It was, Paul knew, a job tailor-made for Manuel's return. He would be able to spend his time at the community level, talking with the elders and the ordinary people about what they understood about aboriginal rights and aboriginal title, learning and politicizing as he went along.

As Paul suspected, George Manuel was immediately interested in the commission idea. Along with putting him back in contact with the people and allowing him to lay the groundwork for a new popular front, the commission would parallel the Berger Commission in the North, which was then holding hearings on the Mackenzie Valley pipeline.

George Manuel had already made two appearances in front of the Berger commission and he was impressed by how the Dene were coming forward to explain their hopes for the future and their fears about a project that could damage their lives and livelihood. He also appreciated the wide press coverage that gave the general public an education about Indian life and their sense of nationhood.

At George Manuel's first appearance in front of the Berger commission in April 1976, he began by welcoming the opportunity to speak and added that "For once, the voice of Indian people is being heard before a final ruling on a major project is made."

In his testimony, he reiterated the need for government recognition of aboriginal rights. He emphasized that "the solution to our land claims is not money. If the answer to Indian land claims and aboriginal rights was merely money, the conflict could be resolved with a minimal degree of haggling. Indians across the country would simply pry as much cash out of the federal coffers as they could, and the federal government would sigh with relief as it washed its hands of Canada's original people."

Once again, George Manuel used the James Bay Agreement as an example of what native peoples did not want. His message was directed to the northern natives as much as it was to his own friend and former Native Brotherhood lawyer, Tom Berger.

"The catastrophic clauses of the James Bay Agreement are those sections which surrender title to the land," he said. "In the case of James Bay, then, the opportunity has been lost for a new relationship to be established between the Indian people and Canadian society as a whole."

That new relationship would be based on "neither apartheid nor assimilation but participation – participation on terms that will recognize our national identity and will ultimately strengthen Canada as a whole." For a more concrete model of that new relationship, George Manuel referred to the Dene Declaration as summing up what he meant by sovereignty and independence within Canada. [13]

George Manuel's second appearance before the Berger Inquiry, in early June 1976, was one of his last major speeches before his retirement from the NIB, and it was one of his best. He began by scoffing at the public relations line put out by the oil companies that the pipeline would be as unobtrusive as a piece of string across a football field.

"If such an analogy is valid, then it can be further said that Aboriginal Rights of Indian people are like the football that is being kicked around by the same oil companies and certain politicians. Perhaps, we Indians need to pick up the ball and simply go home. Then the Almighty Oil Companies would have to shut down the football field and the piece of string would rot away or be blown by the winds to places unknown."

George Manuel then returned, once again, to the James Bay Agreement when he pointed out that the Appeals Court set aside the Malouf decision on the basis of the "balance of convenience," which was a way of saying "the rights of six million white Québecois are more important that the rights of eight thousand Cree and Inuit.

"Extending that argument to its logical conclusion on a global basis means, for example, that the rights of eight hundred and forty million Chinese are more important than the rights of twenty-two million white Canadians.

"And since we are always told that we Indians are really descendants of Asian forebears, maybe we should now ask our Asian brothers to come over in hordes to help us get our land back on the basis of 'balance of convenience'."

George Manuel went on to describe aboriginal rights as a moral issue "because it strikes at the very roots of the religious foundation of the Christian society that Canada purports to be.

"As we understand Christianity it is based on the ten commandments of God.

"The seventh and tenth commandments state: THOU SHALT NOT STEAL and THOU SHALT NOT COVET THY NEIGHBOUR'S GOODS.

"We seriously wonder whether these commandments have been amended to read:

7. THOU SHALT NOT STEAL. (Except in Canada where lands of aboriginal people can be taken at will without compensation.)

And,

10. THOU SHALT NOT COVET THY NEIGHBOUR'S GOODS. (Except in Canada where the riches of the land of the Aboriginal people can be taken for sheer profit.)

"We hope the Canadian people will live according to their own Christian laws which state "THOU SHALT LOVE THY NEIGHBOUR AS THY SELF."

He ended his speech with a warning:

"If Canada cannot or will not live up to its historical, legal, political and moral duties to its aboriginal inhabitants, then this country will stand naked before the world. Canada will become renowned for its historical blindness, its legal squalors, its political cupidity, and its moral emptiness."[14]

When Tom Berger released his report the following year, he agreed that the pipeline should not go ahead before the land claim was addressed. This victory in the North did not make up for the loss of aboriginal title in Quebec, but it did serve to stall the government's drive for a James Bay-style extinguishment of aboriginal rights in the other parts of the country.

To capitalize on the success of the Berger hearings, the NIB's September 1976 Annual General Assembly was to be held in Yellowknife. It was there that George Manuel would formally give up the NIB presidency that he had held for over six years.

When he returned to Ottawa in early September, he was busy trying to arrange his family's move to British Columbia and he also had to find a new home for the WCIP. Marie Marule had decided to leave the NIB when George Manuel's term was up, and she had taken a teaching position at the University of Lethbridge. Since she was still the head of the WCIP Secretariat, it was decided that the head office of the WCIP would move west with her, into space provided by the university.

For his part, George Manuel was still ready to take on the world through the WCIP, and in many ways the more difficult and fractious world of Indian politics in British Columbia.

## CHAPTER SIXTEEN

# Back to BC
# 1976-1977

Agreement with the government will only come after a show of power.

George Manuel on his return to BC
1977

George Manuel once wrote that "the kinds of giving are as many and as varied as the gifts and the givers," but the most difficult person to satisfy is the person "who gives to you because the gift for which he hopes in return is his own identity. It is unlikely that you can give to him what he is seeking. And there is a great temptation to give him your own identity instead."

Exactly what was meant by giving "your own identity" he explained this way: "I was in that position myself when I first came to Ottawa. If cabinet ministers had been willing to meet with me then, I would have been ripe for being absorbed into their high-powered methods. It is so easy to allow a person whose status and power you admire to impose his style and values, whether or not that is his intention."[1]

It was one of George Manuel's personal accomplishments that in his six years in Ottawa, with the occasional lunch at 24 Sussex, his frequent meetings with cabinet ministers and the highest bureaucrats in the land and his meetings with world leaders, he never forgot who he was or who he was representing: the 300,000 reserve Indians of the fifty-two First Nations who depended on him to fight for their rights.

Even in the matter of setting his own salary at the NIB, George

Manuel's integrity was beyond reproach. The first year he earned only $18,000 for his sixty-to-eighty hour-a-week job – no more than he would have been making as a boom man on the river. He put his heart (quite literally) and soul into the job for six years and he never gave himself a raise.

At the same time, he refused the blandishments from outside. By 1976, he had been offered safe seats in Parliament by all three political parties. At any time after that, he could have taken the route of other native leaders like James Gladstone, Len Marchand, Guy Williams, Charlie Watt, and Walter Twin, who were rewarded for their work within the system with the prize of a senate appointment.

Instead, at the age of fifty-five George Manuel was heading back to British Columbia to build his peoples' movement. Ottawa had not absorbed him; it had radicalized him by showing him that reasoned argument and a just cause did not lead to government action. Governments, by their nature, only responded to a show of power and the only power Indian nations had at their disposal was that generated by the commitment and drive of their people. So he would build a movement to harness that energy and, if need be, he would lead that movement to the steps of Parliament.

Although his mind had been made up months before, George Manuel waited until mid-August to announce formally that he was resigning from the NIB. He made the announcement when speaking to a meeting of the Union of Ontario Indians in Toronto and musing about his recent travels to Central and South America. He was still filled with the emotion of the trip, and at one point he remarked that the Indians of the region were there before Columbus, "and I told them they should have eaten him. Latin America is as bad as Rhodesia."[2]

When he announced his decision to leave the NIB, he passed over it quickly by simply stating he would not be running for the presidency at the NIB's upcoming assembly in Whitehorse. In looking back over his three terms, he mentioned only that when he took over the NIB, it was in debt and the phones were disconnected. His contribution to the organization was that six years later, the NIB was in the black and the phones were working.[3]

That was, of course, an extreme understatement. When George Manuel took over, the NIB was still a paper organization. It had no legitimacy in the eyes of the government and no public profile beyond the handful of Indian leaders who had signed the initial protocol. After six years of George Manuel's leadership it was the largest lobbying organization in Ottawa with institutionalized access to cabinet and a reputation for hard but honest bargaining on behalf of the First Nations.

During the six years, the NIB had made significant progress on all fronts – political, social and economic – and the Indian organizations, from the national to the band level, gained a new self-confidence that would allow them to pursue the struggle on a level never seen before. And it was George Manuel's unique combination of vision and political savvy that had launched them on their way.

As the mid-September Whitehorse Assembly approached, George and Marlene were preoccupied with their move to Burnaby, where they had rented a small apartment. But when George flew to Whitehorse to make his low-key farewell, he found that his resignation had not been so easily accepted. At every turn he found old friends and colleagues urging him to reconsider and run one more time. In 1976, just as in 1970, 1972 and 1974, there was no Indian leader in Canada who could have defeated him. In fact, if he had changed his mind and ran, it is unlikely that anyone would even have stood against him.

But George Manuel refused to listen to the One More Timers. In his opening address to the assembly he made a point of thanking those who were encouraging him to run, but insisted he wanted "to return to British Columbia and work with the people there."[4]

Only when it was certain that he was out, did the campaigning for his replacement begin in earnest. It was assumed that the powerful prairie leaders, Dave Courchene and David Ahenikew, would throw their hats in the ring, and that Ray Jackson of the Yukon would be the third man in the race. But after a fierce round of back room bargaining in the hotel suites, Ahenikew stood up in the Assembly and nominated the young director of the Federation of Saskatchewan Indians treaty research department, Noel Starblanket, as George Manuel's replacement.

Ironically, Starblanket, a twenty-nine-year-old Cree, had been working at the NIB office in Winnipeg when George Manuel took over from Walter Deiter in 1970, but because of the NIB's debt, Manuel had been forced to lay him off. Since that time, Starblanket had occasionally criticized Manuel because he believed the NIB president was too pre-occupied with aboriginal rights, to the detriment of the treaty rights of the prairie Indians.

In his acceptance speech, Starblanket acknowledged that he had been one of George Manuel's critics in the past, but he thanked Manuel for the groundwork he had laid at the NIB and said it was work George Manuel "could be proud of."[5]

For most of those who had been involved with George Manuel and the NIB over the previous six years, there was still a reluctance to let go. Manuel found himself back in Ottawa for numerous tributes in his honour, including a "celebrity roast" put on by the Ontario Native Women's Association. Bill Badcock was one of the MCs and most of George Manuel's old friends were there to trundle out the George Manuel stories, including a few that suggested that part of George Manuel's motivations for international travel was an excuse for a little "extra-marital hanky panky."

As an *Indian News* report pointed out, Marlene seemed a bit uncomfortable by the tone and the content of some of the jokes but when it came her turn at the microphone she stood up and told how she first met George standing in the hall of Joey's house "buck-naked" and holding a bottle of whisky. It is likely, though, that despite Marlene's quick recovery, George Manuel had a few pointed questions to answer about his travels when he got home. He later admitted to Phillip Paul that while the roast was going on, he was praying a hole would open up in the floor so he could crawl into it.[6]

Less threatening was an evening in his honour put on by the Native Council of Canada. Harry Daniels, the NCC leader, was a good friend who had recently travelled with George on a brief tour of Scandinavia. Daniels presented George Manuel with a Métis sash and flag for his cooperation with the NCC and the Métis people. It was a honour George Manuel valued since he had great respect for Daniels and the Métis and non-status people he represented.

When the retirement accolades were finally over and George Manuel had said his goodbyes to his friends in Ottawa, he headed back to BC where the Union organizers were still trying to patch the organization together after Chilliwack.

They had had some initial success. After their election to the three-person executive, Bob Manuel and Steve Point managed to have the

Union office moved out of Bill Wilson's apartment to Coqualeetza, near Steve Point's community, in the hope that they could block any further attempt by Bill Wilson to take control.

But while Steve Point and Bob Manuel's strategy was to try to isolate Wilson, Wilson ignored the new executive members and carried on with his plans to amalgamate the Union and BCANSI. This became apparent when Bill Wilson organized a Union assembly in Courtenay for May 1976, without consulting either Manuel or Point. According to some observers, Bill Wilson hoped to recreate the atmosphere of Chilliwack, but this time with the delegates cheering not for the rejection of funds, but for the immediate merger of BC's status and non-status Indian organizations.

To make sure he was in control of the conference, Bill Wilson appointed his sister as coordinator and ran the publicity out of his own office. Bob Manuel and Steve Point were left to watch from the sidelines.

A few days before the conference, Bob Manuel received a phone call from a friend who said that he had heard that the Union had rented his P.A. system for the Courtenay conference but that nobody had put it on paper, or agreed to his price and he didn't know whether he should send his equipment to Courtenay or not.

Bob Manuel could only tell him that Bill Wilson was looking after it. Bob then called Steve Point and told him about the organizational problems surrounding the Courtenay conference and they agreed that they should get together to discuss what they could do to fix things. Bob Manuel hopped in his car and headed south to Coqualeetza, but halfway down the canyon he began to chuckle to himself. So what if Bill Wilson was messing things up? He had gone out on his own with the Courtenay conference and any failure would be laid at his feet. By the time he reached Coqualeetza, Bob Manuel told Steve Point that the best thing they could do was to distance themselves from the conference and let everyone know they had nothing to do with it before it started. If Bill Wilson faltered, they would move in and take the meeting over.[7]

The plan worked. Bill Wilson could muster no enthusiasm among the Union members for the merger with BCANSI, At the point where some of the delegates were beginning to drift away, Bob Manuel and Steve Point walked up to the front and started conducting Union business as if Bill Wilson had never been there. It was a major political defeat for Wilson. But the rejection of the merger also hurt a number of BCANSI activists on a personal level. Once again, they felt their status-Indian brothers were slamming the door in their face.

Bill Wilson's response was to withdraw from the Union executive and eventually, from the Union altogether. Phillip Paul, who had been working with Bob Manuel and Steve Point behind the scenes, put himself forward as Wilson's replacement and was re-elected to the open spot on the executive.

The return of Phillip Paul was a signal that the chaos precipitated by the Chilliwack conference had finally run its course. But the funding issue continued to be a cause of difficulties throughout the province. Most bands had quietly begun re-applying for government grants shortly after Chilliwack and the Department of Indian Affairs, pleased with the break in the solidarity of the BC Indians, was only too happy to find itself in a position of making separate deals with a hundred or so isolated chiefs.

By early 1977, the Union was forced to admit that "the motion to reject has not been a success and the blame for that failure can only be placed upon our shoulders."[8] The hangover after the Chilliwack excesses that had been dragging the Union down for more than a year was beginning to lift; it was time to begin rebuilding the Union.

» «

When George Manuel returned to BC in the fall of 1976, he assumed he would be heading the Aboriginal Rights Commission that Phillip Paul had said he was setting up. But after Chilliwack, the Union had no money to pay for the commission, so George Manuel contacted his former colleagues in the Native Brotherhood to see if they might be interested in making the commission a joint venture. The Brotherhood, which was still angling for the Union's lost government funding, refused.

While George Manuel was looking around for a funding source, Phillip Paul approached him about taking over the leadership of the Union. George's first reaction was to ask Paul about what happened to the Commission. Phillip Paul said something to the effect that in bringing George Manuel back to BC, the Commission "had already served its purpose."

George Manuel, who had done his share of people manipulation for the cause, smiled and said, "Phillip, you're a son-of-a-bitch."[9] Then he went to consult friends, like Doug Sanders, about whether or not he should take the job. Sanders knew George Manuel well enough to know he would never turn down such an offer. He merely pointed out the irony of George finding himself back in the same position he had been in at the beginning of the 1970s – taking over a barely functioning organization that was deeply in debt.

When George Manuel told Phillip Paul he would take the job, he did so with one condition. The three-person executive, he said, had turned the Union into a three-headed monster, with the heads spending more time plotting against each other than looking after day-to-day business. So he told Paul and the executive he would run only if the constitution was changed to allow for a single presidency.

Paul and the others agreed to the changes and called a special assembly in Prince George to hold an election for the new post of Union president.

When word went out that George Manuel was back and running for the presidency, the Union was given an immediate shot of adrenaline as activists who had drifted away after the Chilliwack fiasco suddenly remobilized themselves. The news was greeted with less enthusiasm, however, by those who were planning to build a new organization to compete with the Union.

As the Prince George conference approached, there were rumours of a large number of bands planning to pull out of the Union under the banner of the NB and a breakaway organization called the Alliance of BC Indians. When the delegates arrived in Prince George, they heard that a major show of force was in the works, with the dissidents preparing to stand up and march out of the conference hall.

But the show of force never materialized. Most of the bands that were supposed to leave remained in the hall to listen to George Manuel's speech after he was elected. And even the few delegates who walked out, returned to sit as "observers" until the conference was over. By the end of the conference, it was clear that George Manuel was firmly in control of a re-energized Union of British Columbia Indian Chiefs.

Along with the post of presidency, the new Union constitution provided for four regional vice-presidents, with Archie Patrick representing the Northern Region, Ray Jones representing the Coast, Don Moses representing the Central Interior and Phillip Paul representing the Southwest.

At a later executive council meeting in Kamloops, George Manuel invited the two former executive council members, Steve Point and his son, Bob, for a debriefing. After they had filled the new team in on what they had been doing over the past year, the two young leaders were ready to head home, content in the knowledge that they had provided a transition for the Union from the Chilliwack breakdown to George Manuel's return.

The new Union president, however, saw a continuing role for the two, and created quasi-cabinet posts for them with Bob Manuel looking after the Indian Act, Indian government and youth issues and Steve Point taking over the fisheries portfolio. The vice-presidents were also given portfolios with Phillip Paul looking after education, Don Moses economic development and Ray Jones social development.

For Bob Manuel, it meant that politics would be a full-time occupation. A few months earlier, in January 1977, he had been elected as the Neskainlith band chief, which had given him a political base of his own. In the ensuing years he would play a major role within the Union and build a national reputation that would eventually bring him to the verge of the NIB presidency.

At the time, George Manuel's most immediate concern was to rebuild the organization. His first priorities were the same as when he was building the NIB: putting together a team and acquiring funding.

In the wake of the Prince George conference, the Union opened offices on Hastings Street in Vancouver and George Manuel began to work his Ottawa contacts to have the Union's core and project funding restored. He used all of his skills at playing "the establishment Indian" with the Ottawa bureaucrats to get the money flowing again, and in a short time he had the Union's budget back to and beyond the 1975 level.

As the funding came in, George Manuel was already working on what he called his people machine. Most of the staff he hired during this period were young activists, and a number came from outside of BC.

One of the first hired was Millie Poplar, who was the daughter of Clara Tiyza, the representative from the Yukon on the National Advisory Board in the 1960s. She was given the job of special assistant to the president, and would work closely with him until the end of his life.

George Manuel later hired her sister, Rosalee Tiyza, as the education coordinator and then as his administrator, and she became a valued advisor who performed many of the same tasks Marie Marule had performed at the NIB.

George Manuel then hired Raymond Good, a coastal Salish activist, as his administrative assistant, and brought in Mary Lou Andrew as the specific research and legal coordinator.

Mary Lou Andrew put together her own team of young researchers. One of them recalls that the Union was an exciting place to be in those days, with young men and women with little formal training coming in and being put to work. Because of his national and international reputation, most of them saw George Manuel as a larger-than-life figure, to the point where some of the young Union workers began calling themselves "Manuelistas." The high (and perhaps even exaggerated) esteem in which the young workers held George Manuel added a sense of enthusiasm and self-sacrifice to the cause that would soon give the Union an impact on the national scene that far exceeded its numbers.

George Manuel was also able to make full use of his staff funding by laying off his workers when they had enough insurable weeks in the unemployment system and letting the government pay them while they continued their Union work until their benefit period ran out. Then he would hire them back and go through the rotation again. The wages, however, were never high. He paid himself and his vice-presidents the same wage, $18,000 a year, and during his tenure no one received a raise.

To round out his team, George Manuel brought in two non-Indian lawyers, Leslie Pinder and Louise Mandell. The latter, in fact, came to him. She was in her early twenties and just starting out in criminal and family law when she took a vacation to the Grand Canyon and had some sort of quasi-spiritual experience that caused her to quit her job. She was back in Vancouver and unemployed when she met a friend of hers, Art Pape, who was doing some contract work for the Union. He suggested that she see George Manuel about working for the Union.[10]

A meeting was set up in a coffee shop and Louise Mandell watched with interest as the large brown man limped in. She knew nothing about aboriginal rights or the Indian world but she was instantly impressed with George Manuel. For his part, George showed "a real human curiosity" about who she was.

Others had described Mandell as "a hippy lawyer" and this could account for George Manuel's curiosity. He often spoke of the counter-culture movement with a mixture of admiration and suspicion – admiration because they were eschewing the materialistic values of their parents, but suspicion that they were playing at poverty until they got bored with it and moved on to the lucrative careers that were reserved for people of their class.

In Mandell's case, George Manuel must have decided that she was the real article because he hired her as a lawyer and researcher for the Union.

Mandell was involved in the first concrete battle the Union pursued under George Manuel's leadership. At the time, the government was holding environmental hearings over a proposed oil terminal on the west coast. Two oil companies were competing for the right to build it, and Indian fishermen were opposing it because of the effects an oil spill would have on their livelihood.

The Union took up the fishermen's cause and George Manuel instructed Mandell to take a close look at the two competing bids for the terminal. She did, and she found that the two companies had sharply criticized each other's proposals on environmental grounds. George Manuel then suggested that she take those parts of the competing briefs and present it as the Union's case. She went to the hearings and argued that both the companies were right: the two proposals were dangerous to the environment. The government agreed and shelved the project; Mandell and the Union had their first legal victory under Manuel's stewardship. [11]

George Manuel's main preoccupation during this time, however, was broadening the base of support for the Union and promoting the battle for aboriginal rights among the grass roots. He travelled the province relentlessly, visiting communities and people he had met twenty years earlier in his NAIB days and speaking about the struggle for self-government and independence for Indian people.

Once again those around him were impressed by his single-minded dedication to the cause. If his car broke down or he ran out of gas on the way to a meeting, he would simply abandon it and head out on foot or hitchhike to the meeting and return for the car later.

Manuel also kept his staffers out in the field as much as possible. The land claims researchers were expected to begin their work by going onto the reserves and meeting with the elders to find out what they remembered of the land use in their childhood and from their parents' and grandparents' stories. The researchers were billeted out in the community and given a taste of how the people lived. One research assistant, Winona Stevenson, remembers that she spent her nights sleeping four to a bed with the three young girls of the host family while she was working in one of the northern communities.

When the researchers brought the information back to the office in Vancouver, they began their archival work with the oral histories as a guide. When there were contradictions between the archives and the oral history, it was assumed the archives were wrong until proven otherwise.

As the Union grew, George Manuel also set up a resource centre and in-house clipping service and hired Beth Cuthand as his communication coordinator. One of the primary jobs of the communications branch was to put out the newsletter and publicize local and provincial meetings that began to grow in size and frequency until some assemblies drew crowds of more than three thousand people.

The gatherings always had a strong cultural component and many of them had the same energy that had driven the Chilliwack conference into the premature rejection of funds. But this time the leadership was there to focus the radicalism toward realizable goals at the local and provincial level.

The huge gatherings also served as a warning to the governments in Ottawa and Victoria that Indian power in BC was a reality that, sooner or later, they would have to deal with. As George Manuel explained to his workers, "politics is a public act." The native movement would only succeed if it clearly articulated its goals, then showed the government that the people were willing to back up their demands in the streets.[12]

Manuel signalled this approach when he arrived back in BC and went out to lunch with the regional director of Indian Affairs, Fred Walchli. He told Walchli point-blank that he intended to start a peoples' movement that would have "a consistent ideology of struggle" against the government.

Walchli was equally frank. "It will be my job then," he said, "to fight you every step of the way." When the lunch was finished, two men shook hands and began a five-year battle.[13]

According to some who were close to George Manuel, there was a notable exception to his practice of "public" politics. He and Phillip Paul were planning to use civil disobedience as part of their peoples' power campaign and they feared the movement might face the same type of government repression that had made Indian organizing illegal in Canada from 1927 to 1951.

To protect the movement, they began setting up a parallel underground organization, with separate cells at the community level, so the Union could be kept alive and functioning even if it was declared illegal. Manuel even went so far as to invite an IRA leader to the Union office for private discussions on the politics of the underground.[14]

Eventually, George Manuel's underground organization would be tapped, but for a different purpose: marching on Ottawa to fight the Liberal government's constitutional changes. But rumours of the organization led to the belief among the radical wing of the movement that Manuel was a modern "War Chief" who was ready, if necessary, to lead his people into battle.

While George Manuel was busy building his peoples' movement, he did not neglect his commitment to the World Council of Indigenous Peoples. In fact, with his release from the burdens of national leadership and the endless cross-country travelling, he was able to devote more time to the WCIP.

One pressing problem that had to be addressed by the WCIP during this period was the fate of Constantino Lima, a Bolivian delegate at the Port Alberni conference, who had been imprisoned when he returned to his homeland.

When George Manuel and the rest of the Canadian organizers heard of the arrest, they arranged to have his three daughters flown to Canada. After a great deal of lobbying, Constantino was freed in May 1977, and given refuge in Canada with the rest of his family. Upon his arrival, Constantino's friends discovered that he had been tortured in prison. This information created a growing concern for WCIP contacts in other Latin American countries under the heel of right-wing dictatorships.

George Manuel took the Bolivian with him when he travelled to Panama in February 1977 to attend the WCIP conference that would formally launch the Central American regional organization. The Panama meeting had delegations from Canada, the US, Scandinavia, Guatemala, Nicaragua, and, for the first time, from Costa Rica and El Salvador.

The meeting got off to a rocky start when the Salvadoran delegation protested their exclusion from the Port Alberni assembly, but George

Manuel had no patience for dealing with things that couldn't be changed. He told the Salvadorans they weren't invited because the Port Alberni organizers didn't know they existed. But they had to begin somewhere. "So you are here now. And you are going to be part of whatever decisions we make now. So don't complain about what happened in 1975. Do something now."[15]

Despite the awkward start, the Panama meeting did accomplish its goals of setting up a regional branch with representatives of all of the countries of Central America. After it was over, the WCIP executive met and the Sami delegation offered to host the next WCIP biennial assembly in Kiruna, Sweden, in October.

The theme of the conference was to be "the situation of indigenous peoples and international agreements relating to human rights and the protection of lands." In the lead up to the conference, there was a sense of optimism that the new American president, Jimmy Carter, would provide an opening for pursuing the indigenous rights issue with his promised campaign to promote human rights around the world. As Doug Sanders pointed out, the new interest in human rights in other peoples' backyards could only help the Fourth World movement, which depended on international recognition of their national status.

By the time the Kiruna conference opened, an unexpected issue arose that dominated the proceedings. The apartheid government of Rhodesia was in the process of collapsing and white Rhodesians were flooding into countries like Chile, where right-wing dictators were in power. Other Western countries, like Canada and Australia, were also opening their doors to the white Rhodesians, under the pretext that it would help relieve the pressures of the civil war.

A Chilean delegate brought the matter to the WCIP assembly by complaining that the "ex-African white fascist settlers" were bringing their white supremacist ideology with them into his country. An Australian Aborigine confirmed that the same thing was happening in his country, with some Rhodesians showing up as government agents overseeing reserves in Queensland.[16]

George Manuel picked up the issue, receiving wide coverage in Canada when he condemned his government for giving the Rhodesians special immigration status. He called on the government to set an example by treating the Rhodesians as "common criminals."

George Manuel also blasted the U.S. for refusing to offer funds to the American chapter of the Council. He pointed out that American agencies had promised $92,000 for the founding meeting of the WCIP but had later backed out and refused to consider any more funding requests. The reason for this sudden blanket rejection, George Manuel suggested, was that the American government had "a major interest in what happens in Central and South America," and was trying to block WCIP organizing in the region.[17]

The lack of funding had meant that many of the American delegates had to stay at home, as did more than two dozen other delegations who couldn't afford to make the trip. Still, the thirty-eight delegations that were present passed a resolution urging the UN to take a lead in trying to stop "all violent actions and measures against indigenous peoples."

The UN was also asked "to recognize that indigenous peoples are nations and not tribes," and that "aboriginal land rights never can be extinguished." The delegates also condemned government policies of assimilation and demanded that indigenous people have the right to define who they are.

There was an interesting confrontation at the conference when a United Nations representative from Mexico told the delegates that it must "be good to live in Canada where there is no war and violence." Harry Daniels challenged the remark by saying that "the native people of Canada represent three per cent of the general population and yet fifty per cent of the jail population.

"I do not call this a country," Daniels concluded, "without war and violence."[18]

The Latin Americans then joined in and lambasted the Mexican government for refusing to recognize the Indians as a distinct people in Mexico. The attack widened when Constantino Lima stood up and charged that all Latin American governments were oppressing the indigenous people.

In the aftermath of the conference, George Manuel received quite a bit of personal press when a CP reporter did a couple of profile pieces on him. As the reporter saw it, "George Manuel had a bagful of excuses to sit out his life in self-pity and let the state support him.

"Instead, he set off with a crippled hip and a grade-two education to become one of the world's most respected and influential native leaders." The reporter asked him about rumours that he had originally returned to BC to run for Parliament. George Manuel admitted that he had been approached by all three parties, but said that "It's meaningless to be an Indian MP in terms of helping Indian people."

What the Indian people needed was to gather their own source of political power within their own communities and organizations because the "Canadian government will deal with you according to how much political power you have."[19]

George Manuel's own stature in the movement increased still further when he returned to Canada and it was leaked that the International Working Group on Indigenous Affairs had nominated him for the Nobel Peace Prize for his role in launching and leading the World Council of Indigenous Peoples. The 1977 nomination turned out to be the first of three, as he was renominated in 1978 and 1979. Winning was always a long shot, however. In 1977, the award went to Amnesty International, in 1978 it went to Anwar Sadat and Menahem Begin and the 1979 winner was the international Catholic crowd-pleaser, Mother Teresa. Still, simply being nominated added to George Manuel's aura of political invincibility. Around this time, some of his colleagues in the movement nicknamed him "Shogun" after the Japanese warlord, whose genius for political plotting won him the leadership of the empire, in James Clavell's novel of the same name.[20]

At the same time, George Manuel's personal life became the subject of speculation. Rumours began to circulate that the jokes at the celebrity roast about George Manuel's "extra-marital hanky panky" had been based in fact and it was noted that when he came back from the WCIP assembly in Kiruna, George was followed by a small Sami woman dressed in traditional Sami costume, complete with the turned-up shoes.

She remained his travelling companion in Canada for some time before she returned home, apparently carrying George Manuel's tenth child. The boy was born in Sweden and named Ara Manuel. George Manuel accepted his fatherhood and the affair was a serious but, as it turned out, not fatal strain on his marriage to Marlene.

George Manuel had improved as a husband and father since the 1950s, but apparently he still had a way to go.

## CHAPTER SEVENTEEN

# The Peoples' Movement

## 1977-1979

We will no longer live on our knees . . .

George Manuel
President's address, 1978

When George Manuel arrived in Duncan as a community development worker in the mid-1960s, he used the housing issue to rouse the community into collective action. In his first two years at the NIB, Indian control over education had been used to the same effect. In British Columbia in 1977-78, the lightning rod was Indian fishing rights.

Fishing became a major concern during the summer of 1977 when BC Indians were systematically harassed by provincial agents who raided their fishing grounds with tracking dogs and a back-up force of RCMP officers. Louise Mandell was kept busy in the courts. During the winter of 1977-78 she handled no less than sixty-four Indian fishing cases and to the great chagrin of the fishery agents, she won every single one of them.

Despite Mandell and the Union's success in court, the fact that the province was stepping up patrols of the rivers gave rise to suspicions that something was afoot. These suspicions were confirmed when the provincial government announced that it was going to replace the old Indian Fishing Permit with an Indian Food Fishing Licence.

At the time, Indians were allowed to catch as many salmon as they wanted, but they had to clip the nose and the dorsal fin as soon as they were caught. Fish marked in this way were then ineligible for sale. This implicit prohibition against Indians selling their fish would be made explicit with the new Indian Food Fishing License.

More important, the introduction of the new license allowed Fish and Game officers to challenge someone with a large quantity of fish, whether they were clipped or not, and demand that they prove the fish were for their own consumption. Once fishery agents began questioning the number of fish in an individual's possession, it would be a simple step to introduce quotas for the Indian fishery.

The fishery issue was one that both touched the BC Indian people at the gut level and fit into George Manuel's overall self-government drive. At the time, he and the new Union executive were working on a twenty-four point Aboriginal Rights Position Paper that outlined self-government powers for the First Nations in a wide range of areas.

The Aboriginal Rights Position Paper was an expanded and much more detailed version of Manuel's national Indian philosophy. The document supplied the movement with a detailed political manifesto that spelled out the foundations of Indian government by outlining the "twenty-four separate rights that had been usurped by the federal or provincial governments" and that had to be recaptured by the Indian nations. It was by far the most sophisticated and radical document of its kind ever put together by the Indian movement and it would eventually be adopted at the national level by the NIB as the basic self-government strategy for the First Nations.

On the fishery, the position paper stated that Indians had to recoup exclusive jurisdiction of "all fish resources contained with the waterways that are established as being associated with our Indian Reserve Lands."[1] The key words here were "associated with." Manuel's plan called for absolute control over both the conservation and the possible commercialization of the salmon fishery in broad areas of the BC interior. If the Union won on this front, it would set an important precedent for winning the other twenty-four items of the self-government blueprint.

George Manuel's first move on the fishery was to organize a province-wide Fish Forum in Vancouver in December 1977. The conference was attended by a hundred delegates from the Union and the Native Brotherhood and Manuel opened the meeting by throwing out a challenge. "It is you," he told the delegates, "who are going to decide if fishing is a problem, and if it is a crisis, what we are going to do about it?"[2]

During the conference, the Union leader signalled how important he considered the issue by debating Wally Johnstone, a federal representative at the Forum. After Johnstone's vague opening remarks, George Manuel said he was "appalled at how unprepared you are in coming to this meeting," and he accused the fishery officers of incompetence. BC Indians, he said, were "victims of oppressive laws" and were insulted by the nose and fin clipping regulations, which they saw as an attack on their integrity."[3]

Wally Johnstone sputtered something about not all Indians being perfect either, and then pleaded, "But for God's sake give me a chance."[4]

But George Manuel was not willing to give Wally Johnstone, or any other government official, a chance. He had already set up a Legal Fish Committee headed by Louise Mandell that was following Manuel's two-pronged political and legal strategy, which involved playing as much to the court of public opinion as to the court of justice.

To score public-opinion points, the Committee focused on cases like that of Peter Dennis Peters, an elder from the Hope Indian band, who was charged with fishing on a forbidden day. Under persistent cross-examination in court, the old man broke down and wept, admitting that he had been fishing, but only to get food for his daughter, who had broken her leg and couldn't work.

While a steady stream of similar stories of government harassment were being fed to the press, Mandell and her five researchers were busy preparing a legal defence that would be based on the BC Indians aboriginal rights to the land and waterways.

In preparing her case, Mandell went back to a 1881 Royal Commission that had granted BC Indians the right to fish as a part of their basic "right to a way of life."[5] It wasn't long before she had an opportunity to test the defense. In July, eight members of the Lillooet band, including George Manuel's old friend Victor Adolph, openly defied the fishing regulations with an illegal "fish-in." Fifty band members gathered to offer their support and there was a festive atmosphere until a force of twenty fisheries officers crashed the party.

When the officers moved in to make arrests, a shouting match began, then a scuffle broke out and both sides took their share of lumps.

The next day, George Manuel reacted to what he saw as the fisheries officials' attack on his people by announcing that native violence "in the form of sophisticated civil disobedience" was a real possibility if the governments continued to deny basic aboriginal rights.

When pressed by reporters, he explained that some of his people "have come to me, telling me that negotiations for the past hundred years have not got us anywhere . . . and are saying the only way to go is violence." He admitted that he had been seriously thinking about the same thing.[6]

The Union leader went even further the next day when he charged that the fisheries officials were using terrorist tactics and announced that Indians were prepared "to meet violence with violence." In a reference to the underground organization he and Phillip Paul had set up, he warned that: "An army of BC Indians is standing by to undergo weapons and combat training to defend and assert native rights."[7]

Manuel went on to describe a secret hide-out where the training would take place and said that these foot soldiers of the movement would be sent to trouble spots across the province when they were needed.

The fiery rhetoric and his threat to meet violence with violence had a sobering effect on the fisheries officials who admitted that they were "very worried" by the remarks. But they also brought the Union a new enemy when the influential BC Wildlife Federation entered into the fray.

George Manuel had been trying to win at least the Federation's neutrality on the Indian fishing issue for months. He had twice led Union delegations to the Wildlife Federation's meetings to argue that the BC Indians and the Federation were natural allies in the battle to conserve the salmon stocks. He cited government figures that showed that of the 23.5 million salmon caught in BC waters in the previous two years, the commercial fishery had taken twenty-two million, the sport fishermen one million and the Indians only five hundred thousand. It was the commercial fishery, along with industrial pollution of the spawning grounds and coastal waters, Manuel argued, that was killing off a resource the BC Indians had husbanded for thousands of years.

After his threat of unleashing a sort of Indian militia on the province, the head of the BC Wildlife Federation broke off all dealings with George Manuel and vowed to fight "the Indian rip-off of Canada's resources," no matter what kind of forces the Union was amassing.[8]

The negative effects of George Manuel's rhetoric on the Wildlife Federation was offset, however, by the galvanizing effect it had on BC Indian activists. After Manuel's announcement that he was prepared to meet force with force, Indians across the province began to defy the government regulations with a new wave of fish-ins, and BC wildlife officers were kept busy carting Indian men and women off to jail.

As the court dockets began to overflow, Crown lawyers approached the Union with a deal to use the first Lillooet case, against Bradley Bob, as a test case. The Crown would hold back on all the cases using the same defence as Bradley Bob until after his trial. If the Union won, all other charges would be dropped. If the Union lawyers lost, all of the Indians charged with illegal fishing were to plead guilty.

George Manuel flatly rejected the offer and informed the prosecutor that no matter what the outcome of the Bradley case, Indian men and women charged with illegal fishing would continue to seek every recourse through the courts. If that clogged up the justice system, too bad.[9]

While the Crown prosecutors and the fisheries department watched in exasperation, Manuel continued to turn up the rhetorical flame. In September he described the fisheries department as: "Enemy Number One," because the "Fisheries enforcement officers were treating my people in the same way the Germans treated the Jews in the Second World War." He then accused department officials of trying to by-pass the Union with attempts to make separate agreements with individual bands that would limit Indian fishing. He called on the bands to reject the department's 'Nazi' methods.[10]

Up to this point, George Manuel's battle had been with the provincial government, and at the DIA headquarters in Vancouver, officials were left scratching their heads at what they saw as George Manuel's overkill on the issue. But the Union leader's motives became more clear in the lead-up to the Union's Annual General Assembly in Penticton in April 1978, when George Manuel began to tie the radicalism over the fishery issue to the larger battle for Indian government.

At a press conference in Vancouver, he announced that BC Indians wanted not only the restoration of their traditional fishing rights, but the control of their lands and resources, social programs, health care and justice system. To back up the claim, he once again contrasted Canada's three hundred thousand Indians with the much smaller Prince Edward Island population, and asked why the Indians were left with none of the powers and with half the financial resources of the tiny province.

To rectify this situation, the Union was designing a new Indian Act that would not begin by delegating powers to the Indian nations, but with Indian people deciding what powers they would transfer to the federal government, the provincial government and their own organizations. In other words, the Indian nations' inherent right to self-government, based on thousands of years of independence, would have to be the starting point of any negotiations with the Canadian government.[11]

By the time the Penticton Assembly began, the fishing rights dispute had been neatly melded into the overall fight for sovereignty and the eight hundred delegates were kept busy in workshops exploring every available avenue in that larger struggle. One of the essential elements would be a demand for greatly expanded reserve lands to form self-supporting national communities. George Manuel took the opportunity to once again reject any thought of a cash-for-land settlement with the government, even "if it's a hundred billion dollars."[12]

In his address to the Assembly, he explained that "The work that needs to be done for us to manage our Indian government is a monumental task. But I challenge you to keep pace with the job that we must do as Indian people.

"Self determination has to be our goal in our quest to recover the lands, energy, resources and political authority that we have entrusted to the White political institutions. We are saying that for the past hundred years we gave you, the White government, the responsibility to manage our lands, energy, resources and our political authority. You have mismanaged that trust and responsibility. Now we are taking it back into our hands and we will manage our own resources through our Indian political institutions."

He then urged his people to continue the type of militancy they had shown in the fishing dispute in other areas as well. "I'm going to be a leader in this fight," he said, "and I hope that I will have your support, and that in every band you will take the kind of action that is needed to protect and defend our rights."[13]

Manuel then tabled the Union's twenty-four point Aboriginal Rights Position Paper, and asked the delegates to take the document back to their communities, explain its provisions to the elders and the rest of the people, then listen for feedback. Like the 1960 brief to the Joint Parliamentary Committee, it was to serve as an organizing tool and a focal point of debate as well as a political blueprint for future action.

As it turned out, its introduction could not have been more timely. While the Aboriginal Rights Position Paper was being debated across the province, Prime Minister Trudeau launched his drive to patriate the constitution in a way that would have incalculable effects on Indian rights.

» «

Among the Indian leaders in Canada, George Manuel had the best grasp of the constitutional issue and how central it was to the position of the First Nations. The constitution had been a concern of his since his early days at the NIB when he demanded that Indian people "be given full opportunity to participate in all future federal-provincial deliberations on amending the constitution of Canada."[14]

But Trudeau's new constitutional offensive in 1978 made no reference to aboriginal or treaty rights. His package, titled "A Time For Action," was focused on entrenching the two founding nations concept, but with a strong central government "with real powers which apply to all parts of the country." In addition, Trudeau insisted that the package include a charter of rights and freedoms that would be binding on the federal and provincial governments. His timetable called for the new constitution to be enacted by the end of 1981.[15]

The first thing that George Manuel had noticed when he had looked at Trudeau's proposals was the most obvious – that they contained nothing about aboriginal rights. But he also quickly seized on the inclusion of a binding charter of rights. He remembered Doug Sanders's advice during the Lavell case that if the Bill of Rights had been judged to have more force than the Indian Act, the whole special status of Indian people, including their reserve lands and hunting and fishing rights, could be overturned by the courts.

To get a second opinion, George Manuel phoned Walter Rudnicki in Ottawa and asked him to prepare a brief on the possible effects of the constitution on Indian treaty and aboriginal rights.

Rudnicki told George he hadn't "even read the damn thing," but as soon as he got off the phone he went down to the government book store and picked up a copy. A few days later he sent a detailed opinion to the effect that "aboriginal people were being totally excluded from any consideration within the constitution. No rights were being entrenched and nothing was being elaborated in terms of the existing section 124."[16]

Similar concerns were beginning to be felt at the NIB. Dave Monture was working for Noel Starblanket at the time and he was shown a copy of the preamble to the constitution with everything whited out except the reference to the indigenous people. It consisted of one sentence that acknowledged their existence. That was all they were going to get out of the Trudeau proposal, a sentence in the preamble, while the rest of the document threatened to reduce dramatically their historic rights within Canada.

At the Union offices, there was a sense that Noel Starblanket and the NIB hadn't understood the full impact the constitutional changes could have on treaty and aboriginal rights in Canada. Starblanket had surrounded himself with a young, generally well-educated Indian staff who had acted as competent administrators but lacked both the experience and the creativity needed to take on the federal government on an issue as fundamental as the constitution.

Bob Manuel was the Union's liaison with the NIB at the time and he remembers being unimpressed with Starblanket's leadership. He also suspected that Starblanket and his people in Saskatchewan had played a role in ushering his father out of the NIB leadership and he resented him for that. As the Union rep at the NIB, he had at first tried to make life difficult for Starblanket, but when he told his father about this, George wasn't at all pleased.

"If you're doing that for me," he said, "it's totally wrong. I want you to support him one hundred per cent. I held that position and I know what it's like. We're the last ones who want to make trouble for him."[17]

George Manuel would, in fact, back Starblanket for a second term at the fall 1978 NIB Assembly in Fredericton – although he did it in such a way as to signal that he personally intended to continue to play a role on the national scene. Instead of sending the BC delegates to deposit their ballots one-by-one, he made a show of collecting all of the ballots from the BC delegation and personally depositing them in the ballot box.

The gesture symbolized Manuel's continuing influence on the national scene and this role would once again become a dominant one. By 1978, he was, in many ways, in a stronger position than Noel Starblanket to carry out a national campaign against the constitution. He had at his disposal seventy-five Union staffers, as opposed to the fifty-four who were working for the NIB in Ottawa. But more important, George Manuel had the vision, the political intuitions and the ability to inspire the people at the grass-roots level that Starblanket's NIB seemed to lack.

During the summer and fall of 1978, the NIB was pinning its hopes on the Trudeau package collapsing on its own, or at least with a little help from Canada's ten premiers. The premiers had met in Regina in August, describing the Trudeau proposals as "unworkable and a threat to Parliamentary democracy" and vowing to fight him every step of the way. [18]

George Manuel was sceptical about the premiers' hectoring, however. He knew his way around Ottawa and the provincial capitals well enough to be aware of the kind of deals Trudeau could strike with the individual provinces to bring them on side. He had once suggested that Canadian confederation had been built on a hundred years of back-room deals and he suspected Trudeau was capable of carrying on the tradition. [19] So he continued to search for a legal or political way to fight the patriation drive from his home base.

It was a battle he believed could be won only if the First Nations drew on the strength of their indigenous cultures, because for him the constitution fight was about two radically different conceptions of the country. In a series of speeches, he urged the people to begin the fight for their liberation by rejecting the white man's values, particularly the "value of accumulating material wealth." This individual materialism, he said, could destroy "the heart and soul of our Indian institutions, our languages, our governing authority" and the only way to fight against it was to embrace "collective Indian power" and confront the white man and his constitutional manoeuvring head on.

"We will no longer live on our knees," he said. "From now on we will stand and fight on our feet, if necessary we will die on our feet fighting for our Indian rights." [20]

» «

In 1978, George Manuel was still grasping for a strategy to confront the Trudeau government. He had set the Union lawyers on a word-by-word examination of Trudeau's constitutional package and he was quietly getting in touch with his fellow leaders across the country to sound them out on the issue. But he still had not decided how to use his people machine, which was revved up after the Penticton Assembly, in the constitutional battle.

In fact, his attention during this period was diverted by a small but growing challenge to the Union from the more conservative ranks of the Indian movement. One of the leading figures was, once again, Bill Wilson.

After the Courtenay meeting, when his last ditch attempt to merge the Union and BCANSI failed, Bill Wilson and his BCANSI contact, Bill Lightbown settled on an "if you can't join them, beat them" strategy. If the Union would not merge with BCANSI, then they would try to lure the Union's supporters into a new organization that they themselves controlled.

In June 1976, BCANSI officially changed its constitution to allow status Indians to become members, To accommodate the new membership, BCANSI also changed its name to United Native Nations (UNN), which was later temporarily expelled from the Native Council of Canada for its inclusion of both status and non-status members.

As Paul Tennant explained, Bill Wilson emerged as the most prominent figure in the organization. He had been waiting in the wings during the final BCANSI meeting "even though, as a status-Indian, he could not be a member until the change in eligibility was approved, at which point he joined. With Bill Lightbown's support, he was then elected as first president of the United Native Nations."[21]

Shortly after his rejection by the Union delegates, then, Bill Wilson was back on the BC political scene with his own organization and he was already working with another former Union militant, George Watts, on a plan to replace the Union as the representative organization of BC Indians. For their part, the Union activists saw Bill Wilson's return as part of an orchestrated campaign by the three "W"s: Bill Wilson, George Watts and Fred Walchli, the DIA's regional superintendent, to overthrow the Union.

Wilson had begun working with the second "W," George Watts, a few months earlier, when they bumped into each other in the Nelson Place bar in Vancouver. The two men had never been friends and reportedly had little respect for one another, but when they met in the bar that evening and had a few drinks, they discovered that they had a lot of common concerns.

George Watts had been one of the main proponents of the funding rejection resolution in Chilliwack, but in the aftermath he had quit his position on the Union's executive committee and pulled his Nuchanlith Tribal Council, which comprised three Vancouver Island and coastal bands, out of the Union. In 1977, Wilson and Watts, along with the

Native Brotherhood bands that had been trying to get the Union's funding, joined together in a Coalition of Native Indians and made a number of failed attempts to build an organization that could supplant the Union.

In 1978, George Manuel's stature in BC, along with his considerable pull in Ottawa, was able to stave off any immediate threat to his political base. But he obviously saw trouble in the future, because he told the Union members not to be overly concerned about losing the Union as an institution, reminding them that the role of the Union was to serve the people, not to build a bureaucratic empire. "If we lose it," he told his staff, "we lose it. So be it."[22]

On the constitution issue, George Manuel made a concerted attempt to form at least a working relationship with Wilson and Watts and the Native Brotherhood throughout 1978 and 1979. As early as January 1978, he met privately with the UNN and NB leadership to feel them out on their positions on a wide range of issues.

The meetings were a disappointment. The breakaway leaders criticized the Union's structure because it was built on the power of the bands. What they favoured were tribal-based organizations, which, they argued, were the historical organizational unit of the First Nations.

George Manuel rejected the idea, however. He had often pointed to the fact that the First Nations were overrun by the whites because they were divided into fifty-odd tribes and were unable to coordinate their resistance to the invasion. He also worried that breaking up the movement into purely tribal organizations would have serious implications on the legal and constitutional battles since the Indian lands that were kept in trust by the federal government were not Shuswap lands or Blackfoot lands, but the lands of Canada's six hundred or so individual bands.

In negotiating the land claims, George Manuel believed, the Union had to act on behalf of the bands, who were recognized as the legal holders of the lands and who ultimately had the authority to sign an agreement with the government. The only alternative would be to set up and incorporate an Indian association that would negotiate with the government on a tribal basis. But this corporation would also have to function within the rules of the Provincial or Federal Corporate Act. And this, George Manuel feared, would end up in assimilating the Indians into the white system in the same manner as the James Bay Agreement had.

In fact, in 1974 Andrew Delisle had pointed out that the forced incorporation of the Crees in negotiating their claims with Quebec had been an important tool in the government's bag of tricks. In order to receive legal funds in their battle, the Crees were forced to incorporate. Once that was accomplished, the power went from the people at the band level to the legal corporation, whose directors had sole authority to dispose of the Indian land. It was much easier for the government to pressure the Indian corporate director over dinner at an expensive restaurant than it was for the government to pressure the men and women on the reserve.

Despite George Manuel's fears, he still did not close the door on cooperation with Wilson, Watts and the others. He wrote in UBCIC *News* that the Union "had no intention to persuade or compel any of our people to support our Indian government position. There is room for two land claims positions. As a matter of fact, I would be prepared to support such a position if it was a clearly stated position. Providing, of course, our Indian Government position paper is supported by that group also."[23]

But George Manuel found that "No one from either the Native Brotherhood or the United Native Nations would respond to the Union's position on Indian Government. . . . I have to interpret their silence on "Indian Government" to mean that both organizations do *not* support the position of Indian Government by the Union of BC Indian Chiefs."[24]

The dissidents' refusal to endorse the principles of Indian government re-affirmed the suspicion of many in the Union that the only real aim of the "W"s was to destroy the organization from without, after they had failed to destroy it from within.[25] It is not certain whether George Manuel himself was convinced of this, but Saul Terry, the young Bridge River chief who had been elected as his vice-president, remembers that during the meetings with the breakaway leaders, George Manuel would ask them what their philosophy was in working for Indian people.

He was disappointed when he was unable to get a clear answer to his simple, though fundamental, question. In the end, George Manuel suspected the reason for their silence was either that they had no clear philosophy at all, or that "they had a philosophy for every occasion," which amounted to the same thing.[26]

But with or without a clear direction, it was becoming obvious that Bill Wilson and George Watts were after the Union's funding, an ironic move when you consider that both of them had backed the Chilliwack resolution rejecting government funding on the grounds that it would result in the creation of a passive brown bureaucracy.

Watts and Wilson began to have some success only after they joined forces with the third "W," Fred Walchli, who began to speak on their behalf in Ottawa. Even then, that success wasn't immediate. The regional superintendent discovered an initial reluctance among the politicians to take on George Manuel in BC, where any direct move to fund a rival group to the Union would be interpreted as an attack on the NIB affiliate in the province. The Department of Indian Affairs was also concerned about direct funding of Bill Wilson's UNN, since it included non-status Indians who were not covered under the Indian Act.

To overcome the DIA objections, Wilson and his allies called a province-wide conference of the UNN, the Native Brotherhood and the tribal groups to show their support. When Ottawa objected to funding the conference without the Union, which was, after all, the sole recognized representative of BC status Indians, the organizers agreed to let the Union send two delegates. The Department then agreed to fund the conference and to send a DIA representative.

But George Manuel refused to send any Union people, since the conference was "being organized on a tribal basis and there isn't any recognition of Bands and Band Councils as the governing structures with authority. The UBCIC structure recognizes status Indians by way of their chiefs, and our goal is to strengthen Band Councils. . . . Strong Band Councils are going to be at the heart of our land claims and we are very concerned that our work not be undermined by this tribal structure."[27]

The conference went on without Union participation and at the end the delegates decided to form a new organization, the Aboriginal Council of British Columbia, or as it popularly became known, "Abco." The founding meeting was set for May 1979, but as Paul Tennant observed, it was a lacklustre affair with many of the delegates selected by the meeting's organizers rather than by their own tribal groups. With the exceptions of Joe Mathias and George Watts, the political leaders of the tribal groups seemed unwilling to align themselves with any new province-wide body."[28]

Still, the polarization bothered George Manuel and he tried to make peace with members within Bill Wilson's camp. It was around this time that he called Ron George, a young activist who had moved with Wilson from BCANSI to the UNN and was playing a prominent role in the new organization. George Manuel invited him out to dinner and Ron George remembers he was surprised at the invitation. In UNN quarters, George Manuel was painted as the enemy and Ron George was further surprised during the dinner when he found himself impressed by Manuel's openness and intelligence. Later, it was this impression of George Manuel and his growing dissatisfaction with Wilson and Watts, that led to Ron George throwing his lot in with the Union during the constitutional battle.

» «

While George Manuel was looking for allies within Bill Wilson's own backyard, he continued to carry out his politics of protest at the national level. When the health minister, Monique Begin, announced a cutback of health services to Indian communities, the UBCIC leader joined other leaders of the NIB in calling for a meeting with the minister. Begin agreed and George Manuel flew to Ottawa to meet with her and her advisors.

To illustrate the point that he considered the cutbacks a betrayal of old agreements, George Manuel brought a ceremonial blanket to give to Monique Begin as a symbol of the blankets that had been given to the Indians at the time of the treaties. But when he made the presentation, he also referred to the blankets intentionally infected with smallpox that were reportedly given to some American native people in the nineteenth century.

As he handed over the gift, one of Monique's Begin's officials grabbed her arm and warned her not to take it because he feared that George Manuel had put some kind of poison on it. The minister was momentarily confused while George Manuel stood dumbfounded at the ignorance of the men and women who still held dominion over his people.[29]

To her credit, Monique Begin later called the UBCIC president and apologized for the slight, but by then, Begin and her Liberal colleagues were on their way out. A few months after the incident, Pierre Trudeau called a long-overdue election and Joe Clark led the Progressive Conservatives to a narrow minority-government victory.

During the campaign, George Manuel had backed the NDP, yet he welcomed the Conservative victory because it temporarily halted

Trudeau's constitution drive and because he had made some friends within the Conservative party during their long haul in opposition. The most important was Flora MacDonald, who had been her party's Indian Affairs critic in the mid-1970s and had often visited George Manuel's NIB office for information and advice during the James Bay fight.

After the 1979 election, MacDonald became the Minister for External Affairs and George Manuel and Doug Sanders made a courtesy call to her Parliament Hill office and asked for funding for the World Council of Indigenous Peoples.

Flora greeted them warmly and agreed to have the Canadian International Development Agency supply core funding to the WCIP. The eventual grant of $500,000 over a three-year period put the WCIP on a solid financial footing for the first time in its four-year history. The organization was then able to use the precedent of Canadian government aid as a lever to pry funding from Norway and other Scandinavian governments who agreed to match Ottawa in making regular contributions to the World Council.

In 1978, the executive council of the WCIP held its annual meeting in Argentina. It was a time when the country was ruled by an oppressive military regime, so the WCIP was forced to curtail its public sittings and concentrate on the cultural aspects of the movement. The Canadian delegation had brought a troupe of Plains dancers and they were in turn entertained by South American Indian dances, music and theatre.

This part of the conference was widely televised in Argentina, but the real meetings went on behind closed doors where the Canadian delegates asked what they could do to help their brothers and sisters. Someone suggested a solidarity tour in the north where the country's beleaguered Indian population had been pushed. Despite the danger, George Manuel and Marie Marule readily agreed to go.

They embarked on the eight-hundred kilometre bus trip with a representative of the Indigenous Association of Argentina, but they were met in the region by Argentine security forces, who were then in the process of bringing the "the peace of the graveyard" to Argentina. The military men told George Manuel and Marie Marule point-blank that they were not to speak with any of the *indigenes* of the region.

The warning was taken seriously by the Canadian Embassy, which suddenly offered to fly George Manuel and Marie Marule back to Buenos Aires for their own protection. They refused the offer because they feared that if they left the Argentineans who were with them behind, they would be arrested or simply "disappeared" by the security forces.

While George Manuel and Marie Marule were in the region, the only place they could meet with the local Indian leaders was in the local Catholic churches where a few priests dared to criticize the military dictatorship from the pulpit. But even the churches had lookouts and when they were alerted that the military was in the area, the congregation would immediately begin singing hymns to cover up the whispered voices of protest.

» «

George Manuel made another trip south in 1979, when he travelled to Peru with Doug Sanders and Dave Monture to attend a meeting of the Council's South American branch, which was held in the countryside in Oriente Tambo. Dave Monture remembers that George was still concerned that the leaders of the national Indian organizations were not truly representative of their respective peoples and so he tried to spend as much time as possible with the local people.

One incident in Peru that stuck in Monture's mind happened just before the conference started. He and George Manuel were staying in a neighbouring village about a mile away from the conference site and they were on their way to the meeting when George suddenly strolled off the road toward a group of adobe huts. "It was like the pied piper," Monture recalled, with the children smiling and surrounding the limping stranger.

While he was encircled by the children, George turned to Monture, told him to go ahead to the meeting and said he would catch up later.

Monture watched while George Manuel, who spoke not a word of Spanish, ducked into one of the huts and sat down. His surprised hosts soon produced some food and a cup of home made chi-chi beer. Villagers from the other huts heard about the honoured guest and they began to flock to the house where he was sitting on the mud floor eating and drinking with his new-found friends. He stayed for almost two hours while the leaders and the official delegates grew more and more impatient.

When word got around that George Manuel was visiting with the people, Monture remembers that the local leaders began to get nervous.

As in Scandinavia, the leadership was concerned that Manuel's personal charisma would somehow undermine their local authority and they were wondering what kind of political message he was sending them by delaying the meeting while he sat with the villagers.

While they were still trying to analyze the gesture, George Manuel came into view and limped up to the podium in the centre of the square. He noticed that the women and men were divided, with the men front and centre and women to the side, so before he spoke, he went over to the women and presented them with gifts.

Then, with Rodrigo Contreras translating, he made what Monture described as an "incredibly friendly speech" in which "he won the hearts and minds of everyone there, and had everyone laughing. And totally dispelled a tense situation in which the local leaders were suspicious of him for arriving late and undercutting them politically with the masses."

As Monture saw it, George Manuel "had an absolute instinct, without speaking their language, without being totally briefed on the issue, but having shared a common experience of poverty and sickness and colonialism, he was able to totally win the day politically. And I don't know if anyone else could have done that.[30]

While George Manuel was busy on both the BC and international fronts during 1979, he, along with the rest of the country, was caught off guard by another unexpected development on the national scene. Joe Clark's minority government had been defeated on its first budget in December 1979, and the Liberals returned to power in February 1980. It was back to the old faces and the old battles of the 1970s. The greatest battle would be over Pierre Trudeau's attempt to unilaterally patriate the Canadian constitution.

## CHAPTER EIGHTEEN

# Constitutional Express
# 1980

We can't keep on talking about nations within Confederation. We have
to start acting as nations.

>Bob Manuel to an All-Chiefs meeting
>Nov. 1980

Immediately after the 1980 election, George Manuel called a meeting of
the Union executive to decide on how to fight the constitutional battle.
The first priority, they agreed, would be to ensure that during the debate,
the national Indian movement would speak with one voice on a previ-
ously agreed-upon program. The program they wanted adopted was the
Union's Aboriginal Rights Position Paper, which put the First Nations
on an equal footing with the two other founding nations, the English
and French, and gave them the right to veto any constitutional changes
affecting them.

George Manuel knew that the Position Paper might be a difficult sell
among some of his fellow Indian leaders who were willing to settle for
the much more restrictive Department of Indian Affairs plan that put
Indian governments on the same level as municipalities with their power
delegated from the provinces.

But he was determined to push the Union's position at the upcoming
NIB special assembly scheduled for late April, so he launched an intense
nation-wide lobbying effort to convince the more conservative chiefs to
back his proposals. In the end, he won by default. When the chiefs
arrived in Ottawa they discovered that the NIB leadership had failed to

develop a plan of its own and they adopted the Union's Aboriginal Rights Position Paper with an overwhelming majority. For the first time, the National Indian movement had a coherent, step-by-step plan for implementing Indian governments in Canada.

After the BC position was adopted, George Manuel wanted the Assembly to send a strong message to Pierre Trudeau and the minister of Indian Affairs, John Munro, who had been invited to address the Indian leaders, so he organized a demonstration that would take place on Parliament Hill after the conference.

As it turned out, Trudeau's speech was more focused on the upcoming Quebec referendum on secession than on constitutional issues. He called on the Indian people to unite with "the white men" to defeat the separatists in the referendum because a victory for the *Parti Québecois* option would "bring to a standstill the process of renewed federalism." In addressing the constitutional matter, he made only a vague promise that Indian peoples would be included in the process on matters directly affecting them.

John Munro then took the floor and announced, without warning, that he was going to launch a major review of the Indian Act and invited the chiefs to take part.

George Manuel was immediately on his feet. He accused Munro of trying to deflect Indian energies and resources away from the constitutional battle. "If we take the Indian Act as a priority," he pointed out, "any involvement that we have in the constitution would be diluted."[1]

The Union leader then announced that he would not listen to any more of Munro's speech and led the BC, Alberta, Saskatchewan and Maritime delegations out into the streets and on to Parliament Hill with drums beating and placards reading "Make Us Partners in our Homeland," "We have Rights" and "Indian Participation in the Constitution."

In the series of speeches in front of the Parliament buildings, Bob Manuel mocked the Prime Minister's description of the 1980s as "a decade for action" and said the only action the Prime Minister wanted was the type he could "push down our throats."[2]

Many of the chiefs, however, stayed in the hall and accepted Trudeau's claim that Indians would be represented at the talks on matters that affected them; but interestingly, Noel Starblanket and many of his staff followed George Manuel out into the streets.

In the coming months, this split between the radicals from the west and the Maritimes and those who stayed at the NIB assembly continued to grow. The conservative forces within the NIB believed their silence on the constitution would be rewarded with a seat at the table, while the Manuel faction saw the only way to have aboriginal rights protected was an all-out confrontation with the government, using whatever political and legal means the First Nations had at their disposal. If all else failed, they were prepared to use direct action and civil disobedience to block the Trudeau patriation drive.

The Manuel strategy for confronting Trudeau gained more credibility in early June when the Prime Minister announced twelve points he was prepared to deal with before patriation and said that all the rest would have to wait until some unspecified future round of constitutional negotiations. Nowhere in the twelve points was a mention of aboriginal rights, and Trudeau warned that if the provinces did not agree to his patriation package at a September federal-provincial conference, he would patriate the constitution unilaterally.

When the Union lawyers analyzed Trudeau's proposal, they confirmed what Manuel had been concerned about earlier. The Charter of Rights provided "for the English and French people only" and noted that "Indian nations are not recognized as founding peoples." This could "open the doors for any Canadian to take legal action against an Indian or Indians because non-Indian Canadians do not have the equality and freedom to hunt, fish or have hereditary Indian reserve lands and Indian Band Governments."[3]

In the middle of the confusion over Trudeau's constitutional proposal, the NIB leadership suddenly came up for grabs when Noel Starblanket announced that he would not seek re-election to the NIB presidency at the August Assembly. In a surprisingly frank admission, Starblanket said that he had been "acculturated" by his four years in Ottawa during which time he had developed a taste for "fine French wines, gourmet foods and good restaurants." He liked "to have lunch in a place like the Canadian Grill," he said, where he was likely to bump into a cabinet minister. He no longer had the drive needed to fight the fight and he knew it.[4]

After the announcement, there was talk of George Manuel returning to lead the NIB, but he was committed to building his peoples' movement in BC and to the task of leading the World Council into a new decade, so he quickly let it be known that he would not enter the race.

The Manuel family would be represented in the NIB election, however. In a surprising move, Bob Manuel decided to launch a campaign for the NIB presidency. When he told his father about his decision, George only asked him if he knew what he was getting into. His son told him he had no qualms about running. He had worked in Ottawa in the early 1970s and he had been the Union's liaison with the NIB for the past three years. He felt he was ready to take on the job and believed he could lead the national movement in the direction of the peoples' movement in BC.

Initially, his opponents were Del Riley, the president of the Union of Ontario Indians and Clive Linklater, George Manuel's former vice-president. The race tightened up when Linklater pulled out and refused to officially endorse either of the two remaining candidates.

Going into the assembly, Bob Manuel was backed by the more radical wing of the Indian movement. Many were surprised when Noel Starblanket publicly endorsed him as his successor. Starblanket's move was explained in his opening remarks to the assembly when he described himself as "the last of the negotiators," and warned that "we can not forever hold our young braves in check."[5]

George Manuel kept a low profile during the campaign, working behind the scenes in the hotel rooms trying to promote his son's candidacy. He made it clear, though, that it was Bob's show and his own role was merely that of a campaign worker.

By the time the vote was held on August 13, Bob Manuel had the BC delegation and Riley had the Ontario delegation sewn up. The rest of the country was evenly split, but in the end, Riley squeaked by with a 34-32 victory because Ontario had more votes.

For the Manuels and their supporters, however, the defeat was only a passing disappointment. In his campaign, Bob Manuel had made it clear that he was planning to take the NIB down a militant path and the results showed that the representatives of 150,000 Canadian Indians had agreed to follow.

The movement was gaining steam, and just two weeks after the NIB election, the radical position was further strengthened when Trudeau reneged on his April promise to include Indian leaders in any decisions affecting the future of their people. He backtracked after consulting with the premiers, who were worried that the recognition of aboriginal rights would affect provincial control of lands and resources.

The fact that they had suddenly been dealt out of the negotiations seemed to catch Del Riley and the new team at the NIB off guard, and they began to search for a strategy to regain a seat at the table. But by this time, George Manuel was already leading the national battle from his BC base.

In the summer of 1980, he had filed a legal declaration in the Federal Court "to ensure that no patriation occurs without the consent of the Indian Nations."[6] The suit was in his name and in the name of nine BC band chiefs. The NIB had no choice but to back him on the court challenge as "a necessary step."

As soon as his legal challenge was under way, George Manuel began to work on his political strategy. What he needed, he believed, was a two-by-four he could use to get the government's attention and his thoughts turned to some kind of march on Ottawa. Before he could work out a plan, however, he found himself involved in a similar direct action in British Columbia, but for a different purpose.

In early September, the young Shuswap chief of the Spallumcheen band, Wayne Christian, walked into the Union office and told George Manuel that he was concerned about the Indian children who were being removed from the community by the provincial social services agents and placed with white families. During the past two decades, Spallumcheen had lost more than a hundred of its children and four more kids were about to be removed from the reserve by the provincial government.

The Spallumcheen chief wanted to make some waves on the issue and said he was thinking of leading a caravan of parents from the interior to protest the policy on the streets of Vancouver.

George Manuel immediately backed the plan. The right to protect their children was an essential element of his Aboriginal Rights Position Paper and he appreciated the fact that the impetus for the protest came from the community leaders, rather than Union staffers. He told Christian what he told anybody who advocated radical action, "Go ahead, implement it and I'll back you."[7]

His first move was to send Louise Mandell to Spallumcheen to look after the legal aspects, and Jacob Marule, who was living in Chase at the time, to help with the organization of the caravan. With Jacob Marule's African National Congress experience, the Child Caravan, as it was called, was set up with military precision. It began with a cavalcade of cars and buses that left Spallumcheen and moved slowly through the interior to various staging areas where it gathered people from the local communities and held rallies to publicize their cause.

Among those who joined the protest was George Manuel's first wife, Marceline, who was then the social services worker for the band government (of which Bob Manuel was still chief). Marceline had a personal, as well as professional interest in the issue. As she told a *Globe and Mail* reporter, she had been taken away from her own parents when she was nine years old and she knew the pain "suffered during the time I was away from my people."[8]

The Caravan arrived in Vancouver on Thanksgiving Day and one thousand Indian protesters marched to the house of the Social Credit government Human Resources minister, Grace McCarthy, carrying signs demanding that the government stop "kidnapping" Indian children. They were told that McCarthy was "out to dinner," but as one newspaper columnist put it, "the press was in."

The protesters told the reporters stories of "the heartbreak, alienation and suicide which the government's white-is-right policy" had caused. George Manuel turned up at McCarthy's house and urged the protesters on by charging that "the white man has taken away our lands, our fishing rights, our rights to govern ourselves and now, for a number of years, our children have been stolen."[9]

Such statements won editorial support for the protesters from both the *Globe and Mail* and the major BC dailies, and the press began to put pressure on McCarthy and the Socred government to address the Indians' concerns.

The media attention eventually forced McCarthy to meet with the leaders of the Caravan and sign an agreement that gave the Spallumcheen band jurisdiction over the welfare of their children. The minister of Indian Affairs, John Munro, who had been watching the protest from the sidelines, moved to head off any visits to his own doorstep by agreeing to transfer the authority and funds for child welfare to the Spallumcheen Indian government.

The Child Caravan had been timed to arrive in Vancouver during the Union's General Assembly that was devoted largely to the constitution. George Manuel seized on the success of the Caravan to link it to the constitutional battle.

In his speech to the delegates, he said that aboriginal rights belonged

not only to them, but to their children. The Child Caravan had succeeded in winning the right for the bands to protect their children. "Do
we have the right," George Manuel asked, "to sell them out now? I say
we do not have that right."

In the name of the children and future generations, the First Nations
had to fight against the constitution because it "proposes to exterminate
our hereditary relations with our territorial lands and our rights to self-
determination as Nations of people."

George Manuel then declared a "national emergency." He asked that
everyone devote all of their time and energy to the constitutional battle.
"We must let [the peoples'] voices be heard at this critical time in our
history," he concluded. "Together, we must find a way to drive the wolf
from our door, or make a way with our own hands."[10]

What Manuel had in mind was taking the battle to the steps of
Parliament Hill. He told the delegates of his plan for a Constitutional
Express: the Union would charter trains to take hundreds of BC Indians
to Ottawa to demand that aboriginal rights be included in Trudeau's
patriation package and that those rights take precedence over the
Charter of Rights.

As soon as the announcement was made, the Union office was
transformed into a kind of war room, with George Manuel and his advisors planning the logistics of the Express and setting out the concrete
goals they wished to accomplish. First and foremost was the desire to
unite all Indian people on the constitutional issue and show the government the determination of the First Nations to protect and promote
their historic rights. But George Manuel also saw the Express as a way
"to create such an interest and understanding that when our legal cases
or position are publicized, the Canadian public would have a more
supportive position towards our cause."[11]

This was typical of George Manuel's "an end as a means to an end"
approach. Like a good billiards player, George always tried to position
himself for the next series of shots when he was examining the lay of the
table.

To accomplish his first priority, uniting the people, he had the
lawyers brief the seventy Union staff members on the details of the
constitutional package and then sent them out to communities around
the province to explain the importance of the issue and to urge the
people to join the Express.

To ensure that the publicity surrounding the Express was favourable, he brought in the elders to draw up a Code of Conduct, which prohibited all alcohol and drugs on the trains and called for strict self- discipline "in honour of the spirit of our Grandfathers and children yet to be born."

Then he added one final touch. The government had begun public hearings on the constitution in July and it was assumed that the Union would ask to appear before the Parliamentary committee to confront the politicians. But instead of pleading in front of what he considered a politically handcuffed committee, George Manuel decided to deliver a petition to the Queen's representative in Canada, Governor General Ed Schreyer, urging Her Majesty "to refuse the Patriation of the Canadian Constitution until agreement with the Indian Nations is reached in Canada." The petition also demanded that the Indian Nations, Great Britain and Canada enter into internationally supervised trilateral negotiations in a neutral country to decide the constitution issue and that measures be taken "to separate Indian nations permanently from the jurisdiction and control of the Government of Canada whose intentions are hostile to our people."[12]

The petition would be handed to the Governor General at a ceremony at Rideau Hall. Then, after the ceremony, George Manuel and the Union delegation would refuse to leave. With the press watching, they would take over the Queen's residence and begin to hold their own First Nations hearings on the constitution.

To work out the details of the operation, George Manuel enlisted the help of Walter Rudnicki, who also happened to be a friend and recent colleague of Ed Schreyer's.

Rudnicki had worked for Schreyer for a couple of years in the mid-1970s as the deputy minister of health when Schreyer was premier of Manitoba. Rudnicki returned to Ottawa in 1976 and set up a consulting office. He briefly came to national attention when he discovered a government blacklist naming him as part of a secret Extra-Parliamentary Opposition that included left-wing and community groups from across the country. Rudnicki went public with the blacklist and successfully sued the government for his inclusion on it.

When George Manuel told him about the plan to occupy Rideau Hall in the fall of 1980, Rudnicki thought it was a nice piece of mischief and immediately agreed to help at the Ottawa end. He soon discovered, though, that his friend Ed Schreyer was also privately pleased at the thought of the BC Indians taking over the official residence. Rudnicki was sipping Courvoisier with the Governor General at Rideau Hall in late October when Schreyer told him that he had heard from the intelligence people that an Indian constitutional train was coming to town and that they planned to take over his home.

Rudnicki didn't acknowledge that he was working with George Manuel on the plan, but he asked Schreyer what he thought about it.

"As far as I'm concerned," the Governor General replied with a smile, "they can do it."[13]

As Rudnicki recalled, Schreyer agreed that the best thing he could do was check into the royal suite at the Chateau Laurier with his wife and let George Manuel and the others carry on with their hearings.

While the Schreyers were anticipating the arrival of the BC Indians, the plans for the Express were going on at a frantic pace in both Ottawa and Vancouver. Bob Manuel was in charge of the Ottawa preparations, but he and his team were having trouble lining up food, lodgings and places to hold rallies for the estimated one thousand people who would be arriving in the capital. By the time he returned to Vancouver, all they had was "six bags of groceries and about two billets," and they had decided that they would have to take over the old Indian Affairs building to house the protesters.

Up to this point, George Manuel had been planning to ride the Express to Ottawa along with the others. But two weeks before the departure, a medical check-up showed serious heart irregularities and evidence of a second mild heart attack. His doctors issued a stern warning. Either he sharply curtail his activities or he would dramatically shorten his life. But George Manuel was involved in what he saw as the most important political battle of his life, and his only concession to his doctor was to agree to fly to Ottawa with the advance team, rather than making the four-day trek by train.

When he arrived in the capital, Manuel discovered that even though the train hadn't yet left Vancouver, the Express was already having an effect on politicians and security forces, who were becoming jittery over the rumours that the BC Indians were planning the same sort of all-out assault on Parliament Hill that the young Red Power activists had attempted in 1974.

Their paranoia increased on November 24 when almost one thousand BC Indians showed up at Vancouver's VIA station on Main Street to purchase tickets for the Express. Many of them marked the importance of the event by wearing their traditional dress and others brought their drums to entertain the people during the journey.

The atmosphere on the train was festive as it left the station but in many ways, it would be a difficult four days. The Express was made up of two trains, one that would take the northern route through the interior of BC, up to Edmonton and then down to Winnipeg, where it would link up with the second train that would pass through southern BC, Calgary and Regina. Both trains were jammed. Two hundred elders, who were not up to the journey, had flown to Ottawa, but the elders who decided to take the train were given the beds and the fold-down seats and the luggage racks were converted into makeshift cradles for the smaller children.

To keep order, each car had an appointed Indian security officer, but as it turned out they were not necessary. The train trip became a kind of rolling powwow, with singing, chanting and drumming mixed with Union-organized political workshops on the constitution.

As they wound their way through the interior Rockies, the trains were met at every stop by crowds of local Indians who had come to join the Express or to offer food, money and encouragement to the trekkers. As the land flattened out and they began to roll across the prairies, Alberta Indians were waiting alongside the track to catch a glimpse of the trains and wave at the protesters.

By the time the Express arrived in Manitoba, hundreds of native people were flocking to the stations to encourage their BC brothers. When the two trains arrived in Winnipeg, the crowd had swelled to more than a thousand people and the national press began to take notice.

There was an overnight stop in Winnipeg and a large and enthusiastic rally was held with speaker after speaker denouncing the attempt to undermine aboriginal rights with the new constitutional package. After hours of impassioned speeches and drumming and singing, offers of overnight billets poured in to the point where there were, as one organizer put it, "not enough Indians to go around." [14]

When the train pulled out of Winnipeg the next evening, it became apparent that the authorities were also taking a closer look at the

Express. A couple of the new porters looked suspiciously like RCMP officers and at midnight, four hours out of the station, the train ground to a halt between two giant rock faces at the western edge of the Canadian shield. A contingent of RCMP officers swarmed aboard, announcing that there had been a bomb threat and ordered everyone off the train. Bob Manuel met with some of the officers and protested sending the children, the old people and people in wheel chairs out into the cold, but the RCMP officers insisted they empty the train.

Bob Manuel called the leaders of the Express back to the baggage car and relayed the RCMP's message. The reaction was generally "That's bullshit, they just want to search the train," but they agreed that they had no choice and went back and told the others. The suspicion that the RCMP were using the bomb threat to search for weapons was confirmed when the people saw they were walled in by the rock faces and they were told to open their own bags while the RCMP officers poked around with flashlights.

No weapons, other than ceremonial spears, were found and the train was allowed to go on its way. But the alarm over the Express was continuing to grow in Ottawa as the police began to fortify not only Parliament Hill, but the entire capital with metal riot fences.

As Doug Sanders, who was then working as an advisor to the NIB saw it, only an Indian organization could have created the same "wonderful sense of uncertainty. There is nothing politicians hate more," he said, "than not being able to control information and come to some kind of conclusion about what was going to happen."

Sanders also observed, "It has always seemed that one of the strengths of Indian activism has been the ability to keep government off balance. And one of the ways you keep it off balance is to have a kind of ferment in the organization so you can't tell them what you are going to do anyway . . ."

The government's concern about the Constitutional Express was reflected in a sudden reversal made by the Parliamentary Committee studying the patriation package. The Committee had originally planned to close its hearings on December 6, but as the train chugged toward Ottawa, the fear of a possible Indian assault on the Hill led to the government extending the hearings and inviting the BC Indian delegation to present a brief.

It was the first concrete concession that any Indian group had won on the constitution, but for George Manuel and the other BC leaders it was not nearly enough. The leaders of the Express announced that they would only negotiate with the government on a nation-to-nation basis. If the government refused, they would send a delegation to the United Nations to put their case in front of the world body.

Ironically, there were others in Ottawa who were having trouble coming to terms with the Express; the leaders of the National Indian Brotherhood were not pleased to find George Manuel bringing his confrontational tactics to their doorstep. For Del Riley, who had beaten Bob Manuel by only two votes that summer, the Express, coming out of the Manuels' BC heartland, appeared as a direct challenge to his leadership.

Riley and the NIB kept their distance during the planning stages of the Express and suggested that it would have no effect either as a publicity stunt or as a wedge that could pry concessions from the government. George Manuel found the lack of support from the NIB executive disappointing, since he had continually assured the Ottawa leadership of his support in whatever strategy the NIB proposed. He saw the Express as complementary to, rather than in competition with, any NIB-led initiative.

The suspicion from the NIB officials was in sharp contrast to the support the Express received from the people of Ottawa and particularly from the Mayor, Marion Dewar. A couple of days before the Express was scheduled to arrive in the capital, Dewar called a press conference to announce that a trainload of Indian people was on the way from BC and asked the people to "open your hearts and open your homes" to them and to take the opportunity to learn something about their culture. [15]

The citizens responded. Offers for billets flooded in from nonnatives who had similar concerns about the constitution. Mayor Dewar's plea was also answered by the large unions and the churches and even by the girl guides in Ottawa, who rallied their troops to ensure that the nearly one thousand BC Indians would have food and lodging during their stay in the city.

When George Manuel met with his advance team in his Ottawa hotel room two days before the train was scheduled to arrive, the mood was buoyant. The Express was getting favourable publicity across the country; the omission of aboriginal rights in the constitution had suddenly moved from a fringe concern to one of the central preoccupations of the national news media. The BC action was also being endorsed by many of the key Indian leaders who were gathering in Ottawa for an All-Chiefs Conference and the Union staffers were busy in the hotel suites trying to line up support for the Express from the majority of the chiefs.

But the congratulatory mood of the Union strategists was suddenly broken when the Union leader stood up and said that something was wrong and he wanted someone to drive him to the hospital.

He was taken to the University Civic Hospital and he spent the night conscious, but hooked up to monitors in the intensive care unit. George Manuel was seriously ill with heart disease and his refusal to dismount from the political buckin' horse was ruining his already fragile health. On November 28, however, he was able to watch the Constitutional Express chug into the capital from his hospital bed. It was a remarkable show. When the train arrived in Ottawa, it was greeted by one thousand Indian supporters who had travelled to the area or who were in town for the All-Chiefs meeting. As the trekkers stepped onto the platform, they were met with the sound of drumming and chanting and a delegation of elders in traditional costume who offered a formal welcome.

When Bob Manuel, who was one of the first off the train, spotted Del Riley and John Munro waiting to greet them, he brushed past them to an area in the station that had been set up by Marion Dewar for a press conference.

In a toughly worded speech, he told the gathered Indian delegations and the press that unless Trudeau amended the patriation package to include a guarantee of aboriginal rights, the Constitutional Express would head down to New York to put the Indian case before the United Nations.

When a reporter mentioned a statement made by the prime minister the day before to the effect that he was confused by what the Indians meant by aboriginal rights, Bob Manuel retorted:

"We've been talking about it on the way here. What we want is the re-establishment of our language, our dignity and pride."

He then charged that "Trudeau's vision is one of Indians without a homeland," where the majority of Canada's Indians would "end up in the slums of the city." He warned again that if their demands for inclusion in the constitution were not met, they would not only go to the United Nations to protest, but they would begin to "work toward establishing a seat there."[16]

Most of the people on the Express, tired, hungry and longing for showers, were ushered into buses and taken to a local hockey arena to rest and to sort out the billets. But the leaders, Bob Manuel, Wayne Christian and Archie Pootlas, tapped the shoulders of the team of activists they had selected on the trains and led them back onto a bus for the trip to deliver the petition to the Governor General and to take over Rideau Hall.

When they gathered on the bus, most of the rank and file still knew nothing of the takeover plan. In fact, Bob Manuel only had the plan confirmed when a code word was spoken on the phone during a brief stop of the train in Ontario. On the bus on the way to Rideau Hall, the activists were told only that they were to listen to what the leadership said during the petition ceremony. If they were asked to lie down on the floor and block the doors, they were to do it. It was important that they acted together and acted quickly.

When they arrived at Rideau Hall, they were surprised to find there was another Indian delegation ahead of them, a group of traditional dancers from Vancouver Island who knew nothing of the Union's plans. Schreyer ushered in the Union people and sat them down to watch the performance.

Most of BC activists had eaten very little on the train and hadn't had time to eat in Ottawa, so they were relieved after the performance when they were ushered into a reception room where hors d'oeuvres were served. Bob Manuel recalls that they were so hungry that they were practically gobbling up the little sandwiches with both hands.

When the time finally came to present the Union's petition to the Governor General, an elder stood up to explain the basis of their claim for self-government:

"The Creator has given us the right to govern ourselves and the right of self-determination. The rights and responsibilities given to us by the Creator cannot be altered or taken away by any other nation."[17]

When the ceremony was finished, Bob Manuel took the Vancouver Island people aside and told them about the planned sit-in. They balked. In fact, they said it was the stupidest idea they'd ever heard.

Bob Manuel hesitated. He and everyone in his group were exhausted. He knew he should carry out the plan and tell them to sit down, but then he thought of the impression it would make if the

Vancouver Island people walked out and began to condemn their fellow BC Indians to the waiting press. He decided to leave Rideau Hall after the petition was accepted.[18]

The fact that the sit-in wasn't carried out did not block the momentum of the Express, however. While Bob Manuel and his delegation were at Rideau Hall, the rest of the Union leadership was working long into the night planning their strategy for the All-Chiefs meeting the following day when they would try to pass a resolution to boycott the parliamentary committee hearings and to win support for sending a delegation to the United Nations.

The back-room blitz of sympathetic chiefs bore fruit two days later when the issue was put before the conference. With George Manuel in the hospital, it was left to his son to lead the delegation.

Bob Manuel told the chiefs that waiting until after patriation of the constitution for the inclusion of aboriginal rights was not an option, because after patriation the new amending formula would require provincial consent to any changes, and the provinces had already shown that they "were hostile to native demands to form Indian governments."

At the end of his speech he issued a challenge. "We can't keep on talking about nations within confederation," he said in a booming voice. "We've got to start acting as nations."

He then pointed a finger at John Munro, invited by Riley to be an observer at the conference, and told him: "Munro, tell Trudeau to answer us within three days . . . Don't expect us to play around with some joint parliamentary committee!"[19]

Before the vote on the resolution the following day, there was a sense that things were starting to move in the BC Indians' favour. First, word came from Rotterdam that the Russell Tribunal had condemned Canada, the U.S. and five Latin American countries for "stealing land and suppressing the cultures of fourteen tribal groups."[20]

The NDP government in Saskatchewan then announced it would ask that Trudeau amend the charter to include native rights. At the same time, the national NDP leader, Ed Broadbent, stood up in the House of Commons and condemned the overreaction of the security forces in putting up the riot fences around the city as an insult to the Indian people. A motion was passed with unanimous consent calling for the removal of the barricades.

To the chiefs, it seemed that George Manuel and the Union were succeeding where Riley and the NIB leadership had failed. So when the issue of attending the parliamentary committee came before the assembly, the chiefs backed the Union resolution that called for a boycott of the hearings.

Del Riley took the vote as a personal defeat, but glossed over the Union's role in the debate. He told the press that "it was just a matter of the various band chiefs not fully understanding the parliamentary process" and he blamed himself and the rest of the NIB leadership "for not adequately informing them."[21]

With the boycott in place, the people of the Express were sent out in small groups to Parliament Hill to lobby the MPs and the senators individually about Indian government and the Union's constitutional position. While the members of the governing bodies were being blanketed by Indian lobbyists, the Express was dominating the CBC and CTV national news. It was their lead story for five nights running and it was picked up by the US media, which broadcast the Canadian Indian struggle to an estimated fifty million American viewers.

Most Canadians were reacting favourably to the protesters, particularly to the colourful and dignified ceremonies the native groups were performing on Parliament Hill. By the 1990s, sweetgrass burning, prayers from the elders and circle dances had become part of Canada's political landscape. But in 1980, the cultural expression of the First Nations was still something of a novelty and the BC Indians were transformed into media stars.

George Manuel experienced this feeling first-hand in the hospital when a doctor asked him if he was a member of the Constitutional Express. When he said that he was, he found staff from around the hospital – doctors, nurses and service workers – stopping by to visit him to offer encouraging words about the Indians' constitutional fight and to praise their behaviour in Ottawa. Because of the Express, George Manuel later told his supporters, "I was treated like a king. That is how much you stimulated Ottawa."[22]

When Ottawa is stimulated, the first people to get aroused are the politicians. As the public pressure mounted in the Indians' favour, Ed Broadbent threatened to withdraw NDP support for the patriation package if the protection of aboriginal rights was not included. The NDP was then joined by dissenting voices from the Conservative and Liberal parties. The whole Trudeau package seemed to be unravelling and Jean

Chrétien, who was acting as Trudeau's point man on the constitution, was forced to work frantically behind the scenes with the official NIB, Inuit and Métis leadership to try to strike a deal.

While Chrétien was negotiating with the national leaders, the BC Indians were making good on their promise to take their case to the United Nations. George Manuel and Marie Marule, whom he had also enlisted to help organize the Express, had pinpointed the UN's Decolonization Committee as the best place to lobby, and they had sent Dave Monture and Wayne Haimila, a young Cree law student, to New York to arrange for meetings with the international representatives, and for a demonstration in the square in front of the UN.

During the trip, they must have exaggerated a bit about how many trekkers were on their way down from Canada because when the bus load of fifty-four Union activists pulled up in front of the UN building, they were surprised to see the square surrounded by riot fences and hundreds of New York City police officers. When Saul Terry stepped off the bus he was politely asked by one of the policemen where the rest of the group was. Terry and the others were amused to find that somehow the fifty-four people had been transformed into fifty-four bus loads and had the New York police battening the city down for the thousands of Canadian Indians they expected to come storming down from the North.

The UN trip had a concrete impact on the native cause when four countries representing the Non-Aligned Nations – Tanzania, Cuba, Iran and Yugoslavia – agreed to put their case for independence before the Decolonization Committee and recommended that it later go to the United Nations General Assembly for a vote. For the First Nations, it was another important step toward internationalizing their cause – and toward embarrassing the Canadian government in Ottawa into acting on their demands.

While the official delegation was off to New York, the rest of the BC Indians were invited to powwows at nearby Indian reserves like Akwesasne, where the Longhouse people put on a feast and held traditional dances in their honour. By the second week in December, when the train began the trip back west, most of those on board felt that the event had changed their lives in a fundamental way and they credited their War Chief, George Manuel, for the transformation.

In a very real sense, the Express also changed the constitution. It had led to the press focusing on the Indian cause and to the NDP and a number of Liberal and Conservative members threatening action if native rights were not included in the package. Before the trains left town, Jean Chrétien, Del Riley of the National Indian Brotherhood, Harry Daniels of the Native Council of Canada and Charlie Watt of the Inuit Tapirisat came to an agreement on the inclusion of aboriginal rights in the patriation package.

According to the agreement, the Indian Act would be exempted from the Charter of Rights, and aboriginal rights would be recognized in the body of the constitution. The exact definition of those rights, however, would be decided in a series of federal-provincial conferences that would take place after patriation was complete.

Riley, Daniels and Watt were reported as having had tears of joy in their eyes when the deal was struck with Chrétien. They all agreed to drop their protest against patriation and Daniels even went so far as to offer to carry the constitution home from London himself if it would be of help to the Minister.

At first, most Indian, Métis and Inuit leaders fell into line with words of praise for the deal. It was, after all, a dramatic improvement. But George Manuel was not a better-than-nothing type of leader. Instead of savouring his victory in forcing changes to the fundamental law of the land, he surprised most Indian leaders by denouncing the deal as "an empty box."[23] When all was said and done, he argued, it would still be the premiers who would have the final say in defining aboriginal rights and in delineating the powers of Indian governments. These were the same premiers, he argued, who had traditionally opposed any expansion of Indian rights and who had recently blocked Indians from a seat at the constitutional table.

George Manuel felt no need to keep the national organization's promise to Chrétien to stop lobbying against the deal. Only days after he was released from the Vancouver hospital, where he had been transferred from Ottawa, he called the Union activists together and told them they would have to continue the fight. Alone if need be. If Ottawa wouldn't listen, they would take their case to the world.

# PART FOUR

# Final Days

Our people have been awakened by the spirit of our ancestors and we can continue the beat of our drums throughout our Indian nations.

George Manuel
Oct. 1981

## CHAPTER NINETEEN

# European Express
## 1981–1982

George Manuel looks like a dumb Indian type of guy, but he is a shrewd son-of-a-bitch.

Official at the Canadian High Commission, London.

While George Manuel was in hospital in Ottawa, he was told he would need major heart surgery. The operation was scheduled for early May, but he was determined to continue working in the intervening months.

His first order of business was an assessment of the Constitutional Express. He told his staff that he believed the movement had developed "a political sophistication to face our oppressors with courage and determination. . . . This is no longer one man's battle, or that of a few. We are a movement of a thousand people and more, and it will continue to grow."[1]

The Constitutional Express and its immediate aftermath had, in fact, turned out to be a significant turning point in Canada's relations with the First Nations. It signalled for the first time that Indian leaders were to be dealt in as players in the constitutional game. Under George Manuel's leadership, the Indian people of Canada had pushed themselves into the hall where the constitution was being decided and they would not be pushed outside again.

The next stage of the struggle was to get a place at the table. George Manuel kept the drums beating by planning a European Express that would take the First Nations' case to Germany, then to Holland, France and Britain, where they would lobby the European powers to intervene to protect the rights of the indigenous peoples in their former colonies. While the trip was being organized, the Union held constitutional meetings around the province to keep the people focused on the issue.

George Manuel was also pushing the NIB to withdraw its support for the Chrétien package and he joined with Alberta, Saskatchewan and Manitoba in asking for Del Riley's resignation if the NIB continued to support the government proposal.

Del Riley responded in February 1981, by hinting that he would, indeed, resign to save the NIB from self-destruction. But when it came down to actually leaving his post or reversing his position, he took the latter route by withdrawing his approval of the Chrétien package. He joined George Manuel and the western bloc by stating that he, too, would refuse to accept a provincial role in interpreting the aboriginal rights clause in the constitution.

But once again, George Manuel and the Union were far ahead of the NIB. The Union leader had hired a British lawyer to take the matter to the High Court in London to try to get an injunction against patriation. Specifically, what the Union was asking for was a veto power in the amending formula on any issue that touched on aboriginal or treaty rights.

While the constitutional battle was continuing on the home front, the Union leader was also facing an increased challenge from within his own province as Fred Walchli began to work openly with the breakaway leaders. After calling a meeting of the Union's opponents in Vancouver, Walchli convened a series of regional meetings where he "suggested meeting times, prepared the agendas, co-ordinated travel and hotel arrangements"[2] for the groups that were after the Union's funding.

To counter this threat to the Union's funding base, George Manuel flew to Ottawa in February, to confront the DIA bureaucrats and to argue that his organization was still the only representative of status Indians in British Columbia. After the embarrassment Manuel had caused the government over the constitution, however, the Department was much cooler to him than it had been in the past.

George Manuel's welcome in Ottawa turned even chillier when he refused an invitation by John Munro to sit in the House of Commons gallery while the minister was addressing the constitutional issue.

Instead, George Manuel showed up uninvited at Munro's press conference afterward and virtually took it over. He condemned the minister for failing to offer any prospect of restoring Indian land and self-government rights and he said that he would never support the patriation of the constitution in its present form.

Munro was furious at Manuel's upstaging, and is reported to have yelled, "Come off it, George, we're all politicians here!"

To the amusement of the press, George Manuel yelled back, "I'm not a politician, I'm a statesman!"[3] Munro didn't even crack a smile, and he later wrote Manuel a scathing letter where he described the Union leader's actions as "reprehensible."[4] As George Manuel had warned his C.D. workers in the 1960s, if you are going to make waves, you are going to make enemies.

While George Manuel was coming under attack from all sides, he was forced to make a difficult decision about his future in the international movement. The upcoming WCIP Assembly in Canberra, Australia coincided with the date of his heart surgery. It was an election year at the WCIP, but after assessing his health and looking at the scope of the constitutional battle still ahead, he decided to resign the presidency of the international organization he had founded and shaped over the past six years.

But the future of the WCIP would remain a passion in his life and before his surgery, he found time to make another international trip, travelling to Chile with the backing of a group of Canadian churches to investigate the plight of the Chilean Mapuche Indians who were being persecuted by the Pinochet regime.

In his report on the Mapuche, which was sent directly to Prime Minister Trudeau, George Manuel charged that "Canada's economic policy allows individual bank, corporate and crown investments in Chile to take place while it condemns Chile loudly for violating human rights in very select forums."[5]

His findings were also submitted to the Canberra Assembly and the WCIP agreed to work at the UN for action against the Chilean government.

Even though he was in a Vancouver hospital for his heart surgery, George Manuel's presence was also felt in Australia when Del Riley read his note to the eight-hundred-fifty indigenous delegates and observers.

In the note, George Manuel told them about his medical problems and said he was "deeply saddened" by his absence, but that he was present in his "mind, spirit and heart" as they pursued their indigenous ideology of struggle.[6]

George Manuel was succeeded in the post of the wcip president by a friend from Costa Rica, José Carlos Morales. Before the Assembly ended, George Manuel was named as the wcip's permanent ambassador-at-large, which would allow him to continue to travel for the organization and to represent them at conferences around the world.

In the summer of 1981, George Manuel was still hoping to get back into the constitutional fight, but after his by-pass operation he was hit by a stroke that temporarily paralysed his left side. His legendary determination allowed him to fight back and eventually regain his mobility, but in the minds of many of his friends and colleagues, the stroke was a blow that signalled the end of George Manuel's leadership.

While he was slowly recovering at home, Rosalee Tiyza and the young "Manuelistas" were telling their ailing leader that he should not give up the fight. If he couldn't walk, they told him, they would be his legs. And whatever happened they would carry on the struggle he had launched.[7]

That point was proven during the summer of 1981 when a large group of bc native women marched into the Department of Indian Affairs "Black Tower" office building in downtown Vancouver and demanded a public investigation into the role of the dia in the province and in particular into the manoeuvrings of Fred Walchli.

That action had begun in George Manuel's Neskainlith community when Joyce Willard[8] and a group of Manuel's women supporters founded an organization called Concerned Aboriginal Woman to protest the fact that pro-Union communities, like Neskainlith, were being squeezed for funds by Walchli's department.

They had come up with a plan for a woman's sit-in at the Black Tower and they took the idea to an interior chiefs' meeting in Lytton. The men were sceptical, so the women of Neskainlith held a meeting with the women of Lytton and the plan began to take shape. They decided that they would march into the dia's Vancouver office and stay there until Walchli resigned and the Department promised to investigate his conduct in the province. To ensure international publicity and that the government would negotiate rather than immediately send in the police, they planned the takeover to coincide with the arrival of the world leaders in Canada for the G-7 summit.

As soon as they had the details set, they began to contact native women around the province. Among the first recruits were George's first wife, Marceline, and their daughter, Vera. One of the largest contingents came from the Mount Currie band and as the takeover date approached, they emerged as the leading force in the protest.

At the appointed time, eighty Concerned Aboriginal Women marched into the Black Tower and took over the DIA floor. Walchli was caught in his own office and surrounded by the elders, some in their eighties, who blocked his exit for several hours while they politely stated their grievances. When they had said their piece, they let the regional superintendent of Indian Affairs leave the building while they settled in to deal with the head office in Ottawa.

The first reaction of the DIA in Ottawa was to go to the courts and try to get an injunction ordering the women out. The courts, however, imposed a mediator, Nelson Small Legs Sr., who was the father of an Albertan Indian who committed suicide in 1976 to protest the DIA's mishandling of the lives of Indian people.

Nelson Small Legs Jr. had become a symbol of resistance to DIA oppression, but when his father arrived to mediate between the women and the Department, they politely declined the offer. What they wanted was a meeting with Ottawa, and they repeated their demand for Walchli's resignation.

When the mediator was turned back, the courts granted the government injunction, but the women refused to budge. As the days wore on, they found themselves winning support from various ethnic and women's organizations in the city. The government finally sent in an Ottawa DIA official, Ray Perrault, to negotiate. After the meeting, Perrault flew back to Ottawa to speak to the minister about their demands.

Supporters of the sit-in continued to bring in food and drink for the women and the children who were with them, and some of the supporters, like Rosalee Tiyza, came in and out of the building frequently. Others remained the whole time and defied the police to move in and arrest them.

Eventually, that is what happened. Late at night, a week after the occupation began, the police stormed the building and dragged the women down the freight elevators and into waiting paddy wagons.

Some, like Marceline Manuel, were injured in the expulsion and had to be taken to hospital, but when Louise Mandell was called to the police station she found the protesters in high spirits with the older women exclaiming that they should have made that gesture of defiance years ago.

Mandell was able to get all of the women off when she argued that the women were allowed to enter and leave the building during the occupation, and this constituted implied consent on the part of the government. In the end, the women did not succeed in getting a public investigation into the DIA operations in the province, but they did, in effect, end the career of the third "W," Fred Walchli, who was later shifted aside and eventually squeezed out of the Department.[9]

While the women were occupying the Black Tower and George Manuel was resting at home, the younger generation of leaders was running the Union. The number one priority was still the constitution, and they were carrying out George Manuel's plans for the European Express. George had already sent Dave Monture and Wayne Haimila to Europe on a thirty-day advance tour to make initial preparations. In Vancouver, Union activists spent the fall publicizing and fund raising for the European trip, including holding a benefit concert that attracted musicians like Buffy Saint Marie.

The delegation was slated to leave for Hanover, Germany on November 1. But before they left, there was the question of the Union leadership to settle. The General Assembly was scheduled for October and there was a feeling that for health reasons George Manuel should step aside from the rigours of day-to-day leadership and work for the Union as a strategist and advisor.

George Manuel was slowly regaining his strength and he was considering serving for one more term as the Union president, but his mind was changed during a meeting in Vancouver's Dufferin Hotel with Phillip Paul, Saul Terry and his son, Bob. All three suggested he step down. For George Manuel, the fact that his old friend and ally Phillip Paul was among them, was probably the deciding factor.

At the time, Paul was disillusioned about what he termed "Walchli's buy-back program" of Indian leaders and he had decided to return to his reserve in Saanich to fight the government at the community level. George Manuel and Phillip Paul had shared a combative ideology and a friendship since the early 1960s and George always took Phillip's advice seriously. So after a long discussion about what was best for the Union, George agreed not to run for re-election.

The Union's Assembly took place on 28-30 October 1981. George Manuel was in a reflective mood as he gave his farewell address. He spoke about the need to create viable Indian institutions to avoid being assimilated into the dominant society. He called for "real soul searching in terms of what to do in the future. We are going to have to decide for ourselves whether we want to be absorbed into the institutions of the white man. We've got to think about that because that's where the government wants to take us in the Resolution to Patriate the Constitution, to assimilate our people into their society and absorb us into their institutions. Is that what we want?"

He feared some Indian leaders would accept assimilation, but he insisted that "our people don't want to be assimilated, they want to grow and develop as Indians and be proud as Indians . . . We have an ideology. An ideology is something that never dies, it goes on and on and it will outlive many lives." [10]

It took time for many BC Indians to understand that George Manuel, for the first time since 1957, was no longer the leader of an Indian organization. But the fact that the Manuel era was still not over was personified in the election of the new president.

In the Dufferin Hotel room, Saul Terry and Phillip Paul had decided to back Bob Manuel as the new president and when the vote was held on the floor of the Assembly, he received massive support from the chiefs. In his acceptance speech, Bob Manuel pledged to continue what his father had begun, leading the Union on the path to sovereign Indian government.

Two days after the Assembly ended, the new Union president led a group of one hundred BC Indians to Europe in a last ditch attempt to try to block the Trudeau patriation drive. As in the Ottawa Express, those travelling to Europe were encouraged to bring their traditional costumes and drums; this cultural display had a strong impact when they got off the plane in Germany. The Germans had a long fascination with North American Indians and the press reflected this interest with intense and sympathetic reporting of the Indian cause. Even the former German Chancellor, Willie Brandt, got into the act by meeting with the Canadian Indian delegation to discuss his North-South Dialogue initiative.

The Express was just leaving on the second leg of the trip to France when news came of a last-minute agreement by the federal government and nine of the provincial premiers on a patriation package. As a price to pay for the agreement, Chrétien had dropped all reference to aboriginal and treaty rights.

The news that the limited recognition of Indian rights had been removed was a shock to all those on the trip. But it made them even more determined to press their case. In Paris, the Union organized a march from the Canadian embassy to the British embassy to protest Canada's genocidal policies against their people and the march was briefly joined by a well-disciplined contingent from the IRA carrying banners in support of the First Nations' cause in Canada.

By the time the Express reached Belgium, crowds of three thousand people were turning out to show support. The Belgium military even supplied an honour guard for a sweetgrass-burning ceremony the BC Indians held in Flanders Field to commemorate their fathers and grandfathers who had died in European wars.

The main part of the protest would take place in Britain, however. When the Union delegates arrived in London, they moved into an office the NIB had set up and virtually took it over. Then they began an intense lobbying effort of every single British MP and member of the House of Lords to convince them to block patriation of the BNA Act.

They had their greatest success with the British Labour Party, which assured the Canadian Indians that they would put on "a three-line whip" in the British House of Commons to block Trudeau's patriation bid if native rights were not restored to the constitution. The Labour Party's only condition was that their opposition to the package be approved by their fraternal party in Canada, the NDP. [11]

A measure of their success in Britain can be made from the number of External Affairs diplomats who were sent into the various countries to engage in damage control in the wake of the Express. The Union leaders also had a taste of the Canadian government's irritation at them when a Canadian official at the High Commission in Trafalgar Square was overheard commenting that George Manuel, the instigator behind the Express, "looks like a dumb Indian type guy, but he is a shrewd son-of-a-bitch." [12]

Unlike William Pierrish's sojourn to London more than a half century before, the BC Indians would not be depending on the High

Commission to deliver their message to the Crown. They had already received an invitation to Buckingham Palace where they were received by the Queen's representatives. It was a heady moment for all concerned, although Wayne Christian recalls they were a bit nervous that their sweetgrass ceremony would set off the smoke alarms in the palace as it had in the practice run at the hotel the night before.

While the European Express was in London, the protest against the exclusion of native rights from the constitution was also growing in Canada, not only from native organizations, but from all sectors of society. Editorialists showed particular disdain for the short shrift given to native rights, with most papers describing the premiers as "shameful" and "narrow minded" for trying to remove recognition of the First Nations in the country's fundamental law.

The same views were being expressed in the British press. The complaints of Bob Manuel and the members of the Express over the new patriation deal found a willing audience and renewed the opposition of many of the British MPs to patriating the constitution without the recognition of native rights.

Back in BC, the Union was showing its opposition to the patriation process by working with the Nuxalk people in staging a formal declaration of independence. Under the glare of television lights, a Nuxalk spokesman announced that "Through our Creator, we now assert our sovereignty, independence and self determination as the Nuxalk nation, recognizing and practising our own laws to govern all Nuxalk land, water, air and resources."[13]

The Nuxalk chief and Union activist, Archie Pootlas, then warned that "blood would be spilled" if Canada refused to recognize the inherent self-governing rights of all of the country's First Nations.

The clamour within the country and the embarrassment abroad caused by the European Express finally began to show results. The federal New Democratic Party and MPs from other parties threatened to vote against the patriation resolution unless recognition of native rights was restored. Prime Minister Trudeau had heard that patriation would likely be refused by the British if the Canadian House of Commons was divided along party lines on the issue, so he was forced to go back to the premiers and ask them to reinstate the two aboriginal rights clauses to his package. But with another hitch. The original agreement between

Chrétien and the national native leaders had called for a recognition of "aboriginal rights," but to win the support of Alberta's Peter Lougheed, Chrétien inserted the word "existing" in front of "aboriginal rights."

In the final draft, the aboriginal rights section in the constitution, Section 35, was titled Rights of the Aboriginal Peoples of Canada. It read:

(1) The existing aboriginal rights and treaty rights of the aboriginal peoples of Canada are hereby recognized and affirmed.

(2) In this Act "aboriginal peoples of Canada" includes the Indian, Inuit and Métis peoples of Canada.

Exactly what "aboriginal rights" meant would be left to the series of constitutional conferences between the federal government, the provincial premiers and leaders of aboriginal organizations. What was being offered in one hand, George Manuel and the Union activists feared, would soon be taken away with another.

The Union activists had an opportunity for one parting shot at Trudeau when he was in Kamloops on a speaking tour and a group of 150 Indians gathered to protest his constitutional initiative. Wayne Christian elbowed his way through the security men and, standing only a foot away from the Prime Minister, objected to "the lies you have been telling the world about Indian people."

"What lies?" Trudeau demanded, and then he asked who Christian represented. When Christian told him he represented the Shuswap nation, Trudeau continued. "Five thousand? Well, there were many more Indian leaders in Ottawa last February representing many more than you and they were happy with the resolution."

Trudeau is then reported to have glared at the chief and said, "Perhaps you'd better meet with them and settle your lies between yourselves and don't accuse me of lying."[14]

The agitated Trudeau was then hustled away by his security men, and soon after his constitutional package was approved by the British Parliament. The Canada Act was signed into law by Queen Elizabeth on 17 April 1982.

George Manuel, whose Constitutional Express had done more than anything else to get the government to include the promise of the federal-provincial talks in the constitution, would not be directly involved in them. But the talks did have an unforeseen effect on BC politics as the various warring factions realized they would have to pull together in a common front against the premiers.

In January 1983, representatives of the Union and virtually every Indian organization and Indian band in the province attended the British Columbia Aboriginal Rights Conference in Penticton to hammer out a common constitutional position. It was the most representative BC Indian gathering since the beginning of the Union in 1969. Many personal wounds between the Manuel and Wilson camps remained, but by 1983 there was also a growing sense that the internal battles had only served to exhaust the players, to the benefit of the government.

The Union's constitutional battle had, in fact, left it $380,000 in debt, and Bob Manuel was forced to drastically curtail its activities. During his term of office he managed to get the debt down to $30,000, but in doing so he had to pare the staff and programs to the bone and then convince some creditors to take fifty cents on the dollar for the money they were owed.

The changes in British Columbia were also influenced by changes on the national scene when the NIB was restructured into the Assembly of First Nations, with its membership made up of approximately six hundred bands, rather than provincial and territorial organizations. It was a structure that George Manuel always preferred; it fit in with his conviction that a band-based organization was in the best position to fight for aboriginal rights on both the legal and political fronts.

Yet with the bands directly represented in the Assembly of First Nations, the existing band-based provincial bodies suddenly seemed redundant and the organization of Tribal Councils rapidly began to fill the void of local leadership.

The Shuswap nation organized itself into the Shuswap Nation Tribal Council in 1985 and Bob Manuel left the Union and began to work with the new organization. Saul Terry took over the Union and tried to expand its mandate so it could include tribal councils, but with only limited success.

While pleased with the changes at the national level, George Manuel remained sceptical about tribal organizations. Along with Nyerere's warning, he was still concerned about the James Bay example and he feared that the government would eventually try to break the Indian movement by making separate deals with the fifty-two small

Indian nations rather than face the united national organization representing the 600 bands and over 300,000 people.

George Manuel's personal struggle was coming to an end, however.
He had recovered slowly from his previous stroke and was considering
moving back onto the active political scene, but his hopes were dashed
by a second and much more serious stroke that left him in a wheelchair
for most of his remaining days.

His incomplete recovery would still have allowed him to take on the
role of the elder, the grandfather of the movement, but that was a role he
was not prepared to assume. In his final years he found himself locked in
a political battle which, like almost all the other political battles he had
undertaken, he won. This time, though, it was a battle that his family,
and many of his friends and allies in the movement, wished he had not
undertaken.

» CHAPTER TWENTY «

# Passing the Torch
## 1982-1989

The torch George Manuel inherited was barely aflame. The torch he passed on was burning bright.

> Harold Cardinal, on the legacy of George Manuel.

The man of the people returned to the people. And George Manuel would leave the world as he had come into it: battling poverty and illness.

To a great extent, his poverty was caused by his principles. Unlike many other native leaders, George Manuel refused offers of a genteel retirement into the Senate. He turned them down because he believed it would be a betrayal of his struggle for First Nations sovereignty if he allowed himself, at the end of his days, to be absorbed by the Canadian government structure he had spent his life trying to overturn.

At the same time, though, the peoples' movement could not provide its aging warrior with the luxury of a pension. George Manuel's only income came from a small and, as it turned out, temporary consultant's salary from the Union. Even more disappointing, he found he could not rely on housing from his band. The house he had built in the early 1950s was no longer habitable, and despite the fact that his son was the band chief, there wasn't any reserve housing available for him and Marlene and their children. George Manuel was forced to live out his days in a small duplex across the river in Chase.

Still, he had managed to make one last trip as the ambassador of the

World Council of Indigenous Peoples, and it was one of the most emotional he ever took. During late 1981, there had been rumours of a brutal military campaign in the Guatemalan Highlands against the local Mayan Indians. George Manuel was well enough in July 1982 to attend an international indigenous peoples conference in Regina and he took the opportunity to alert the delegates to the wave of military violence that was breaking over the Guatemalan Indians.

When George Manuel later heard stories of the Guatemalan Maya struggling through the country's northern jungles and into hastily assembled refugee camps in Mexico, he resolved to go down to see what he could do to help.

He travelled to southern Mexico, and through local contacts he was taken into the isolated jungle camps where the Guatemalans were gathering. At the age of sixty-one, suffering from progressive heart disease, he found himself sitting on the dirt floor of a shack in the rain forest, watching a mother and her two-year-old baby slumped in a darkened corner. "When this weakened mother has no more milk for her child," he was told, "the child will die," because there was no food in the camp.

In another shack, thirty people were jammed together, and George Manuel was told by one woman how "the Army dragged her husband from their home and killed him in the most cruel fashion, before burning their home and cornfield."[1] Others told him of soldiers descending on villages and bashing the heads of children against adobe walls and of soldiers gathering men, women and children into village squares and mowing them down with machine-gun fire.

The Mayan survivors in the Mexican camps lacked food, drinking water and decent shelter and the rate of Dengue fever and malaria was reaching epidemic proportions. George Manuel was witnessing first-hand the genocidal policies that had devastated the Indian peoples of North America centuries earlier. In the faces of the dying and the grieving, he saw the Shuswap people his grandfather had told him about during the smallpox epidemic. Massacres by bullets, decimation by disease: the Indian wars had never stopped in the Americas.

Still, George Manuel learned that in the Mayan language, there was no word for "conquest." After four hundred years of Spanish and Ladino presence on their lands, the Maya still spoke only of "occupation." Along with the rest of the Fourth World George Manuel had helped to shape, they still dreamed of liberation; and amid the ashes of defeat they were preparing to renew the fight.

They would not be alone. The refugees who struggled across the border were given initial shelter, small bags of corn, yucca, chickens and seeds by the Mexican Indians of the Chiapas rain forest, who were themselves desperately poor. George Manuel was deeply touched by the fact that the poor Mexican Indians were willing to stretch out their hands and their meagre resources to help their brothers and sisters, and he viewed this act of solidarity as a model for the Fourth World movement.

When he returned to Canada, he issued a plea for Canadian Indians and their supporters to join with the Mexican Indians in aiding the Guatemalans. He asked for "food, medicine and tools so they can support themselves. A plastic sheet to put over their heads. A spoon. A cup. Seeds . . ." Anything to help the beleaguered Maya. [2]

While George Manuel was raising funds and awareness about the Guatemalan tragedy, he found himself receiving a number of late-life honours at home. They began when he was still in the hospital recovering from the stroke. The University of British Columbia announced that it was awarding him an Honorary Doctor of Laws. The irony of a man with barely two years of formal education receiving such an award was not lost on George Manuel, but because he was still in the hospital, the oldest son of his second marriage, George Jr., was sent to the UBC convocation to accept it.

In 1984, when he had recovered sufficiently to be pushed around in a wheelchair, the Union held a ceremony where George Manuel was given the title of Grand Chief. Friends and Indian leaders from across the country gathered in Neskainlith to mark his contribution to the cause. George was able to meet again with colleagues from the days when he was organizing for the NAIB and people he worked with at the NIB, the Union and the World Council of Indigenous Peoples.

In 1986 he was awarded the Order of Canada. He accepted it with reluctance because he did not think it right that he accept accolades from a government that still refused to acknowledge the sovereignty of the First Nations. His friends pointed out that it came from the Crown and not the Canadian government, so he finally agreed to attend the ceremony. But when he arrived in Ottawa, he changed his mind and decided to stay in his hotel room. At the last minute, he was convinced to go through with it, but he later told reporters that he didn't know why he had bothered to accept it. When he was back in his room he described the medal as being worth less than a fifty-cent piece and tossed it into the wastebasket.

Even though his health was deteriorating, Manuel was still determined to escape the retiring statesman's role of being buried alive in honours. He wanted to spend his last days working for the movement with whatever strength he could muster, and in January 1985, he ran and won a seat on the Neskainlith band council along with his son Bob, who was elected for his fifth straight term as chief.

George Manuel's election to the council ensured that his voice would be heard. But the job of councillor came with only a token salary and his financial position became precarious a few months later when Saul Terry sent George a letter informing him that he had to cut off his Union consultant's salary. Facing increased government cutbacks, the Union no longer had the money to pay it.

In his last years, George Manuel also had time to spend with his family. His last child, Ida, had been born in 1978 when George was busy with the fish wars and was beginning his constitutional battle. Marlene remembers that when he arrived at the hospital shortly after Ida was born, he was so tired that he fell asleep on the bed beside them. In the mid-1980s, he finally had a chance to get to know his children. Young George Jr. recalls that before his father "was in his wheelchair, we hardly ever talked. He was always gone to meetings."

Now George Jr. got to know the man whose name he carried, and was able to watch a western on television with him or have his father teach him how to make fish-head soup.[3]

Occasionally, Marlene would take George to Vancouver where he would meet with old friends and go out for Chinese food and talk about the current political struggles and about the old days, thirty years earlier, when he and Jacob Kruger travelled the province trying to rouse the people into action, and spent the nights in haystacks in their travels between communities.

Even though he was enjoying his time with his family, there was still a sense of restlessness about George Manuel. He wanted to serve the cause, but his body would not allow it. By 1986, his mental sharpness was also beginning to waver. Guy Lavallee, who was living in Vancouver at the time, saw George Manuel three or four times a year and he remembers that "sometimes his conversation would be inconsistent so we had to repeat often with him. And his memory was also beginning to fail a little bit."

Mary Thomas also noticed the change. When she visited George Manuel in Chase "he would start talking about something and he'd end up talking about something else. He wasn't the George I knew. He was paralysed and I don't think all of his brain was functioning."

Wayne Christian found his visits with George Manuel during this period difficult, and he realized that at the end of a life devoted to politics you "were left with nothing."

It was in this gradually weakening mental and physical condition that George Manuel found himself in his last, and least satisfying political battle. It began when an issue came up at a band council meeting that had to do with a DIA self-government initiative. Bob Manuel saw an opportunity to expand the council's power and he agreed to take over the DIA responsibilities, but George Manuel opposed the move. He thought that Bob was caving in to the Department and he accused him of betraying the principles of Indian government that the Union had set out under his leadership.

He confronted his son on the issue, but the two could not sort out their differences. So George Manuel, an aging and ailing political warhorse, set out on his last campaign. He organized a takeover of the Neskainlith band office and released a scathing written attack on his son's leadership.

It was a difficult moment for the family and the whole community; the difficulty was increased when George Manuel announced that he was going to run against Bob for the chief's post. True to his word, he ran in the 1987 band election and won the job he had held thirty years earlier.

George Manuel would barely live out his term. As his health continued to fail he spent his last months in the traditional way: taking a rigorous personal inventory. "The old people used to tell us," he told a friend visiting him at the hospital, "that when you come to the end of your life, you have to think of all the people you hurt. And this is the time for me."

In the fall of 1989, George slipped into a coma from which he never recovered. He died on 15 November 1989.

News of George Manuel's death travelled quickly through Indian country and beyond. In Ottawa, Dave Monture picked up his phone and heard Bill Badcock telling him that "Shogun is dead." Rodrigo Contreras was in Belize attending the first meeting of the Caribbean branch of the wcip when the call came. The meeting was halted while tributes were paid to their founding president. The news also travelled across the ocean and into the camps of the Sami reindeer herders and a boy who knew George Manuel as a distant father made an attempt to get in touch with the family but was hampered by the lack of a mutual language.

The funeral was a fairly low-key affair. Senator Len Marchand tried to arrange to have a friend bring a horse-drawn wagon to carry the coffin, but the friend was snowed in in the high country and couldn't make it. In the valley where the services were held, the snow turned to a cold November drizzle and the three hundred friends and colleagues from across Canada stood quietly in the rain while Wayne Christian read the eulogy that had been written by George and Marceline's oldest daughter, Vera.

"The trail he forged for Indian people is well marked," Vera Manuel had written. "Many doors have been opened; many children were born and grew up in the wake of this man's vision . . . And he never asked of anyone any sacrifice that he was not willing to give himself. As a leader he truly walked with the people. He was the biggest Chief of all times – a War Chief."[4]

Dressed in his buckskins, George Manuel was laid to rest on a windy hillside above Neskainlith on 20 November 1989, a few hundred metres from the spot where he was born.

# Epilogue

George Manuel, the War Chief, and the greatest Canadian and international indigenous leader of his generation was gone and the torch was passed. As Harold Cardinal had observed, the torch that George Manuel had inherited had been barely aflame. When he entered the political fray in the 1950s, the only access most Indians had to power was to sit outside the Indian agent's office, hat in hand, and plead for gifts from a low-level government appointee who reigned over them like a Roman governor over the defeated Gauls.

As chair of the Indian Advisory Board in the 1960s, George Manuel had led the Indian movement to the door of the minister of Indian Affairs. In the early 1970s, as the president of the National Indian Brotherhood, he gained access to the cabinet room and the prime minister's office. With the Constitutional Express, the Indian leadership was able to bring the Indian cause to the table with the eleven men who made the decisions on how to carve up the political and economic power of the land.

On the international scene, his vision shaped the Fourth World movement and gave it a voice and a place at the United Nations through the World Council of Indigenous Peoples. In a very real sense, George

Manuel's death was mourned in the jungles of Central America, the mountains of Peru, the deserts of Australia and the far reaches of Scandinavia.

In the end, only death was able to throw George Manuel off the buckin' horse of the First Nations' struggle, but that struggle has continued unabated.

For most of the 1980s, the Indian movement in Canada was preoccupied with the negotiations between the federal and provincial governments to define the meaning of the aboriginal rights clause in the 1982 constitution.

As George Manuel had predicted, the negotiations ended in deadlock when the premiers refused to recognize the inherent right of native peoples to govern themselves. But the negotiations were not a waste of time. While the premiers were turning a deaf ear to the Indian cause, the heavily publicized conferences provided the Indian leadership with a platform to make their case directly to the Canadian people, and support for the native cause continued to increase throughout the decade.

The Indian movement was given another boost during the so-called "Indian summer" of 1990 when the Manitoba MLA, Elijah Harper, succeeded in blocking the Meech Lake constitutional accord with its provisions that threatened the First Nations' position in Canada. A few months later, Canadians were alerted to the seriousness of the native commitment to their historic rights when they were confronted by an armed stand-off at Oka, Quebec between the Mohawk Warriors and the Canadian army.

In BC, during that tense summer, the peoples' movement was once again in full swing with Bob Manuel bringing the Indian nations of the interior together to co-ordinate a series of road and rail blockades in solidarity with their Mohawk brothers and sisters under siege in Kanesatake and Kanawake.

Just as George Manuel had used the radicalism at the base to push the Indian cause with government leaders, one of his successors at the Assembly of First Nations, Ovide Mercredi, and Manuel's ally Ron George, who was elected president of the Native Council of Canada, used Oka and the widespread Indian opposition to the Meech Lake Accord to win major concessions for the First Nations, including the recognition of their inherent right to self-government, in the 1992 Charlottetown Accord.

In the end, that Accord was defeated in a nation-wide referendum on 26 October 1992, but the defeat did not mean that First Nations lost ground. The Indian movement, from George Manuel's time to the present, has always been able to use each ceiling as a floor as it climbs toward emancipation. And today, the recognition of the inherent right to Indian self-government has become the new floor in the continuing struggle to rebuild the First Nations economically, socially and culturally.

The movement's greatest leader, George Manuel, offered a legacy of struggle and a blueprint for attaining sovereignty that informs the present and, undoubtedly, the future. As Rosalee Tiyza put it, George Manuel said that he wanted us to be so "radically charged, that no matter where we went, change would follow. And I suppose he's right. After working with him, I can't go back to the way I was. I can only go forward." The ceiling becomes the floor. The struggle continues.

# NOTES

## Chapter One

1. Minutes of the Proceedings of the Joint Committee of the Senate and House of Commons on Indian Affairs, 26–27 May 1960, p. 643.
2. Ibid.
3. Ibid., p. 642.
4. Ibid.

## Chapter Two

1. Michael Posluns Collection, York University, T17.
2. Amy August interview.
3. Pierre Manuel came from the Skeechestn band, one hundred-fifty kilometres to the west of Neskainlith, while Louis Manuel came from the Kamloops band.
4. Bob Manuel interview.
5. Amy August interview.
6. George Manuel and Michael Posluns, *The Fourth World: An Indian Reality* (Toronto, 1974), p. 40.
7. Celia Haig-Brown, *Resistance and Renewal: Surviving the Indian Residential School* (Vancouver, 1988), p. 36.
8. Posluns Collection, York University, T14.
9. Mary Thomas interview.
10. Manuel and Posluns, *The Fourth World*, p. 35.
11. Cited in Paul Tennant, *Aboriginal Peoples and Politics: The Indian Land Question in British Columbia, 1849–1989* (Vancouver, 1990), p. 92.
12. *Kamloops Standard Sentinel*, 12 Nov. 1921.
13. Amy August interview.
14. Shuswap Nation archives.
15. Cited in Minutes of Proceedings of the Joint Senate and House of Commons, 25 May 1960, p. 583.
16. Cited in Proceedings of the Joint Senate and House of Commons Committee on Indian Affairs, 25 May 1961, p. 583

17. Manuel and Posluns, *The Fourth World*, p. 52.
18. Mary Thomas interview.
19. Ibid.
20. Manuel and Posluns, *The Fourth World*, p. 63.
21. Haig-Brown, *Resistance and Renewal*, p. 44.
22. Manuel and Posluns, *The Fourth World*, p. 67.
23. Rosalee Tiyza interview.
24. Haig-Brown, *Resistance and Renewal*, p. 54.
25. Manuel and Posluns, *The Fourth World*, p. 36.
26. Ibid., p. 65.
27. Tennant, *Aboriginal Peoples and Politics*, p. 126.

## Chapter Three

1. House of Commons Debates, 9 Apr. 1937, p. 2867.
2. Ibid., 2 May 1932, p. 2537.
3. Manuel and Posluns, *The Fourth World*, p. 100.
4. Ibid., p. 67.
5. Ibid., p. 101.
6. Bob Manuel interview.
7. Manuel and Posluns, *The Fourth World*, p. 2.
8. *The Canadian Forum*, Oct. 1944, p. 153.
9. *The Native Voice*, Apr. 1951, p. 14.
10. Mary Thomas interview.
11. Bob Manuel interview.
12. Manuel and Posluns, *The Fourth World*, p. 107.
13. Ibid.

## Chapter Four

1. Manuel and Posluns, *The Fourth World*, p. 109.
2. Tennant, *Aboriginal Peoples and Politics*, p. 126.
3. Joe Manuel interview.
4. Arthur Manuel interview.
5. Manuel and Posluns, *The Fourth World*, p. 112.
6. Joe Manuel interview.
7. Cited in Proceedings of the Joint Senate and House of Commons Committee on Indian Affairs, 25 May 1960, p. 599.

8. Cited in *Indian News,* May 1956, p. 2.

9. Cited in *The Vancouver Sun,* 3 May 1958, p. 3.

10. Posluns tapes, T14.

11. Posluns tapes, T12.

12. Henry Castilliou interview.

13. Bob Manuel interview.

14. Henry Castilliou interview.

15. Bob Manuel interview.

16. Henry Castilliou interview.

17. Len Marchand interview.

18. Tennant, *Aboriginal Peoples and Politics,* p. 128.

19. Ibid.

20. *Kamloops Standard Sentinel,* 27 Apr. 1959, p. 1.

21. Tennant, *Aboriginal Peoples and Politics,* p. 129.

22. Posluns tapes, T12.

23. Henry Castilliou interview.

## Chapter Five

1. Indian-Eskimo Association bulletin, Autumn, 1961.

2. Proceedings of the Joint Parliamentary Committee on Indian Affairs, 26 May 1960.

3. At the time, Indian Affairs was a branch of the Citizenship and Immigration Ministry.

4. *The Native Voice,* Dec. 1962.

5. *The Native Voice,* Nov. 1961, p. 7.

6. Ibid.

7. *The Native Voice,* May 1962, p. 7.

8. Arthur Manuel interview.

9. Bob Manuel interview.

10. Mary Thomas interview.

11. *The Native Voice,* Apr. 1963, p. 1.

12. *The Native Voice,* Nov. 1963, p. 1.

13. *The Native Voice,* Feb. 1964, p. 2.

14. *Maclean's,* 6 July 1963.

15. Walter Rudnicki interview.

16. Ibid.

17. Ibid.

*Chapter Six*

1. Phillip Paul interview.
2. Walter Rudnicki interview.
3. Manuel and Posluns, *The Fourth World*, p. 132.
4. Ibid., p. 133.
5. Michael Posluns tapes, T11.
6. Harkewel Singh Basi report to the British Columbia Social Services Dept.
7. Manuel and Posluns, *The Fourth World*, p. 136.
8. Wes Modeste interview.
9. Manuel and Posluns, *The Fourth World*, p. 141.
10. Manuel and Posluns, *The Fourth World*, p. 144.
11. Wes Modeste interview.
12. Report by George Manuel to the Department of Indian Affairs and Northern Development, Feb. 1969, p. 6.
13. Phillip Paul interview.
14. Minutes of the first meeting, National Indian Advisory Board, Ottawa, 10-12 Jan. 1966.
15. Ibid.
16. Ibid.
17. *The Native Voice,* June 1964, p. 3.
18. House of Commons Debates, 2 Oct. 1964, p. 8697.
19. Len Marchand interview.
20. Minutes of the second meeting of the National Indian Advisory Board, 19-23 Sept. 1966, p. 55.
21. Minutes of the fifth meeting of the National Indian Advisory Board, 2-4 Aug. 1967, p. 59.
22. Ibid., p. 65.
23. Ibid., p. 69.
24. Ibid., p. 60.
25. Speeches by the Hon. Arthur Laing, p. 4.
26. An Address by the Hon. Minister of Indian Affairs and Northern Development, 25 Feb. 1967, p. 22.
27. *Indian News* insert, Apr. 1967.
28. Walter Rudnicki interview.
29. Text of remarks by the Hon. Arthur Laing to Indian Day, Expo '67, p. 3.
30. Phillip Paul interview.
31. Ibid.

32. *Victoria Colonist,* 27 Oct. 1966.
33. *Calgary Herald,* 25 Nov. 1968.
34. Notes for an address by the Hon. Arthur Laing, 12 Feb. 1967, p. 3.
35. Phillip Paul interview.
36. *Canadian News Facts,* 1-18 Jan. 1968, p. 7.

## Chapter Seven

1. Harold Cardinal, *The Unjust Society,* (Edmonton, 1969) p. 1.
2. *Maclean's,* Dec. 1969, p. 20.
3. Cardinal, *The Unjust Society,* p. 118.
4. Harold Cardinal interview.
5. Ibid.
6. Report by George Manuel on Indian Leadership Development Workshops, Feb. 1969, p. 13.
7. Ibid., p. 13.
8. Arthur Manuel interview.
9. House of Commons Debates, 5 Dec. 1969, p. 3527.
10. Cardinal, *The Unjust Society,* p. 107.
11. Harold Cardinal interview.
12. Ibid.
13. Christine Deom interview.
14. Arthur Manuel interview.
15. Jean Chrétien, *Straight from the Heart,* (Toronto, 1985) p. 57.
16. Cited in speech on Indian Day at Expo '67 by Walter Currie, 7 July 1967.
17. Arthur Laing's introduction to *Choosing a Path,* Department of Indian Affairs, 1967.
18. Cardinal, *The Unjust Society,* p. 119.
19. House of Commons Debates, 23 Jan. 1969, p. 4738.
20. Report of the Indian Consultation meeting, Nanaimo, 30 Oct. 1968, p. 36.
21. Rapporteurs' account of the National Conference on the Indian Act, 28 Apr.-2 May 1969, p. 20.
22. Manuel and Posluns, *The Fourth World,* p. 179.

## Chapter Eight

1. An address by the Hon. Jean Chrétien to the Indian-Eskimo Association, 20 Sept. 1968, p. 7.

2. Canadian Facts on File, 16-20 June 1968, p. 289.

3. Cardinal, *The Unjust Society*, p. 1.

4. Manuel and Posluns, *The Fourth World*, p. 126.

5. Prime Minister Trudeau, Remarks on Aboriginal and Treaty Rights, 8 Aug. 1969, p. 1.

6. Ibid.

7. Harold Cardinal interview.

8. House of Commons Debates, 6 Mar. 1969, p. 6310.

9. House of Commons Debates, 11 July 1969, p. 11132.

10. Cited in *Indian News*, Nov. 1969, p. 4.

11. Pauline Comeau and Aldo Santin, *The First Canadians: A Profile of Canada's Native People Today* (Toronto, 1990), p. 9.

12. *Indian News*, Mar. 1959, p. 3.

13. *Indian News*. Aug. 1969, p. 4.

14. Dave Monture interview.

15. Minutes of the National Indian Brotherhood General Assembly, 17-19 July 1969.

16. Ibid.

17. *Indian News*, Aug. 1969,p. 6.

18. Minutes of the National Indian Brotherhood Executive Council Meeting, 23 March 1969.

19. Phillip Paul interview.

20. Cited in Tennant, *Aboriginal Peoples and Politics*, p. 154.

21. Paul Tennant has pointed out that Phillip Paul was often referred to as the "chairman" of the UBCIC even though the post did not officially exist. *Aboriginal Peoples and Politics*, p. 155.

22. Cover page of *Citizens Plus*, the Indian Association of Alberta, June 1970.

23. Ibid, p. 1.

24. Harold Cardinal interview.

25. *Indian News*, Sept. 1970, p. 6.

26. *Indian News*, June 1970, p. 1.

27. Ibid.

28. Ibid., p. 7.

29. Harold Cardinal interview.

30. Ibid.

31. Henry Castilliou interview.

## Chapter Nine

1. Minutes of the National Indian Brotherhood meeting, 20-23 Aug. 1970.
2. Ibid.
3. Communication from the National Indian Brotherhood, 20-23 Aug. 1970.
4. Minutes of the meeting of the Union of British Columbia Indian Chiefs, 16-19 Nov. 1971, p. 34.
5. Minutes of the Executive Council meeting, 25-27 Sept. 1970, p. 53.
6. Doug Sanders had become involved in the Indian movement while working with Thomas Berger in British Columbia and in 1970 he published *Native Rights in Canada,* a detailed legal study of the First Nations' historic rights in Canada.
7. Minutes of the Executive Council meeting, 25-27 Sept. 1970, p. 54.
8. Resolutions from the Executive Council meeting, 25-27 Sept. 1970.
9. Letter from H.B. Robinson, deputy minister of the Department of Indian Affairs, to George Manuel, 8 Oct. 1970.
10. *News of the North,* 19 Nov. 1970.
11. Marie Marule interview.
12. Phillip Paul interview.
13. Michael Posluns interview.
14. Presentation by George Manuel to the National Indian Brotherhood Executive Council, 10-12 Mar. 1971.
15. President's Report to the General Assembly, 14-16 July 1971.
16. Ibid.
17. Cited in *Indian News,* June 1971, p. 1.
18. Minutes of the UBCIC Second Annual Convention, 16 Nov. 1970.

## Chapter Ten

1. George Manuel speech on Economic Development, Oct. 1972.
2. NIB press release, President's Response to Education Report of the Commons Committee of Indian Affairs, June 1971.
3. Harold Cardinal interview.
4. Speech to the 8th Annual School Committee Conference of Indian Teachers, 8 Nov. 1971.
5. Cited in Harold Cardinal, *Rebirth of Canada's Indians* (Edmonton, 1977) p. 80.
6. Ibid., p. 66.
7. George Manuel speech on Economic Development, Oct. 1972.

8. Letter from George Manuel to the Hon. Jean Chrétien, 5 June 1971.

9. Speech by George Manuel to Iroquois and Allied Indian Association, 17 Apr. 1971.

10. Cited in *Indian News,* Jan. 1973, p. 1.

11. Letter from George Manuel to the Right Hon. P.E. Trudeau, 24 Oct. 1972.

12. Notes for a speech to the BC Association of Non-Status Indians by George Manuel, 17 Nov. 1971.

13. Jamie Deacey interview.

14. Ibid.

15. Minutes of the UBCIC Meeting, 16-19 Nov. 1971.

## Chapter Eleven

1. Report on the New Zealand and Australia tour by George Manuel, 1971, p. 4.

2. Ibid., p. 6.

3. Telegram #167 from the High Commission, Wellington, to the Under-Secretary of External Affairs, Ottawa, 19 March 1971.

4. Michael Posluns tapes, T14.

5. Report on the New Zealand and Australia tour by George Manuel, 1971, pp. 7-8.

6. Len Marchand interview.

7. Report on the New Zealand and Australia tour by George Manuel, 1971, p. 15.

8. Ibid.

9. *The Whitehorse Star,* 27 May 1971.

10. Ibid.

11. Canadian Press report, Calgary, 13 May 1971.

12. *Indian News,* Vol.14, No.11, p. 1.

13. NIB press release, Celebration of Uhuru, Jan. 1972.

14. Cited in Telex from DSLAM to EXTOTT, 13 Dec. 1971.

15. Telex to Under-Sec. of State for External Affairs from the Canadian High Commission, Dar Es Salaam, 31 Dec. 1971.

16. Telex to Under-Sec. of State from High Commission, Dar Es Salaam, 17 Dec. 1971.

17. Cited in Telex from DSLAM to EXTOTT, 15 Dec. 1971.

18. Telex to Under-Sec. of State for External Affairs from the Canadian High Commission, Dar Es Salaam, 28 Dec. 1971.

19. Ibid.

20. Cited in speech by George Manuel, 25 Oct. 1974, p. 13.

21. Posluns tapes, T18.

22. Speech by George Manuel, 25 Oct. 1974, p. 11.
23. Letter from George Manuel to the Hon. Jack Davis, min. of the environment, 11 Feb. 1972.
24. George Manuel's Report on the UN Conference on the Environment, p. 2.
25. Ibid., p. 3.
26. Ibid., p. 4.
27. Ibid., p. 5.
28. Ibid., p. 7.
29. Jamie Deacey interview.
30. Ibid.
31. George Manuel's Report on the UN Conference on the Environment, p. 8.
32. Ibid.
33. Ibid., p. 11.

## *Chapter Twelve*

1. George Manuel's speech to the UBCIC Annual Meeting, Nov. 1972, p. 1.
2. Cardinal, *The Rebirth of Canada's Indians* (Edmonton, 1970), p. 148.
3. Doug Sanders, Land Claims Report to the NIB, 1974.
4. Cited in Cardinal, *The Rebirth of Canada's Indians,* p. 137.
5. Len Marchand interview.
6. NIB press release, Jan. 1973.
7. Roy MacGregor, *Chief: The Fearless Vision of Billy Diamond* (Toronto, 1989), p. 54.
8. Cited in MacGregor, *Chief,* pp. 67-68.
9. Speech by George Manuel at Man and His World, 22 Aug. 1971, p. 7.
10. Jamie Deacey interview.
11. MacGregor, *Chief,* p. 101.
12. Ibid., pp. 101-2.
13. Ibid., p. 104.
14. Cited in *Maclean's,* May 1973.
15. Press release, George Manuel's Response to Recent Federal Position Regarding James Bay, Jan. 1974.
16. *Indian News,* Special Issue, Vol.17, No.7.
17. Canadian News Facts, 15 Feb. 1974, p. 1149.
18. *Indian News,* Special Issue, Vol.17, No.7.
19. Marie Marule interview.
20. NIB president's annual report, 1974.

21. Guy Lavallee interview.
22. Rodrigo Contreras interview.

## Chapter Thirteen

1. *Calgary Herald,* Apr. 1971.
2. Ibid.
3. Bob Manuel interview.
4. Vern Harper, *Following the Red Path,* (Toronto, 1979), pp. 52-3.
5. Ibid., p. 78.
6. Minutes of the Joint NIB–Cabinet Committee Meeting, 3 Oct. 1974.
7. Cited in *Indian News,* Sept. 1973, p. 6.
8. George Manuel travel report, Aug. 1973 to July 1974.
9. Doug Sanders interview.
10. Doug Sanders, *The Formation of the World Council of Indigenous Peoples,* p. 8.
11. Speech by George Manuel on Education, 28 Aug. 1973, pp. 3-4.

## Chapter Fourteen

1. Cited in *Indian News,* Summer 1975, p. 1.
2. Cited in letter from George Manuel to Judd Buchanan, 21 Mar. 1975.
3. Cited in CP wire service report, Kiruna, Sweden, 3 Oct. 1977.
4. *Maclean's,* Mar. 1975, p. 48.
5. Letter from George Manuel to James Richardson, 4 Mar. 1975.
6. Canadian News Facts, 31 May 1975, p. 1391.
7. Ibid., p. 1392.
8. Minutes of Joint Cabinet/NIB Meeting, 12 Dec. 1975.
9. Cited in letter from George Manuel to the Hon. Judd Buchanan, 1 Oct. 1975, p. 2.
10. Text of Clive Linklater's address to Regional Directors' Meeting.
11. Letter from George Manuel to the Right Hon. Pierre Trudeau, 8 Oct. 1975.
12. Warren Allmand interview.
13. Ibid.
14. Minutes of the UBCIC Land Claims Conference, Terrace, BC, 2 Apr. 1975, p. 6.
15. Ibid.
16. Ibid.
17. *Indian News,* June 1975, p. 5.
18. Bill Wilson interview.

19. Tennant, *Aboriginal Peoples and Politics*, p. 177.
20. Ibid., p. 176.
21. Phillip Paul interview.
22. Tennant, *Aboriginal Peoples and Politics*, p. 179.
23. Bob Manuel interview.
24. Phillip Paul interview.
25. Bob Manuel interview.
26. Ibid.
27. Ibid.
28. Dene Declaration, 1975.
29. Bob Manuel interview.
30. Dene Declaration, 1975.
31. Speech by George Manuel to the Anglican Synod of the Diocese of Niagara, 3 Oct. 1975.

## Chapter Fifteen

1. Doug Sanders, *The Formation of the World Council of Indigenous Peoples*, p. 11.
2. Ibid., p. 13.
3. Ibid.
4. Dave Monture interview.
5. Ibid.
6. Rodrigo Contreras interview.
7. Ibid.
8. Report by George Manuel to the wcip, Jan. 1977.
9. Rodrigo Contreras interview.
10. Report by George Manuel to the wcip, Jan. 1977.
11. Rodrigo Contreras interview.
12. Ibid.
13. Presentation of George Manuel, President of the nib, to the Mackenzie Valley Pipeline Inquiry, 13 Apr. 1976.
14. Presentation of George Manuel, President of the nib, to the Mackenzie Valley Pipeline Inquiry, 3 June 1976.

## Chapter Sixteen

1. Manuel and Posluns, *The Fourth World*, p. 265.
2. *London Free Press*, 14 Aug. 1976.

3. Ibid.

4. Cited in *Indian News*, Vol.17, No.9, 1976, p. 1.

5. Ibid. p. 2.

6. Phillip Paul interview.

7. Bob Manuel interview.

8. Union of British Columbia Indian Chiefs Policy Statement, 1977.

9. Phillip Paul interview.

10. Art Pape was a non-native married to Maxine Pape, who was a Union staffer.

11. Louise Mandell interview.

12. Millie Poplar interview.

13. Bob Manuel interview.

14. Phillip Paul interview.

15. Rodrigo Contreras interview.

16. C.P. report, Kiruna, Sweden, 25 Aug. 1977.

17. Ibid.

18. Ibid.

19. C.P. report, Kiruna, Sweden, 27 Aug. 1977.

20. Bill Badcock interview.

## Chapter Seventeen

1. Cited in President's Message, UBCIC *News*, Dec. 1978.

2. UBCIC Special Report, 20 Jan. 1978.

3. Ibid.

4. Ibid.

5. Louise Mandell interview.

6. *Vancouver Province*, 26 July 1978, p. 4.

7. *Vancouver Province*, 27 July 1978, p. 1.

8. Ibid.

9. Louise Mandell interview.

10. President's Report, UBCIC *News*, 8 Nov. 1978.

11. Cited in UBCIC *News*, Vol.1, No.5, 1978, p. 9.

12. UBCIC *News*, Spring 1978.

13. UBCIC *News*, May 1978.

14. *Indian News*, Feb. 1971, p. 1.

15. Cited in *Canadian News Facts*, 1-15 June 1978, p. 1959.

16. Walter Rudnicki interview.

17. Bob Manuel interview.

18. *Canadian News Facts*, 1-31 Aug. 1978, p. 1993.

19. Posluns and Manuel, *The Fourth World*, p. 218.

20. President's Annual Report to the UBCIC, 1978-79.

21. Tennant, *Aboriginal Peoples and Politics*, p. 186.

22. Rosalee Tiyza interview.

23. UBCIC *News*.

24. UBCIC *News*.

25. Paul Tennant, *Aboriginal Peoples and Politics*, p. 188.

26. Saul Terry interview.

27. Ibid.

28. Tennant, *Aboriginal Peoples and Politics*, p. 192.

29. Walter Rudnicki interview and Millie Poplar's *George Manuel, an Indian Biography*, UBCIC, 1984.

30. Dave Monture interview.

## Chapter Eighteen

1. Cited in the *Montreal Gazette*, 30 May 1980.

2. Ibid., 5 May 1980.

3. Cited in the UBCIC Constitutional Communique, 16 Oct. 1980.

4. *Ottawa Journal*, 7 Mar. 1980, p. 2.

5. *Montreal Gazette*, 13 Aug. 1980, p. 17.

6. Cited in George Manuel's Address to the UBCIC's 13th Annual Assembly, Oct. 1981.

7. Wayne Christian interview.

8. *The Globe and Mail*, 17 Nov. 1980.

9. *Montreal Gazette*, 22 Oct. 1980, p. 7.

10. UBCIC Constitutional Communique, 11 Oct. 1980.

11. Cited in Constitution Report of the UBCIC, Oct. 1981.

12. Ibid.

13. Walter Rudnicki interview.

14. Bob Manuel interview.

15. *The Globe and Mail*, 27 Nov. 1980.

16. Ibid., 27 Nov. 1980.

17. Ibid., 8 Dec. 1980.

18. Bob Manuel interview.

19. *The Globe and Mail*, 1 Dec. 1980.

20. Ibid., 2 Dec. 1980.

21. Ibid., 8 Dec. 1980.
22. George Manuel's Address to the UBCIC's 13th Annual Assembly, Oct. 1981.
23. Bob Manuel interview.

### Chapter Nineteen

1. George Manuel's Address to the UBCIC's 13th Annual Assembly, Oct. 1981.
2. Tennant, *Aboriginal Peoples and Politics,* p. 197.
3. Michael Posluns interview.
4. Millie Poplar, *Indian Profile of George Manuel,* May, 1986, p. 19.
5. George Manuel, *The Mapuche of Chile and the Threat of Law* 2568, p. 14.
6. *Kainai News,* Apr. 1981, p. 1.
7. Rosalee Tiyza interview.
8. Joyce Willard later married Bob Manuel, who was the Neskainlith band chief at the time.
9. Louise Mandell interview.
10. George Manuel's Address to the UBCIC's 13th Annual General Assembly, Oct. 1981.
11. Bob Manuel interview.
12. Ibid.
13. Bella Coola Declaration, UBCIC archives.
14. *The Globe and Mail,* 24 Nov. 1981.

### Chapter Twenty

1. George Manuel's open letter to the people of Canada, 1982.
2. Ibid.
3. George Manuel Jr. interview.
4. Vera Manuel, Eulogy for George Manuel.